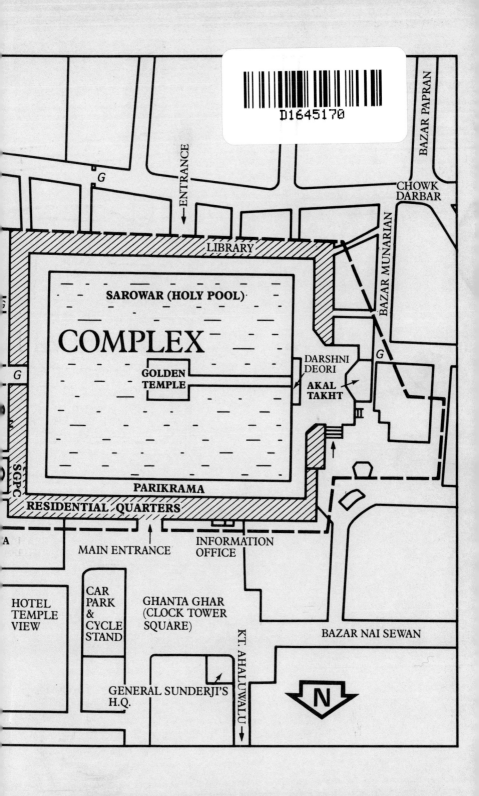

AMRITSAR

AMRITSAR
Mrs Gandhi's Last Battle

MARK TULLY &
SATISH JACOB

JONATHAN CAPE
THIRTY-TWO BEDFORD SQUARE LONDON

First published 1985
Copyright © 1985 by Mark Tully and Satish Jacob

Reprinted 1986

Jonathan Cape Ltd, 32 Bedford Square, London WC1B 3EL

British Library Cataloguing in Publication Data

Tully, Mark
Amritsar: Mrs Gandhi's last battle.
1. India – Politics and government – 1977-
I. Title II. Jacob, Satish
954.05'2 DS480.853

ISBN 0-224-02328-4

Typeset by Inforum Ltd, Portsmouth
Printed and bound in Great Britain by
Biddles Ltd, Guildford and King's Lynn

Contents

Illustrations

Picture Credits

The authors and publishers are grateful to the following for permission to reproduce copyright illustrations: Camera Press Ltd (nos 1 and 22); Patrice Habans, John Hillelson Agency Ltd (no. 2); *India Today* (no. 5); Sandeep Shankar (nos 3, 4, 6, 7 and 9); the *Telegraph*, Calcutta (no. 21). All other photographs come from the authors' own archives.

Note to Readers

Amritsar, Mrs Gandhi's last battle, was not a battle against the Sikhs, a community Mrs Gandhi always regarded with great affection. It was a battle in which infantry, armour and artillery were used against a small group of Sikhs who had fortified the Golden Temple complex and used it as a base from which to defy the authority of the Indian government. The tragedy is that many Sikhs do not accept this definition. They maintain that it was indeed a battle against their community. Satish Jacob and I followed the events which led up to the army action in the Golden Temple very closely, reporting every twist and turn for the BBC's External Services, which have a vast audience in India itself, and for BBC radio and television.

We started work on this book before Mrs Gandhi's assassination because we were convinced that 'Operation Blue Star' would have the gravest consequences for the unity of India if it was not recognised that the Sikh leadership was as much responsible as the government for that disaster. The tragedy of Mrs Gandhi's assassination proved us right. She was killed because some Sikhs were convinced that she had deliberately and unjustifiably waged war on their most sacred shrine. The danger of the alienation of a large section of the Sikh community was magnified by the government's failure to control the

violence unleashed against Sikhs after Mrs Gandhi's assassination. We therefore felt there was all the more need to tell the
story of Bhindranwale and the mistakes which led up to the
disaster in the Golden Temple.

If this book leads to a greater understanding among Sikhs
and Hindus of the forces that were at work, it will surely
strengthen the hope of reconciliation. We have tried to show
that neither side wanted that final confrontation.

When it came to telling the story, Satish and I faced a
problem. We had worked so closely together that it was un-
thinkable that Mark Tully or Satish Jacob alone should tell the
story. At the same time we soon found that two people cannot
actually write a book. The Indian government's decision to ban
all foreigners from Punjab provided us with a satisfactory
division of labour. We decided that Satish, being an Indian
citizen, should spend his time in Punjab talking to army
officers, Sikhs and others who had been eyewitnesses of Operation Blue Star and the events which followed, while I got on
with the writing. That is why I have written in the first person.
The work itself is in every sense a joint work, from the original
outline to the final corrections. At every stage I have been
dependent on Satish Jacob for facts and interpretation.

We are both deeply indebted to Gillian Wright for her many
invaluable contributions and suggestions. She did much of the
historical research, saw the book through the publishers while
we were in Delhi, and compiled the index. We also wish to
thank the many Indian journalists who unselfishly shared their
information. We are particularly grateful to Harbir Singh
Bhanwer, Sanjeev Gaur, Raju Santhanam, Tavleen Singh,
Rahul Bedi and D.K. Vashisht. Five of our friends read the
manuscript and prevented us from falling into many traps.
They were Ian Jack of the *Sunday Times*, Viqar Ahmad of the
BBC External Services, Abdul Gafoor Noorani, lawyer and
journalist of Bombay, Sant Bux Singh, politician and philo-
sopher, and the Sikh historian and head of the Guru Nanak
Foundation, Mohinder Singh. Of course, they bear no respon-
sibility for the views expressed in the book.

Satish and I hope that this book will not be seen as perversely
critical. It is an honest attempt to relate, before memories dim

and the actors in the drama scatter, an important chapter in the history of a country we both love deeply.

On 20th August 1985, after this book went to press, Sant Harchand Singh Longowal, the President of the Sikh religious party, the Akali Dal, was shot dead in a *gurudwara* near his home village. His death threatened the accord he had signed less than a month before with the Prime Minister, Rajiv Gandhi. Longowal was killed by young Sikh fanatics who wanted to prevent a reconciliation between their community and Hindus. Part of the establishment in Delhi, which felt threatened by Rajiv Gandhi's modern style of government, was not unhappy at this apparent setback. The *Times of India*, for instance, saw the assassination of Longowal as evidence of the need for 'political skills of the highest order and not what the Americans call knee-jerk reactions and public relations exercises.' The Prime Minister ignored the establishment and continued to implement his settlement. It is to be hoped for India's sake that he, not the forces of reaction, will eventually win the day in Punjab.

Delhi
August 1985   MARK TULLY

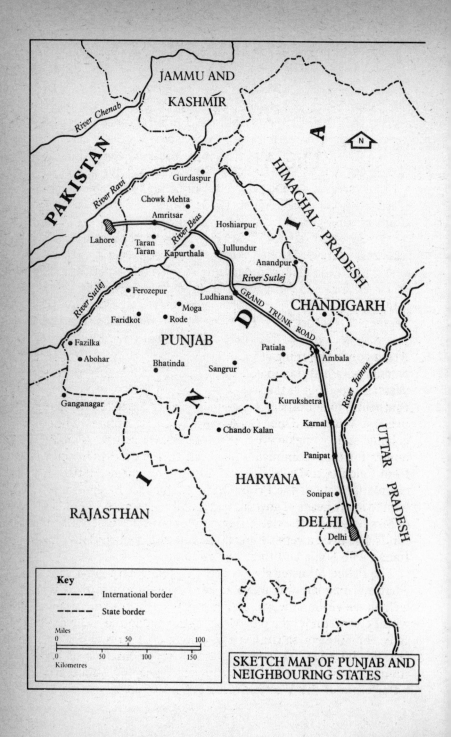

SKETCH MAP OF PUNJAB AND
NEIGHBOURING STATES

I

The Assassination of
a Prime Minister

At 9.15 on the morning of 31st October 1984 Indira Gandhi, the woman who had dominated Indian politics for nearly twenty years, stepped out of the side-door of her bungalow to cross the compound to her office. Throughout her Premiership she had lived at Number One, Safdarjang Road, a simple, white, colonial-style bungalow built by the British as one of many homes for their administrators when they moved the capital from Calcutta to Delhi. There was nothing vulgar, garish or ostentatious about the Prime Minister's house. In sharp contrast to many heads of government, good taste was the hallmark of Mrs Gandhi's lifestyle. Although she controlled vast political funds, she lived a very simple home life with her son Rajiv, his Italian wife Sonia and their two children.

The Prime Minister always chose her saris with great care. That morning she was wearing saffron because it showed up well on television. She was on her way to a television interview with Peter Ustinov, the playwright, actor and humorist. Ironically, in Sikhism saffron is the colour of martyrdom. Mrs Gandhi did have her vanity. She was very conscious of her status as a world leader, and enjoyed it hugely. Although a bitter critic of the Western media, she responded to visiting celebrities' requests for interviews with remarkable alacrity.

Most days the Prime Minister started her public engage-
ments with a *darshan*, or audience, at which selected groups,
often very poor and from remote parts of India, were taken into
the compound of Number One, Safdarjang Road to meet her
'informally'. No *darshan* had been arranged for 31st October.
Mrs Gandhi had returned the night before, cutting short a tour
of Orissa. In her last public speech, made on that tour, Mrs
Gandhi appeared to foresee her own death. She said, 'I do not
worry whether I live or not. As long as there is any breath in me,
I will go on serving you. When I die, every single drop of my
blood will give strength to India and sustain united India.' Mrs
Gandhi had come back early because her grandchildren had
been involved in a car accident in Delhi. The whole of her
family had been receiving threatening letters from Sikhs enraged by the army attack on the Golden Temple in Amritsar and
Mrs Gandhi feared the accident might have been an attempt on
her grandchildren's lives.

The compounds of Mrs Gandhi's home and her office were
separated by a fence with a wicket-gate. As the Prime Minister,
accompanied as usual by her Personal Assistant, R.K. Dhawan, approached that gate, she smiled at Beant Singh, the Sikh
Sub-Inspector of Police on duty there. As she did so he drew his
revolver and fired at her. She fell to the ground and Constable
Satwant Singh, the Sikh on duty on the other side of the gate,
emptied his sten gun into her body. Many of his bullets missed
and ricocheted off the concrete path.

After shooting the Prime Minister he had been appointed to
guard, Beant Singh hung his walkie-talkie on the fence, lifted
his hands above his head and said, 'I have done what I had to do.
Now you do what you have to do.' He had taken revenge for the
Indian army's attack on the Golden Temple in Amritsar, the
shrine which stands at the heart of Sikhism.

The two bodyguards were bundled into the police post in the
office compound where an altercation started with the commandos from the Indo-Tibetan Border Police who provided the
outer security ring for the Prime Minister's house. Beant Singh
was shot dead and Satwant Singh was seriously wounded.

Ironically, Beant Singh was a Mazhabi Sikh, a descendant of Untouchables who had been converted to Sikhism and were despised by the dominant caste of that religion.

There were no ambulance, no blood supplies and no special medical team on standby; so Dhawan and Mrs Gandhi's Italian daughter-in-law, Sonia, had to put the Prime Minister into an Indian-made Ambassador car for the three-mile drive to the All India Institute of Medical Sciences. There she was received by panic-stricken junior doctors. When their seniors arrived Mrs Gandhi was put on heart/lung bypass machinery, and blood was pumped into her. The doctors did not declare her dead until 2.20 in the afternoon, but she was in fact clinically dead when she arrived at the hospital. The Superintendent of the All India Institute of Medical Sciences later said that more than twenty bullet wounds had been found in her body. They punctured her liver, kidney and arm, and some arteries and veins on the right-hand side of her body. The government-controlled All India Radio did not receive permission to announce the death until 6 in the evening, five hours after millions of Indians had learnt from local news agencies and the External Services of the BBC that their Prime Minister had been shot dead.

One of those who listened to the BBC for news of the Prime Minister's assassination was her only surviving son, Rajiv. On 31st October he was campaigning for the Congress (Indira) Party in the Hooghly Delta below Calcutta. A police patrol stopped his cavalcade and told him that he must return to Delhi immediately because something very serious had happened. Rajiv Gandhi drove to a helipad from where he flew to Calcutta airport. There he tuned in to the twelve-thirty bulletin of the BBC's World Service to hear Satish Jacob report that Mrs Gandhi's condition was grave. A few minutes later Satish Jacob confirmed to London that the Prime Minister had died. Rajiv Gandhi flew from Calcutta to Delhi where he was met by, among others, his close friend Amitabh Bacchan, the top-ranking Bombay film star.

According to the film star, Rajiv Gandhi's first concern on landing at Delhi airport was for his own family. 'First of all he wanted to know whether his wife and children were all right.

Then he tried to find out something about the security. From the airport we drove straight to the hospital where his mother had been taken. When he reached the gates of the hospital and could not get through the vast crowd he turned to me and asked me about my illness. "How are you?" he asked. "When I was in Calcutta I met someone who said he had a cure for your illness. I want you to meet him. I will tell you about him." It is a marvellous thing that he was able to think about the person next to him, about his friend in spite of everything that had happened to him. His spirit was unbowed and he could still think about his friend.'

There was a report that Rajiv Gandhi did in fact break down when he first heard that his mother had died. He denies this. 'Let me say that some newspapers or magazines reported that when I heard the news I went to the loo and had a bawl. That's all rubbish. I was fairly upset but that is not the way I give expression to my emotions . . . I was sitting in the cockpit with the pilots actually when they took off; it was an Indian Airlines plane. When I heard this (that Mrs Gandhi had passed away), I came back and told Dikshit Ji [Uma Shankar Dikshit, present Governor of West Bengal] and others. And I just sat down one seat apart.'[1]

Mrs Gandhi was the first Indian Prime Minister to be assassinated but the third to die in office. When her father, Pandit Nehru, and his successor, Lal Bahadur Shastri, died, a senior minister was sworn in as interim Prime Minister until the Congress Party could elect a new leader. This time senior Congress leaders, including the Finance Minister Pranab Mukherji, who had been campaigning with Rajiv Gandhi that day, decided that the succession must be assured immediately. So the 39-year-old former airline pilot, who had been involved in politics for only four years, was sworn in that evening in the Darbar Hall of the Presidential Palace by the Sikh President of India, Giani Zail Singh. Although opposition leaders criticised this breach of custom, it proved to be a very wise decision.

Mrs Gandhi had deliberately decimated the leadership of her own party. She had brooked no rival, and so there was no member of her Cabinet with the stature to see India through the dangerous and uncertain days ahead. The only hope of maintaining stability was the charisma of the Nehru/Gandhi family and Rajiv, although he held no post in the government, was heir to that dynasty.

The evening after Mrs Gandhi died, anti-Sikh riots broke out along the main road leading to the All India Institute of Medical Sciences. The next day India seemed to be going up in flames. Almost the only state which was not affected by the communal frenzy was the Sikhs' homeland, Punjab. There Hindus waited anxiously for the Sikhs to take their revenge, but extensive deployment of the army and the responsible behaviour of many Sikh leaders prevented the backlash.

In the capital for two days gangs of hooligans, often led by local Congress Party workers, roamed the streets, killing, burning and looting at will. In some cases the police actively joined in the mayhem, in others they turned a blind eye. Reports of Sikh railway passengers being butchered were ominous reminders of the holocaust of partition. Reporting by police stations to headquarters was so limited and inaccurate that the Commissioner of Police did not know what was going on. Deliberate rumour-mongering by some Hindus created further confusion designed to enflame feeling against the Sikhs. Exaggerated stories of Sikhs rejoicing at Mrs Gandhi's death were spread, although there is no doubt that in some cases Sikhs did infuriate Hindus by celebrating her assassination. One senior official insisted that a train from the Punjab had arrived at Sahibabad just outside Delhi with hundreds of dead bodies on it. He said the passengers had all been butchered by Sikhs. I sent a journalist to Sahibabad and he found that there was absolutely no truth in the report.

In the midst of all this uncertainty Satish Jacob stumbled on one of the worst massacres which did take place in Delhi. On Friday 2nd November he crossed the income-tax office bridge over the River Jumna and drove to Trilokpuri, a sprawling new working-class housing area. A small group of agitated residents told him to go to Block 32. They said, 'Something dreadful has happened.' When he reached the block the first thing he saw was three charred bodies laid out on the verandah of a small brick house. As he walked down the narrow lane he found bodies on the verandahs of almost every house. They were obviously Sikhs because their long hair had been cut after they had been killed and it was still lying beside their bodies. Satish Jacob could smell the fumes of the kerosene which had been used to burn the bodies. Some of them had been pierced with iron bars. Most of the houses had been ransacked. The dazed women and children of the Sikh families were still in their houses. Many of them were weeping. Most were too stunned to talk. However one elderly Sikh woman related her experience. She said, 'Hordes of people, mobs in their hundreds invaded this block. They killed and burned all Sikh men they could find. There was no way of escaping. They were like wild beasts, not humans. We had done them no harm.' A crowd of Hindus gathered as Satish Jacob was talking to that elderly Sikh woman. They told him they were residents of Trilokpuri but had had nothing to do with the massacre. They said that gangs of *goondas* (hooligans) had swarmed into the suburbs and committed the atrocities.

Then Dr Ashfaq, an elderly Muslim Satish Jacob knew from his home in the old city of Delhi, called him aside. He told Satish that the slaughter had lasted for four hours and confirmed that gangs from outside Trilokpuri were responsible for much of the bloodshed. He added that some local residents had also taken part. Apparently the gangs had first attacked the nearby Sikh *gurudwara*, or temple, and then moved into Block 32. The Sikhs put up a fight but were hopelessly outnumbered. Dr Ashfaq said that the police officer in charge of the area and three other policemen had stood and watched all this happening.

Satish Jacob went to the police station where he asked Sub-Inspector Suryavir Singh why he had not taken any action. The police officer replied, 'We were helpless. We only had batons to protect ourselves.' Just as Satish was leaving, Deputy Inspector-General Hukam Chand Jatav arrived from police headquarters. He was beside himself with anger and shouted at the local police officer, 'Why didn't you report what was happening in your area to headquarters?'

'Sahib, what could we do?' replied Sub-Inspector Suryavir Singh. 'We were hopelessly outnumbered. We couldn't defend ourselves.'

'What do you mean? All right, you had lost your guts. Had you lost your voices too? Don't you have a wireless or a telephone?'

'Sahib, we did not know what to report. We didn't know what was happening. How could we give details?'

'That's not true. You were either too frightened or too involved yourselves to let us know the true position. Everyone else here knew what was happening. Why didn't you?'

'Sahib, it isn't that easy . . .'

'Shut up, you are under arrest,' shouted the Deputy Inspector-General and ordered his men to take the Sub-Inspector away.

Rahul Bedi, a reporter for the *Indian Express*, also entered Trilokpuri on the afternoon of 2nd November. He was told by residents that the slaughter had lasted for thirty hours. At one local police station he was told that nothing of consequence had happened. When he asked about a lorry with charred decomposing bodies in it parked in the yard, a police officer said, 'The Station House Officer Sahib knows about these deaths but he is in Delhi and will deal with them on his return.' Bedi did not find the armed forces any more helpful. He informed two army officers about the ghastly happenings in Trilokpuri and they promised to send help, but three and a half hours later there were still no soldiers in the area. An airforce officer stationed on the bridge over the Jumna flatly refused to help. A second-lieutenant on the city's main ring-road said, 'I have no orders to intercede in any emergency.'

The government itself admits that throughout India more than 2,717 people were killed in the anti-Sikh riots. Almost all of them were Sikhs. Some 2,150 of them died in Delhi. There the rioters were mainly brought in from the slums to the areas they attacked. Many Sikhs said that local Hindu residents sheltered them from the mobs. Still, according to official estimates, 50,000 Sikhs fled from the capital of their country to Punjab for safety. Another 50,000 took refuge in special camps set up by the government and voluntary agencies.

In the absence of an official inquiry, three different groups of eminent citizens conducted their own inquiries. They found evidence that local policing had collapsed and that in five places local leaders of the Congress Party had instigated the violence. One of the groups, the Citizens' Commission, consisting of a former Chief Justice of India, a former Home Secretary, a former Secretary of the Commonwealth, and a former Secretary of the External Affairs Ministry, said, 'The remarkable uniformity in the pattern of crimes committed, with some local variations, strongly suggests that at some stage the objective became to teach the Sikhs a lesson.' The report also spoke of 'the incredible and abysmal failure of the police, the instigation [of riots] by dubious political elements, the equivocal role of the information media [the government-controlled radio and television services] and the inertia, apathy and indifference of the official machinery.'

The People's Union for Democratic Rights and the People's Union for Civil Liberties were even more specific in their report. It said, 'In the areas which were most affected, such as Trilokpuri, Mangolpuri and Sultanpuri, the mobs were led by local Congress Indira politicians and hoodlums of that locality.'

Rajiv Gandhi came under strong pressure to hold an official inquiry into those allegations. He eventually agreed in April, five months after the violence took place. Members of the Sikh religious party, the Akali Dal, claim that he delayed the announcement of the inquiry until after the general election and the elections to state assemblies which he needed to win convincingly to establish his position as Prime Minister. According to the Sikh politicians, Rajiv Gandhi feared that an inquiry would be unpopular with Hindu voters. The government at first maintained that an inquiry would be dangerous because it would 'reopen old wounds'. When the Home Minister did eventually announce the inquiry, it was said to be part of a package of concessions designed to restore normality in Punjab. By that time the riots had left a deep scar on relations between Sikhs and Hindus. In his book *India: The Siege Within*, M.J. Akbar has written that Mahatma Gandhi's assassination by a Hindu 'shocked the country out of its communal madness'. Mrs Gandhi's assassination by two Sikhs might well have shocked the community out of its anger over the attack on the Golden Temple. The Delhi riots put an end to that hope.

There is no knowing how long the anti-Sikh violence in Delhi would have continued if Rajiv Gandhi himself had not visited the worst affected areas very early on 3rd November, only hours before the start of his mother's cremation. That visit appears to have convinced the new Prime Minister that serious and co-ordinated measures were necessary to restore the writ of the government.

The Information Minister told me that the new Prime Minister himself ordered the Chief of the Army Staff to take some drastic steps to restore order. By midday tracked armoured personnel carriers were parked by the India Gate in the centre of New Delhi and lorry-loads of soldiers were patrolling the streets. But the army had arrived too late for Mrs Gandhi's funeral.

Vast crowds had turned out to see Mahatma Gandhi, Nehru and Shastri's funeral processions, but the streets of New Delhi were almost empty as Indira Gandhi's body, laid out on a gun carriage with the face exposed, wound its way slowly to the cremation ground. Indians used to flock to see their Prime Minister, but fear kept them away from her last journey.

As Rajiv Gandhi, a sombre and dignified figure, stood by his mother's pyre, he must have wondered how he was to cope with the legacy she had left him. He was aware of his mother's weaknesses as well as her strengths, and he knew that the weaknesses had, in no small measure, been responsible for her death. He already knew that there had been glaring omissions in the security arrangements for his mother, amounting almost to criminal negligence. For instance, according to the police guidelines on the Prime Minister's security, Mrs Gandhi should have been surrounded by a ring of security men on the morning she died. This was not the case. Satwant Singh had no business to be on duty inside the Prime Minister's house that day. He had just returned from two months' leave in the Gurdaspur district of Punjab, a hotbed of Sikh extremism on the border with Pakistan. He should therefore have been kept on the perimeter until his superiors were confident that he had not been affected by the violent hostility of many Sikh villagers, who felt that Mrs Gandhi had committed the grossest form of sacrilege by sending the army into the Golden Temple complex. Satwant Singh had arranged to be put on duty beside his accomplice simply by claiming to have an upset stomach and so needing to be near a lavatory. Beant Singh's superior officers knew that he had been meeting Sikh extremists in one of Delhi's main Sikh temples, and had removed him from the Prime Minister's security squad of the Delhi Armed Police; but Mrs Gandhi herself had insisted that he be reinstated. Rajiv Gandhi had become suspicious of Satwant Singh's behaviour and had once even had him removed from the inner guard at the Prime Minister's house. Four months after the assassination, in an interview with M.J. Akbar, Rajiv Gandhi said, 'You see, I used to have meetings at Akbar Road [the Prime Minister's office] at night, and often as we were walking back to the living quarters at one o'clock or two o'clock – a couple of times I wondered at his behaviour. He would stand there with his gun pointing straight (at me). I used to think, you know: I have my security chaps around me, but if he presses that trigger, nobody can stop him at this range, he is already in position. After that he was shifted from that place. But then he did this fiddle and came back.'[2]

Mrs Gandhi had been receiving a flood of letters threatening her life and the lives of her family. Threats to her life were also sent to the BBC's office and to our knowledge no attempt was made to investigate them. The fact that the two assassins, who were the key witnesses, were shot by the company of the Indo-Tibetan Border Police did not say much for the latter's discipline either. They had been brought in to help guard Mrs Gandhi when the threats on her life became too serious to leave to the Delhi police alone. Inevitably some have drawn a parallel with the shooting of Lee Harvey Oswald, President Kennedy's assassin. The police map of the assassination, drawn by a Sikh, Balbir Singh, the Assistant Draughtsman (Crime), shows three bullet marks on the roof of Mrs Gandhi's house. The marks also indicate that the plot went deeper than just the schemings of Satwant and Beant Singh. According to P.N. Lekhi, Satwant Singh's lawyer, the post-mortem report says that Mrs Gandhi was also shot seven times in the back; that is, she was shot from behind as well as in front. But it is possible that shots from the two guards hit the Prime Minister in the back when she was lying crumpled on the ground.

It was not only the security surrounding the Prime Minister's person which had become disgracefully lax. A few months after Mrs Gandhi's death her Principal Secretary resigned when it was discovered that junior members of his staff had been photocopying secret documents and selling them to foreign embassies. This laxity had come about because Mrs Gandhi had fallen into the trap of so many oriental potentates: she had surrounded herself with sycophants who told her what she wanted to hear, not what she ought to have heard. Although a democratically elected Prime Minister, she in fact presided over an old-fashioned *darbar*, or court, the perfect breeding ground for gossip and intrigue. Rajiv Gandhi was well aware of the problem. I once asked him what he thought about the wide-spread criticism of his mother's courtiers. He replied, 'You cannot do without a caucus. Anyone in power will have to have one, but it depends on who is in that caucus.' He also knew that the attack on the Golden Temple could have been avoided if his mother had acted earlier against the Sikh fundamentalist Sant Jarnail Singh Bhindranwale, who had been spreading violence, hatred and communal poison in Punjab, India's most prosperous state. The *sant*, or holy man, had turned the sacred Sikh shrine into a fortress from which he had defied the might of the Indian government and the Indian army. The Prime Minister's son had publicly criticised the government's failure to arrest Bhindranwale before he fortified the Golden Temple complex, but his mother had not listened.

Why did Mrs Gandhi not act earlier? There are plausible political explanations. During her last period in office Mrs Gandhi abandoned her party's traditional supporters – Muslims and Harijans or Untouchables – and tried to forge the majority Hindu community into one solid vote block. This had never been achieved before because of the deep divisions of caste. The catalyst for this new political synthesis was the Hindu revivalism sweeping through India. Hindus were beginning to see themselves as the victims of more than thirty years of secularism in which Muslim family law had been protected. Sikhs had been given a state of their own and Harijans or Untouchables had been given special opportunities for education and employment, all at the expense of caste Hindus. As

M.J. Akbar put it, 'Hindu revivalists began saying that in Hindu-majority India it was Hinduism, not Islam, that was now in danger.'[3]

Such was the impact that even Mrs Gandhi began to believe there was bound to be a 'Hindu backlash' against further pampering of the minorities. Far from challenging such revivalism, she decided to ride it as far as it would take her. Mrs Gandhi's change from secular to Hindu politics has led some to suggest that she delayed taking action against Bhindranwale because she was happy to have such an obvious challenge to Hinduism by a minority community. It helped her to weld the Hindu community together.

Some proponents of this theory would have us believe that Mrs Gandhi only took action when the Bhindranwale factor turned against her and when Hindus started to doubt her capacity to protect them. Others take an even more cynical view. They believe that Mrs Gandhi actually wanted to inflict a crushing defeat on the Sikh community in order to win applause from the Hindus. A general election was due at the end of 1984. It was argued that Mrs Gandhi needed a spectacular achievement to restore her image as Durga, the Hindu goddess of destruction, an image she had acquired by defeating the Pakistan army in 1971 and breaking that country in two.

The possibility of Mrs Gandhi ordering another attack on Pakistan to refurbish her image was being discussed in the press. We never believed this to be a serious possibility. Mrs Gandhi, who was by then the Chairperson of the Non-Aligned Movement, was far too conscious of her international role to attack Pakistan without first carefully building up world opinion, as she had done in 1971. General Zia, the military ruler of Pakistan, was much too clever to give her *casus belli*. In fact he did the exact opposite. He went on what he called 'a peace offensive'. So, the cynics argue, Mrs Gandhi had to look elsewhere for an election spectacular, and she found it in Punjab.

Satish Jacob and I have a far less sinister explanation for the attack on the Golden Temple which led directly to Indira Gandhi's death. Indians may have called Mrs Gandhi 'Durga' and the Western press may have called her 'the Iron Lady' or 'the Empress of India', but looking back over the preceding twenty years it is possible to argue that Mrs Gandhi was not a decisive woman, that she was very reluctant to act, and that she only fought back when she was firmly pinned against the ropes. The first great crisis of her Premiership came in 1969 when she split the Congress Party to free herself from the chains with which her father's senior colleagues had shackled her. During her first three years in office she had made very little effort to escape from her imprisonment. It was only when it looked as though 'the grand old men' of the Congress Party might actually be going to throw her out that she reacted. Then she reacted with such political violence that she destroyed the Congress Party, creating in its place a rootless body of time-servers, dependent entirely on her charisma. It was an organisation quite incapable of providing that most invaluable commodity for any ruler – information about the implementation and effect of her policies.

Mrs Gandhi did handle the Bangladesh crisis with a superb sense of timing, but within four years she was on the floor again. This time the corruption and inefficiency of her government had so damaged her credibility that, when she was found guilty on a charge of electoral corruption, even her own enfeebled party made an attempt to get rid of her. The charge was little more than a technicality, and Mrs Gandhi could easily have withstood the pressure on her to resign if she had not allowed the reputation of her government to sink so low. When she did fight back she risked Indian democracy itself by declaring a state of emergency, muzzling Parliament, the courts and the press, and arresting all her leading opponents. Once again with Mrs Gandhi it proved to be a case of not 'too little, too late', but 'too much, too late'.

Thanks to the incompetence and overweening ambition of some of her opponents, Mrs Gandhi did manage to recover from the defeat inflicted on her when she asked India to endorse her Emergency in a general election. But when she returned to power in 1980 she once again showed a strange reluctance to act decisively.

By 1984 her reputation had slumped once more. Unrest over illegal immigration in the north-eastern state of Assam had been allowed to drift to disaster, with three thousand people being massacred in an election Mrs Gandhi forced on the Assamese people. In Uttar Pradesh, the heartland of India, Muslims had been the victims of some of the worst violence since independence. Punjab appeared to be ruled by a fanatical fundamentalist preacher who was being talked of as the 'Khomeini of the Sikhs'. By-elections were going badly for Mrs Gandhi's Congress in spite of her son Rajiv's attempts to revive her party. Mrs Gandhi appeared uncertain how to tackle the many problems she faced. Marie Seton, the English writer and film critic, had been an intimate friend of Mrs Gandhi for more than thirty years. Miss Seton, who herself died early in 1985, last saw Mrs Gandhi in Delhi shortly before the attack on the Golden Temple. When they met over a family lunch, Miss Seton sensed in Mrs Gandhi a mood of fatigue and helplessness. 'She seemed like a woman who'd run out of steam,' she later told Ian Jack of the *Sunday Times*. 'She's always been a private person, an introvert rather than an extrovert, instinctive rather than empirical, but now she seemed to be genuinely at a loss and more melancholic than I'd ever known her. I took away the impression that she no longer knew whom to trust, or what advice to act on. I think she'd begun to doubt her own judgment. I felt worried and sorry for her.'

She was not the only person to sense that Mrs Gandhi might be losing her grip. There was much talk in the Central Hall of Parliament, where members gather to exchange political gossip, of the possibility of an electoral defeat for the Congress. The press were not optimistic about Mrs Gandhi's prospects either. So, we believe, Mrs Gandhi, facing disaster once again, was forced to take drastic action against Bhindranwale. This time, tragically, she did not get away with 'too much, too late'.

By her death Indira Gandhi had ensured the succession, but she left her son a nation more bitterly divided than at any time since partition. The Sikhs, the most prosperous and progressive community in India, had been humiliated. Mrs Gandhi had played into the hands of the Sikh fundamentalists, and many of them were now openly separatist. The riots which followed her death caused many Sikhs who had never thought of secession to wonder whether they were safe within India.

2

The Sikhs

The population of Delhi has mushroomed since independence. Then it was 300,000; now it is nearly seven million. This alarming population explosion started with the arrival of Sikh and Hindu refugees from Pakistan at the time of partition. Until 1984 they had always lived in complete amity. Ever since independence there have been Hindu-Muslim troubles, but no one ever thought of the possibility of Hindu-Sikh clashes. The two lived as one community.

Nowhere was this more apparent that outside our office on the tarmac square set back from the main road to Agra. It is an open-air automobile workshop, petrol station and taxi stand. Bhim Sen Pollai, a Hindu, runs the mechanical workshop, but for electrical repairs we go to a Sikh, Harbans Singh Saini. Our punctures are also repaired by a Sikh, Jarnail Singh. The taxi drivers spend most of their days sitting on *charpoys* or string beds, playing cards or gossiping. Fares are hard to come by. Some of the taxi drivers are Hindus, others Sikhs. Among the Sikhs are three brothers, Hardev Singh, Sukhdev Singh and Baldev Singh Bhinder. On the morning of 1st November 1984, the day after Mrs Gandhi's assassination, Hindu mobs went on the rampage in the nearby markets of Bhogal and Ashram.

Seeing the smoke rising from the burning shops and houses of the Sikhs, Hardev Singh decided to remove his taxi from the stand before the mobs came down the Agra road. Discretion being the better part of valour, he had the first haircut and shave of his life so that he would not be recognisable as a Sikh. Sukhdev Singh valued his religion more than his livelihood, so he took refuge in a nearby house, leaving his taxi to the mercy of the mobs. They burnt three taxis on our stand that day.

By good fortune Baldev Singh was in the family's village home in Punjab; so he too still wears the beard and turban of a Sikh. His youngest brother Hardev Singh was the only member of the family who had to bear the taunts of his mother and father for denying his faith. He said, 'I felt utterly miserable and guilty. My father was shocked when he saw me in the evening. He abused and cursed me. My mother and other relatives were appalled when they saw me in our village of Mominwal. But what could I do? I had to save my life. Baldev's brother-in-law was roasted alive in Nand Nagri [East Delhi], so were two young cousins. My cousins' grandfather, when he saw his two young grandsons being thrown in the fire by mobs, jumped into the pyre himself from the roof of his house.'

The three brothers are all back on the taxi stand with their Hindu friends. The Hindu mechanic, the Sikh electrician and the puncture-mender are back at work too. But none of them will ever forget the day when Hardev Singh deserted the symbols of his faith, decreed by the last of his Gurus.

The Sikhs are the people of the Gurus. The word 'Sikh' means disciple, and their religion was evolved by a succession of ten teachers, the first of whom, Guru Nanak, was born 500 years ago, comparatively recently for the founder of a major religion. He was born into an era of violent political change in a part of India, the Punjab, long familiar with the passage of invading armies intent on either loot or capture of the capital Delhi. During Nanak's lifetime the first Mughal Emperor ascended the throne and the last Guru died only a year after the last great Mughal, Aurangzeb.

In the days of Guru Nanak, Islam, the religion of the Mughals, was in the hands of backward-looking clerics. Hinduism, the historic religion of India, was caste-bound and dominated by Brahmin priests and their rituals. However, religious orthodoxy was not unchallenged. Several Islamic and Hindu movements had grown up which stressed mysticism rather than ritual. The first Sikh Guru was deeply influenced by that mystic tradition. Mysticism is the search for the heart of religion, and so there is inevitably much in common between mystics of all beliefs. After all, when the trappings of dogma are cut back, every faith seeks to meet the same desire of man, his desire for a god to worship and give purpose to his life. Guru Nanak was a mystic and so he inevitably combined much of those two apparently irreconcilable religions – monotheistic Islam and Hinduism with its pantheon – into his teaching. The Sikh scriptures, the Guru Granth Sahib, contain the verses of Guru Nanak, who wrote prolifically in Punjabi, and his successors, but they also include verses by Hindu and Muslim mystics.

Guru Nanak took the doctrines of reincarnation and karma from Hinduism. According to Hindu beliefs, a man's condition in this life is governed by his actions in his past life, or, as Guru Nanak put it, 'one reaps what one sows and one eats what one earns.' But he took the Islamic doctrine of brotherhood, rejecting totally the Hindu caste system. The Guru also appears to have been influenced by Islam in his firm commitment to monotheism. In fact the central teaching of Sikhism is the oneness of God. He is eternal, ineffable and never incarnate like the gods of Hinduism or, indeed, the God of Christianity. Nanak described God as '*nirankar*', or formless, and condemned the Hindu practice of worshipping images of the deity. But imagery has a way of creeping back into religions; that is perhaps why Sikhs pay such reverence to their shrines and copies of their holy book. The Guru believed in approaching God through devotion and meditation, and had no time for ritual observances, as this story about his visit to one of the most sacred Hindu pilgrimage centres clearly shows.

When he visited Hardwar on the Ganges, he saw Hindus throwing water towards the east for the relief of the '*manes*' [spirits] of their ancestors. He joined his hands so as to form a cup, and began to throw water to the west. The crowd was astonished, and inquired what manner of man it was who, contrary to all ancient custom, threw water towards the setting instead of towards the rising sun. He told them he was throwing it to irrigate a field he had sown in his native village. The spectators thought he was crazy and told him the water could never reach his field, which was too far away. He replied that their departed ancestors were much further away, and the water he threw was more likely to reach his field than the water they threw was to reach their ancestors. 'You call me a fool,' he said, 'but ye are much greater fools yourselves.'[1]

Guru Nanak also strongly rejected the caste system. He instituted the *Guru ka langar*, or Guru's kitchen, where his followers would all eat together in order to break down the barriers of caste.

For all the differences between Nanak and brahminical teaching, Hindus have always regarded the Sikhs as part and parcel of Hinduism. They believe that anyone born a Hindu remains a Hindu throughout all his lives, no matter what doctrines he may profess. This is one reason why Sikhs have always striven so hard to establish their separate identity and feared that their religion might be reabsorbed by Hinduism.

Guru Nanak travelled widely, visiting Hindu and Muslim holy places, but he was himself a Punjabi; he wrote in Punjabi and it was in the Punjab that his teachings took root. Within forty years of his death Nanak's followers had grown into a body of believers recognised by the Mughal Emperor Akbar. With a grant of land donated by the Emperor, the Sikhs set about building a shrine, around which grew their holy city of Amritsar. Amritsar means 'pool of nectar' and refers to the sacred pool, or *sarowar*, excavated by the fourth Guru. The Golden Temple itself, the Hari Mandir or Temple of God, was built in the middle of the *sarowar* by the fifth Guru, Arjun. Although 'Hari' is a name of the Hindu god Vishnu, the Hari Mandir was, and still is, very different from a Hindu temple. The foundation stone was laid by a Muslim mystic, the Sufi Mian Mir of Lahore. The temple had four doorways instead of the usual one, to indicate that it was open to all the four main caste divisions of Hindu society. Devotees had to step downwards to enter the temple, to remind them of the humility necessary to come close to God.

Guru Arjun realised the necessity of providing an authorised version of the scriptures to enshrine Guru Nanak's teaching. He it was who compiled the holy book of the Sikhs, the 'Adi Granth', or first book, which later became known as the Guru Granth Sahib, and installed it within the Golden Temple. Amritsar and its Golden Temple are as central to Sikhism as Mecca and the Ka'aba are to Muslims. That is why the Indian army's attack caused such profound shock throughout the Sikh community.

Guru Arjun, the builder of the Golden Temple, was also the Sikhs' first martyr. He fell foul of the Emperor Akbar's successor, Jehangir, who suspected the Guru of being in league with his rebellious son and sentenced him to death. The Guru was imprisoned in the city of Lahore where he was tortured to death. Sikhs have always set great store by their martyrs and it was particularly unwise of the Indian army to surround Guru Arjun's Golden Temple on the anniversary of his martyrdom. The Emperor Jehangir did not foresee the potential of Arjun's legacy. He wrote of him:

> In Gobindwal which is on the river Biyah (Beas) there was a Hindu named Arjun, in the garments of sainthood and sanctity, so much so that he had captured many of the simple-hearted Hindus, and even of the ignorant and foolish followers of Islam, by his ways and manners, and they had loudly sounded the drum of his holiness. They called him 'Guru', and from all sides stupid people crowded to worship and manifest complete faith in him. For three or four generations (of spiritual successors) they had kept this shop warm. Many times it had occurred to me to put a stop to this vain affair or to bring him into the assembly of Islam. [2]

That 'vain affair' and those 'stupid people' grew into one of the world's major religions, long outlasting Jehangir's Mughal Empire.

Guru Arjun's young son and successor, Hargobind, constructed the other important shrine within the Golden Temple complex, the Akal Takht or Eternal Throne, to be a symbol of the temporal power of Sikhism. As a gesture of defiance to the Mughal Emperor, he held court there from a throne higher than that of the Emperor's. The martyrdom of Guru Arjun changed Sikhism into a more militant and militaristic faith. From then on Sikhs maintained, literally, an army of the faithful.

This army was welded into a formidable fighting force by Guru Gobind Singh, the tenth and last of the Gurus, who also commanded his followers not to cut their hair or shave their beards, thereby giving Sikhs a distinctive physical appearance. It was in 1699 that he took measures to protect the Sikhs' identity, not only from reabsorption into Hinduism, but also from the religious persecution of the Muslim rulers, who were by now openly hostile to the Sikhs. He summoned a grand assembly at Anandpur in Punjab where he announced the formation of a new order of Sikhs called the 'Khalsa' or pure ones. To distinguish them from other men and women, the Guru ordered members of the Khalsa not to cut their hair (*kes*) or shave their beards, to carry a comb (*kangha*), to wear a steel bangle (*kara*), and breeches (*kach*), and to carry a dagger (*kirpan*). These became the five 'k's' by which an orthodox Sikh can still be identified today. The Guru instructed all men who joined the Khalsa to take the name 'Singh' or lion. Women were also baptised into the Khalsa, taking the name 'Kaur' or princess. Sikhism has always respected women's independence and there are several formidable Sikh women politicians today.

The pure ones became the core of the Sikh army. Their cry was 'Raj karega Khalsa' − 'The Khalsa shall rule!' Sikhs still repeat this cry which, if taken literally, inevitably leads to a conflict of loyalties in a modern secular state like India. One of the central tenets of Sikhism is that spiritual and temporal power, religion and politics, are indivisible. The Khalsa did not succeed in ruling the Punjab or defeating the Mughal Emperor. During the eight years between the formation of the Khalsa and the death of Emperor Aurangzeb they fought a series of desperate but indecisive battles with Mughal armies.

When Guru Gobind Singh was assassinated in 1708, he left behind him the legend of a poet, preacher and guide, skilled in warfare, courageous, defiant and unbowed, to fire the imagination of future generations of Sikhs. When followers of Bhindranwale were asked why they found him so attractive a leader, they said, 'He is just like another Guru Gobind Singh.' Before he died the Guru decreed that there would be no other Guru after him. The holy scriptures, the Guru Granth Sahib, would provide spiritual guidance in place of a living Guru, while the temporal affairs of the community would be in the hands of the 'Panth', the community of the Khalsa and their representatives.

Gobind Singh taught the Sikhs that they must preserve their identity at all costs. In his time the beard and long hair were symbols to identify those Sikhs who were prepared to fight the Muslim challenge to their faith. To Bhindranwale the five 'k's were the symbols of those Sikhs who were prepared to fight the Hindus.

By the middle of the eighteenth century the Mughal Empire was in decline and had become so weak that the Emperor ceded the Punjab to the Afghan ruler Ahmad Shah Abdali. The Mughal rulers could not even defend their capital against the Afghan marauders. But Ahmad Shah Abdali found the Sikhs a very different matter. As one Indian historian put it: 'The simple, untrained peasant of Guru Hargobind had now become a regular, well-equipped soldier of the Khalsa, adept in the use of arms and trained in the methods of guerrilla warfare. The Khalsa had further tasted the sweets of victory and acquired a love of plunder.'[3] The Khalsa found justification for plundering the Afghans in the saying of their last Guru that 'Robbing the robber is no sin.'

The Sikhs' attacks on his troops and baggage trains led the Afghan king to take revenge by raiding Amritsar. He blew up the Golden Temple, which represented the spiritual power of God, and filled the holy pool with the carcasses of slaughtered cattle. The Akal Takht, which stood opposite the Golden Temple and represented the temporal power of God, was razed to the ground. Each time the Sikhs, undaunted, rebuilt their holy places and maintained them until the Afghan power was spent and Abdali retreated from the Punjab for ever. From that day onwards no army has entered the holiest shrines of Sikhism – until, that is, Mrs Gandhi sent in the troops in June 1984 to remove the fundamentalist preacher Bhindranwale who had turned the Akal Takht into a fortress.

George Thomas, an English adventurer, who established his own private kingdom at Hansi in the modern state of Haryana not far from Delhi, wrote an eye-witness account of the Sikh warriors who had been the scourge of the Afghans.

After performing the requisite duties of their religion by ablution and prayer they [the Sikhs], comb their hair and beard with peculiar care, then, mounting their horses, ride forth towards the enemy, with whom they engage in a continued skirmish advancing and retreating, until man and horse become equally fatigued; they then draw off to some distance from the enemy, and, meeting with cultivated ground, they permit their horses to graze of their own accord, while they parch a little grain for themselves, and after satisfying nature by this frugal repast, if the enemy be near, they renew the skirmishing; should he have retreated, they provide forage for their cattle, and endeavour to procure a meal for themselves . . . Accustomed from their earliest infancy to a life of hardship and difficulty, the Sikhs despise the comforts of a tent; in lieu of this, each horseman is furnished with two blankets, one for himself, and the other for his horse. These blankets which are placed beneath the saddle, with a gram-bag and heel ropes, comprise in time of war, the baggage of a Sikh. Their cooking utensils are carried on *tuttoos* [ponies]. Considering this mode of life, and the extraordinary rapidity of their movements, it cannot be a matter of wonder if they perform marches, which to those who are only accustomed to European warfare, must appear almost incredible.[4]

The departure of the Afghans left the field open for the Sikhs. One of their *misldars*, or chieftains, Ranjit Singh, helped by the decline of all major military powers – except the British – in the north-west of India, became Maharaja of Punjab at the age of twenty-one, and went on to prove, in a way unique in Sikh history, that the Sikhs could create and rule an empire.

Illiterate and blind in one eye after a childhood attack of

smallpox, Ranjit Singh extended his empire from Kashmir and the borders of China and Tibet to the Khyber Pass and down to the frontiers of Sindh in the south-west. The British, by then ensconced in Delhi with the Mughal Emperor as their pensioner, prevented Ranjit Singh from expanding his empire to the south but they never had the temerity to attack the Sikh monarch. Their relationship with Ranjit Singh was one of equals. During the last years of his reign the Governor-General of India, Lord Auckland, paid an official visit to the court in Lahore.

By that time Ranjit Singh was an eastern potentate with a court of a splendour that would have matched the Mughals at their best. Lord Auckland's sister, Emily Eden, wrote that the Maharaja looked 'exactly like an old mouse, with grey whiskers and one eye' and observed that although he arrived with two stockings on he contrived to remove one so that he could sit comfortably, his foot in one hand, cross-legged on a chair. Her brother's military secretary, William Osborne, was more impressed with the old man when he met him.

> The *coup d'oeil* was most striking; every walk in the garden was lined with troops, and the whole space behind the throne was crowded with Runjeet's chiefs, mingled with natives from Candahar, Caubul, and Affghanistan, blazing with gold and jewels, and dressed and armed in every conceivable variety of colour and fashion.
>
> Cross-legged in a golden chair, dressed in simple white, wearing no ornaments but a single string of pearls round the waist, and the celebrated Koh-y-Nur, or mountain of light, on his arm − (the jewel rivalled, if not surpassed, in brilliancy by the glance of fire which every now and then shot from his single eye as it wandered restlessly round the circle) − sat the lion of Lahore.[5]

Ranjit Singh had a passion for fine jewels, and had managed to extract the Koh-i-Noor from the deposed king of Afghanistan, Shah Shuja, in return for freeing him from imprisonment in Kashmir. The Maharaja wore it on all public occasions and carried it wherever he went. But the Koh-i-Noor was soon to be lost to the Punjab. Queen Victoria gained the diamond when the British captured the Punjab. She had it cut and polished to less than half its original size.

Ranjit Singh was not only fond of beautiful jewels. He engaged some of the prettiest women of the Punjab, Kashmir and Persia to be soldiers in a regiment he formed solely of women who regularly drilled before him in uniform. William Osborne refers to them as the 'Amazons'. He said the Maharaja admitted to him with a laugh that they were the only regiment he couldn't manage and gave him more trouble than the rest of the army put together.

Elephants were kept for ceremonial occasions at court but the Maharaja himself was much more interested in horseflesh. His own horses were caparisoned in a finery which seemed almost outrageous to sedate English tastes. Emily Eden recounts that at one elaborate presentation ceremony a particular horse took his fancy and 'he quite forgot all his state, and ran out in the sun to feel its legs and examine it.'[6]

The glitter of the Lahore *darbar*, or court, was the embodiment of a formidable empire built upon the personality of Ranjit Singh and the might of his armies. His ministers included Hindus and Muslims. The Maharaja was well aware that the majority of his subjects and much of the army were non-Sikh, and out of respect for them he celebrated the festivals of all the main religions. It was all very far from the theocracy of Guru Gobind Singh. In his personal life Ranjit Singh was not an irreligious man; he regularly listened to recitations from the Guru Granth Sahib, for instance. But he certainly did not follow the tenth Guru's injunction on alcohol, being extremely fond of a certain 'fire water' he had especially prepared and which reputedly contained ground pearls. He candidly admitted that he drank for excitement and developed a partiality for Scotch whisky.

The Maharaja was as secular in his choice of wives as in his choice of ministers, several of the twenty-two being Muslims. The bachelor status of the Governor-General, Lord Auckland, attracted his curiosity. Emily Eden recorded a conversation with Lord Auckland on the subject. The Governor-General explained that he did not have a wife because, 'only one was allowed in England, and if she turned out a bad one, he could not easily get rid of her. Ranjeet said that was a bad custom; that the Sikhs were allowed twenty-five wives, and they did not dare to be bad, because he could beat them if they were. G. replied that was an excellent custom, and he would try to introduce it when he got home.'[7]

The Maharaja inspired devotion in his many wives. When he died, exactly forty years after conquering his capital Lahore, four of them together with seven of his 'slave girls' chose to burn themselves alive on his funeral pyre – committing *sati* in accordance with the old Hindu tradition forbidden by the Gurus of the Sikh faith.

Under this strong and secular ruler, the priests of the Akal Takht had to content themselves with curbing Hindu practices which were always creeping back into the shrines at Amritsar. They demonstrated their notional control over the Maharaja by occasionally punishing him for such crimes as marrying a Muslim woman who refused to embrace Sikhism or presenting a decorated cloth to the Akal Takht when it had already hung in his court for a couple of days. They could not complain, however, that he neglected Amritsar. The town became a flourishing trading centre because the Maharaja encouraged merchants to settle there. He constructed the upper three floors of the Akal Takht and altered the design and decoration of the Hari Mandir, turning it into the 'Golden' Temple we know today. He made a grant of half a million rupees for the Temple, and invited the most skilled craftsmen of the age, many of them Muslim, to work on it.

Ranjit Singh's army was the backbone of his empire. Sikhs recall its exploits with pride even today. The Khalsa army before Ranjit Singh had been mainly cavalry, armed with matchlocks and using undisciplined hit-and-run techniques. Sikh soldiers despised the infantry. Ranjit Singh soon realised that, with the advent of European-style armies in India, well-drilled infantry, coupled with artillery, was the secret of a successful army. He set about reorganising his forces from top to bottom on European lines, giving financial incentives to overcome Sikh prejudice against the infantry. He invited able European officers like Allard and Ventura, of Napoleon's defeated armies, to train his men. The policy of incentives worked and by the end of Ranjit Singh's reign Sikhs had taken to infantry soldiering and were becoming the dominant community in the regular army.

Within ten years of the death of Ranjit Singh, the British, helped by endless squabbling over the succession, had defeated the Sikh Empire and annexed the Punjab. During the hundred years they ruled the Punjab there were many forces undermining the Sikhs' separate identity.

The most formidable foe of Sikhism was the Hindu revivalist, Swami Dayananda Saraswati, the Luther of Hindu Protestantism. He founded the Arya Samaj or Aryan Society in 1875. Its slogan was 'Back to the Vedas', the first and most ancient of the Hindu scriptures. The Arya Samaj was that rare phenomenon in a religion as tolerant as Hinduism, an energetic proselytizing force. The Arya Samajis maintained that both Punjabi Muslims and Sikhs had been converted from Hinduism in one of their earlier lives and so it was perfectly legitimate to win them back to their original faith.

The social customs of those times would seem to have justified the Arya Samajis' contention that Sikhs were really just Hindus. There was a great deal of intermarriage between the two faiths, and Hindu families often brought up their eldest sons as Sikhs. Hindus would adopt Sikhism in one generation and drop it in the next. The Mehras are now one of the great Hindu business families of Amritsar, but the grandfather of the present head of the family started life as a Sikh. At the age of seven his head was attacked by a 'plague of boils'. The barber who in those days doubled as a surgeon, advised that the boy's hair should be cut off so that the boils could be treated. His father, who was a first-generation Sikh, took the barber's advice and the Mehra family lapsed gently back into Hinduism. Besides close family ties with Hindus, many of the *mahants* or priests in charge of Sikh temples were more Hindu than Sikh. They helped to bring many Hindu customs back into Sikhism, customs like the practice of Untouchability, idol worship and reverence for the cow.

Of course there were Sikh leaders who took vigorous action to defend their faith from what they saw as the insidious threat of Hinduism. The outstanding Sikh movement of the time was that of the Singh Sabhas (assemblies), founded in 1873 by a group of rich, landed and orthodox Sikhs. Their aim was to educate Sikhs and make them more aware of their religion, to free them from Hindu practices and to remind them of their cultural heritage. They declared war on the Arya Samaj by actively trying to convert Hindus. The Sikh community at the time was scattered and predominantly rural. It was not only miles of countryside that separated them. Caste divisions had arisen in a religion founded to eradicate caste. Several new unorthodox sects were also drawing Sikhs from the path of the Khalsa. But the Singh Sabha movement grew rapidly, setting up a network of Khalsa schools where the study of the Guru Granth Sahib and Gurmukhi, the Punjabi language written in a script devised by the second Guru, Angad, were compulsory. In 1902 the first specifically Sikh political organisation was founded – the Chief Khalsa Diwan. It started as a co-ordinating body for the Singh Sabhas and was controlled by a loyalist élite.

The British had a vested interest in encouraging Sikhs to preserve their identity. In the Anglo-Sikh wars which led to the annexation of the Punjab, the British had discovered what excellent soldiers the Sikhs were and, within a decade of their final defeat, the Sikhs were helping the British to put down the Indian Mutiny. This strange transformation came about partly because the Sikhs had nothing but contempt for the sepoys of the East India Company who, under British officers, had formed the major part of the army which had defeated them. As Philip Mason put it in his book on the Indian army, the Sikhs 'resented the presence of Eastern troops in the Punjab; their embryo nationalism had been Punjabi, not Indian, and they were eager to take any chance of getting their own back on the Bengal sepoy, this time with the British on their side.'[8]

When the Mutiny broke out, however, it was far from certain that the Sikhs would remain loyal to their masters. Karl Marx, reporting on the Mutiny for the *New York Daily Tribune*, argued that 'the Sikhs, like the Mohammedans, were making common cause with the Brahmins, and that thus a general union against the British rule, of all the different tribes, was rapidly progressing.' He was proved wrong. With the British thrown out of Delhi, the last Mughal Emperor placed unwillingly at the head of the rebels and most of northern India in turmoil, Frederic Cooper, the Deputy Commissioner of Amritsar during the Mutiny, admitted that he too had his doubts. However he had to hide them at the time to maintain the citizens' confidence in British rule.

> The urgency of the situation had to be explained frankly, while the hope of the eventual triumph, under Providence, had to take the garb of human certainty . . . The population, swelled by the sudden stoppage of the current of traffic from the north, must have increased to nearly one hundred and fifty thousand souls. Every class, creed, grade, and clime of Asia were represented. The trade operations were intimately mixed up with Delhi; the great commission brokers and capitalists who never thought of politics beyond how it affected the money market and who had always steadily backed the . . . Government, experienced a rude shock when it was announced that the Grand Trunk Road was (for the first time since British rule) impassable . . . It remained to be seen whether the poisonous matter, which had for the first time produced temporary cohesion and unity of action among Hindoos and Mahomedans, would be absorbed in the Sikh system. But not withstanding the thriving mission school and church [*gurudwara*, or Sikh temple] close abutting on the holy temple . . . from first to last no symptom of wavering betrayed itself.[9]

The Sikhs were rewarded for their loyalty with a special place in the British Indian army which was radically reformed after the Mutiny. The British insisted that all recruits from the community wore the five 'k's and swore an oath of loyalty on the Guru Granth Sahib. The army regulation said:

> The *paol*, or religious pledges, of the Sikh fraternity, should on no account be interfered with. The Sikh should be permitted to wear his beard, and the hair of his head gathered up, as enjoined by his religion. Any invasion, however slight,

of these obligations would be construed as a desire to subvert his faith, lead to evil consequences, and naturally inspire general distrust and alarm. Even those who have assumed the outward conventional characteristics of Sikhs should not be permitted, after entering the British army, to drop them.[10]

The intention was to build up the Sikhs' identity as a separate martial race which was loyal to the crown.

Sikh participation in the British Indian army reached a peak in the First World War, as Khushwant Singh wrote in his *History of the Sikhs*:

> The number of Sikhs in the services rose from 35,000 at the beginning of 1915 to over 100,000 by the end of the war, forming about a fifth of the army in action . . . Sikh soldiers fought on all fronts of the war in Europe, Turkey and Africa, and did credit to their race by their bravery. Of the 22 military crosses awarded for conspicuous gallantry to Indians, the Sikhs won 14.[11]

After the Great War the loyalty of the Sikhs to the British crown became strained. Punjab's response to Mahatma Gandhi's first civil disobedience movement was enthusiastic. When the Mahatma was arrested on his way to the Punjab the violent protests followed, culminating in the tragic Jallianwala Bagh massacre, a landmark in the history of India's freedom movement.

On 13th April 1919 General R.E.H. Dyer, a member of a well-known family of north Indian brewers, marched a platoon of infantry to the Jallianwala Bagh — a dusty, brick-walled square only a minute or two's walk away from the Golden Temple itself. A large gathering had assembled in the Jallianwala Bagh to attend a political meeting, defying a ban imposed by Dyer. He blocked the only entrance with his troops and ordered them to open fire. Some 379 people were killed and more than 1,200 injured. Among the dead and wounded were many innocent Sikh villagers visiting Amritsar to celebrate the festival of Baisakhi, the anniversary of the creation of the

Khalsa. Weeks of severe martial law followed. In Amritsar, British troops forced Indians to crawl on their bellies down a lane where a British missionary lady had been assaulted. The Jallianwala Bagh massacre and the subsequent martial law brought British relations with their Indian subjects to the lowest ebb since the Mutiny. They also did irreparable damage to the name of the Chief Khalsa Diwan which supported the British action. Dyer was initially hailed as a hero by the British and, to the shock and disgust of the Sikh community at large, by the priests of the Akal Takht and the Golden Temple. By now the two holiest Sikh shrines were in the hands of government nominees. They presented General Dyer with a robe of honour and initiated him into the Khalsa. The following conversation, quoted by Mohinder Singh in his book *The Akali Movement*, is reported to have taken place in the Golden Temple on that occasion.

> 'Sahib,' they said, 'you must become a Sikh.' The General thanked them for the honour, but he objected that he could not, as a British officer, let his hair grow long. Arur Singh (the Sarbrah or manager of the Golden Temple) laughed. 'We will let you off the long hair,' he said. General Dyer offered another objection. 'But I cannot give up smoking.' The priest concluded, 'We will let you give it up gradually.' 'That I promise you,' said the General. 'At the rate of one cigarette a year.'[12]

The Jallianwala Bagh massacre and the fêting of General Dyer by priests loyal to the British, led to the agitation for the reform of Sikh temples, or *gurudwaras*. The agitation, which continued over five years between 1920 and 1925, shattered the myth of the loyal Punjabi once and for all.

The movement's aim was to wrest control of temples from the hands of corrupt and Hinduized *mahants* or priests, many of whom had managed to make themselves the legal owners of the shrines of which they were originally merely guardians. Mohinder Singh gives a description of the reputed goings-on inside the Golden Temple at the turn of the century:

Costly gifts to the temple slowly found their way to the homes of the Sarbrah and other priests. The precincts began to be used by pundits and astrologers; idols were openly worshipped in the Gurudwara premises. According to contemporary accounts, on Basant and Holi festivals the whole place degenerated into a rendezvous for local thieves and bad characters. Pornographic literature was freely sold, and brothels were opened in the neighbouring houses where innocent women visiting the holy temples were made victims of the lust of licentious Sadhus (ascetics), Mahants and their friends.[13]

In 1920 prominent Sikhs started organising groups of protestors to demonstrate against the corrupt priests. Their first major victory came that year when, in the face of a threat by the agitators to hold a mock funeral procession for him, the manager of the Golden Temple submitted his resignation. The other British nominees soon followed and the protesters were left in possession of the holiest Sikh shrine.

This success produced the two institutions which dominate Sikh politics in the Punjab today – the Shiromani Gurudwara Prabandhak Committee and the Akali Dal. The SGPC was created as a committee to manage the newly liberated Golden Temple. It developed into a kind of Sikh parliament, with control over temples in the Punjab and their huge annual incomes. The Akali Dal, later to become a fully fledged political party, began by training and organising volunteers to fight for the cause of the SGPC.

In 1925 the British government surrendered to the Gurudwara agitation, giving the SGPC control of over 200 shrines in the Punjab. That number has now risen to 700, and their revenue provides the finance for the political activities of the Sikh religious party, the Akali Dal. It was the Akali Dal leaders' surrender to Bhindranwale which was to lead to the attack on the Golden Temple complex fifty-nine years later.

The Gurudwara movement also taught the Sikhs the value of Mahatma Gandhi's non-violent tactics, tactics they were to use so effectively against the Indian government during the days of Bhindranwale. The Rev. C.F. Andrews, an Anglican priest and follower of Mahatma Gandhi, described the British reaction to the Akalis' non-violent protests in this account of an incident he himself witnessed.

There were four Akali Sikhs with black turbans facing a band of about two dozen policemen, including two English officers. They had walked slowly up to the line of police just before I had arrived and they were standing silently in front of them at about a yard's distance. They were perfectly still and did not move further forward. Their hands were placed together in prayer and it was clear that they were praying. Then, without the slightest provocation on their part, an Englishman lunged forward the head of his *lathi* [stick] which was bound with brass. He lunged it forward in such a way that his fist which held the staff struck the Akali Sikhs, who were praying, just at the collar bone with great force. It looked the most cowardly blow as I saw it struck and I had the greatest difficulty in keeping myself under control . . . The blow which I saw was sufficient to throw the Akali Sikh and send him to the ground. He rolled over and slowly got up and at once faced the same punishment again. Time after time, one of the four who had gone forward was laid prostrate by repeated blows, now from English officers and now from the police who were under their control . . . The brutality and inhumanity of the whole scene was indescribably increased by the fact that the men who were praying to God had already taken a vow that they would remain silent and peaceful in word and deed. The Akali Sikhs who had taken this vow, both at the Golden Temple before starting and also at the shrine of Guru-ka-Bagh were . . . largely from the army. They had served in many campaigns in Flanders, in France, in Mesopotamia and in East Africa. Some of them at the risk of their own safety must have saved the lives of Englishmen who had been wounded. Now they were felled to the ground at the hands of the English officials serving in the same government which they themselves had served.[14]

After the Akalis had triumphed in the Gurudwara movement, they were faced with a dilemma. On the one hand, they felt bound to continue supporting Mahatma Gandhi and the freedom movement. On the other, they did not want to be swallowed up by the Congress Party. The Mahatma saw the Congress as the party of all Indians — Hindus, Muslims, Sikhs and believers in the many other faiths which flourish in the subcontinent. Like Jinnah and the Muslim League, many Akalis saw this as a ruse to establish Hindu Raj (rule) in India. This should have made the Akalis and the Muslim League natural allies, but Sikhs still retained their antipathy to Muslims, brought up as they were on stories of the Mughal persecution of the Gurus. So Akalis for the most part supported Mahatma Gandhi and the Congress Party's struggle for independence.

One of the legendary martyrs of the independence movement was a Sikh, Bhagat Singh. He was executed by the British for the murder of a British police officer who was believed to have brutally beaten one of the stalwarts of the freedom movement, Lala Lajpat Rai. Lala Lajpat Rai died a few weeks after the assault and Bhagat Singh, as one of the three young men who avenged his death, captured the imagination of the Indian people. As Jawaharlal Nehru wrote:

> Bhagat Singh . . . did not become popular because of his act of terrorism, but because he seemed to vindicate, for the moment, the honour of Lala Lajpat Rai, and through him of the nation. He became a symbol . . . and within a few months each town and village of the Punjab, and to a lesser extent in the rest of northern India, resounded with his name. Innumerable songs grew up about him, and the popularity that the man achieved was something amazing.[15]

The outbreak of war posed a dilemma for the Sikhs. With so many of their community in the armed forces, how could they support the Congress stand of non-cooperation with the government? Many chose not to. One of them was Master Tara Singh, who had dominated Akali politics since the 1920s. Born into a Hindu home, he converted to Sikhism at school. After taking his B A he became a schoolmaster. He soon deserted the classroom for the Akali rostrum, although he never lost his title

'Master'. Master Tara Singh broke with the Congress over the war issue and backed Britain, even being photographed with a steel helmet over his turban to boost recruitment.

In spite of the Akali stand, Sikhs in the army were influenced by nationalism. Belonging to a comparatively prosperous, go-ahead community with strong links with their villages in the Punjab, they were, according to Philip Mason, 'conscious of politics to a higher degree than any other element in the Indian Army'.[16] The mutiny of the Central India Horse in 1940 showed this. A Sikh squadron of the Central India Horse was on its way to Bombay for posting overseas. At Bombay the squadron's train was shunted into a siding for twenty-four hours. This gave four soldiers, who had come under the influence of the Kirti Lehr, a group preaching incendiary peasant communism, an opportunity to encourage the others to mutiny. The squadron refused to go overseas, was court-martialled and its leaders deported to the Andaman Islands. The incident seriously disturbed army headquarters and there was even talk of disbanding all Sikh units. Sikhs were to mutiny again after the Indian army action in the Golden Temple complex.

Sikh soldiers also played a prominent role in the Indian National Army. The INA was raised by a Sikh, Captain Mohan Singh, from Indian army prisoners of war taken by the Japanese in Singapore. According to Mohan Singh, a third of the 20,000 men who joined the INA to fight the British and free India were Sikhs.

As the war drew to an end the Akali leaders faced a bleak prospect. It was clear that Britain was going to offer independence but it was equally clear that Britain was going to insist on satisfying Muslim demands for a homeland of their own, either by granting them provincial autonomy or full independence. One possibility was that the whole of the Punjab would be Muslim-ruled. This was an anathema to the Sikhs. The other alternative was that the Punjab would be divided. As the Sikhs were spread throughout the province, this was an even worse prospect. It would mean their community would be split and they would be an enfeebled minority in both halves. That would be a threat to the very existence of the Sikh religion.

The Akalis pressed for their own homeland; but the Sikh

leaders were so divided and confused about what they actually meant by homeland that their demand was seen as nothing more than an attempt to prevent the creation of Pakistan. As Khushwant Singh wrote in his *History of the Sikhs*: 'The way the Sikh spokesmen worded their demand for a Sikh state — not as something inherently desirable but simply as a point in an argument against Pakistan — robbed the suggestion of any chance of serious consideration.'

When the British ended their brief role in the long drama of Indian history, they divided the Sikhs, the community to which they had offered their special protection. Around 40 per cent were on the Pakistan side of the border and 60 per cent on the Indian side. Indian Punjab was left with thirteen districts, including the whole of the Jullundur and Ambala divisions and Amritsar, which amounted to 40 per cent of the land area. A bitter blow to the Sikhs was the loss of Lahore, Maharaja Ranjit Singh's capital, to Pakistan.

Partition itself unleashed a holocaust unparalleled in history. The Sikhs living in Pakistani Punjab were among the worst sufferers, but they took their revenge on Muslims living in East Punjab. Nobody will ever know how many people died, although the estimate of half a million has not been effectively contested. Millions of people fled their homes on both sides of the new border. Muslims all but disappeared from East Punjab and Sikhs and Hindus from the West. The Akali leader Master Tara Singh's home became part of Muslim Pakistan — so did several historic Sikh shrines including Guru Nanak's birthplace, Nanakana Sahib. The Congress, which now ruled India, had played just as decisive a role in denying the Sikhs a homeland as the Muslim League. However, at least the vast Sikh migration into East Punjab had consolidated the community. The Akali Dal leaders now saw it as their task to win rights and privileges for Sikhs which would safeguard their religion in independent India, which they believed would be a Hindu-dominated nation.

This crisis of identity was the sore from which Bhindranwale squeezed such hatred of Hindus. His fundamentalism was founded not on love or fear of God, but fear of Hinduism.

3

The Grievances
of the Sikhs

In spite of all their doubts about the Congress, and the losses they suffered at partition, the Sikhs made a rapid recovery and flourished in independent India. In the years following independence the rest of India saw them as models of energy and initiative. They became the most prosperous of the major communities, raising Punjab's per capita income to the highest in the country. They also made Punjab India's most progressive and productive state agriculturally and spread on to the new lands being opened up by deforestation and irrigation in the neighbouring states. The tractor and combine harvester replaced the bullock and the wooden plough. First the cinema, then transistor radios and then videos spread the message of modernity throughout the Punjab. Sikh farmers responded to it. As the journalist M.J. Akbar said, 'The enterprise of the farmer has lifted Punjab away from the quagmire of third world prosperity into at least second world comfort.' Sikhs who had moved to other parts of India, and indeed to other parts of the world, added to Punjab's prosperity by sending remittances back home. Sikhs had always been travellers and had thus established themselves in almost every corner of India before independence. They had also emigrated to other parts of the

Empire, to places such as Burma, East Africa and Canada. After independence they were in the forefront of the emigration boom which ended when Britain, Canada and Australia closed their doors.

So why did the Sikhs become so disenchanted with life that they felt they had to take on the Indian government? The short answer is that most Sikhs did not. But there was an important section of the Sikh community, identified with the Akali Dal, which saw the modernism that came with prosperity as a menace to their faith, a threat to their identity. Terry-cotton shirts, jeans, motor cycles and whisky do not go with the observance of the five 'k's. Modern life is too fast for cumbersome processes like tying turbans, and washing waist-length hair. So to many Sikhs the safety razor became the symbol of modernity, and this alarmed the orthodox.

Then, of course, there was the old threat of Hinduism. Orthodox Sikhs had good reasons to fear Hinduism. The Sikhs are a small community, about eleven million strong, that is less than 2 per cent of the total population of India. An estimated 80 per cent of Sikhs live in Punjab but even there they are barely in a majority. Elsewhere, like Delhi, as they found to their cost after Mrs Gandhi's assassination, the Sikhs are a tiny minority. Hindus, on the other hand, make up 80 per cent of the population of India. Although caste and other factors divide the Hindu community, Hinduism has shown a remarkable ability to influence and sometimes to absorb rival faiths. After all Buddhism has virtually disappeared from India, the land of its birth. Hinduism absorbed the Buddha, converting him into an incarnation of the creator god Vishnu. Jainism, also born in India, has fared little better. Sikh society is divided on caste lines. Outcaste Hindus whose forefathers were converted have still not been fully accepted by other Sikhs. Christian missionaries have found Hinduism hard going. What little progress they have made has been marred by their inability to persuade converts to drop their caste prejudices. In the Roman Catholic archdiocese of Pondicherry churches used to have screens to divide Untouchables from the rest of the congregation until the 1930s, when the crusading French Archbishop Colas threatened to close all churches which did not remove their screens. Some preferred to close. The Jesuits did not recruit Untouchable novices until after the First World War and in Goa, the bastion of Roman Catholicism, caste still divides the Church. Even Muslim clerics have to fight a continual battle to prevent Hindu practices creeping into their worship and their social customs.

From the start of independence the Akali Dal leader Master Tara Singh decided that the only way to prevent modernism and Hinduism drowning the Sikhs' identity was to demand official recognition as a separate community. He told the new government, 'If you are true nationalists then, for the sake of the nation, you must let the Sikhs live honourably. You will err in attempting to extinguish, in the name of nationalism, the distinctive entity of the Sikhs. We value our honour. If we have no separate existence, we shall have nothing to be proud of . . .'

Other Akali leaders also consistently warned Sikhs of the dangers of Hindu communalism. In 1952 a leading Akali, Hukam Singh, even attacked the credentials of that arch secularist, Pandit Jawaharlal Nehru. Hukam Singh, who was later to become a member of the secular Congress Party and Speaker of Parliament, wrote: 'Pandit Nehru is, to say the least, the spearhead of militant Hindu chauvinism who glibly talks about nationalism, a tyrant who eulogises democracy and a Goblian [i.e. like Goebbels] liar − in short, a political cheat, deceiver and double dealer in the services of Indian reaction.'

The Akalis did have evidence to support their campaign against Hindu communalism. Hindu and Sikh refugees from West Punjab had to fight to re-establish themselves in the truncated Indian Punjab, and their struggle aroused communal prejudices, as the *Tribune*, the leading English language Punjab newspaper, reported in 1948.

It is useless to pretend that what is described as communal poison has suddenly developed . . . Let us be honest and admit that it has been there and it has been growing. Its presence and its growth have impeded rehabilitation. Displaced persons are not settling down for fear that they may again be displaced. Communal feeling has not only retarded rehabilitation, it has given it a false accentuation. The two

communities that have come across the border are thinking
and acting in terms of competitive rather than co-operative
rehabilitation. They stand in fear of each other and in fear of
the local population.

Militant Hinduism took political shape with the formation in
1951 of the Bhartiya Jan Sangh, a right-wing Hindu party
which stressed the Vedic origins of Indian civilisation. Its
membership flourished among Punjabi Hindus because of the
influence of the Arya Samaj.

But the Akalis' claim that Sikhism was in danger received its
greatest boost from the movement for a Punjabi-speaking state.
In 1953 Pandit Nehru set up the States Reorganisation Commission in order to consider demands from many parts of India
that state boundaries should be redrawn on a linguistic basis.
Some linguistic groups received satisfaction, but not the Akalis.
The Commission rejected the Sikh claim for a Punjabi-speaking
state, on the grounds that Punjabi was not sufficiently distinct
from Hindi, and that furthermore the movement lacked 'the
general support of the people inhabiting the area'.

Punjabi Hindus claimed that the demand was communal.
The three main languages of the undivided Punjab had been
Urdu, Hindi and various forms of Punjabi. Of the three,
Punjabi was by far the most widely spoken by all communities,
including Hindus. But the Akalis argued that the state's language should be Punjabi written in the Gurmukhi script. This
was the script devised by the second Guru for the Sikh scriptures. It was not widely taught or used outside Sikh religious
institutions. Hindus were therefore able to maintain that the
demand for the Gurmukhi script was a religious demand.
Because of the Punjabi Suba movement and the link between
language and communalism, in the 1961 census many Punjabi-
speaking Hindus declared Hindi as their mother tongue. Bhindranwale used to refer to them scornfully as 'people prepared to
deny their mothers'. The Prime Minister, Nehru, remained
resolutely opposed to the creation to a Punjabi Suba or state
until the end of his life. He too was convinced that the Akalis'
demand was communal. He told Parliament: 'There is no doubt
that it [Punjabi Suba] has grown up not as a linguistic issue but

as a communal issue.' Whether the demand was communal or not, there is no doubt that the Akalis' political ambition was to have a state they would always rule. But they had forgotten that by no means all Sikhs are Akalis, and that they could not hope to rule a Sikh majority state without the support of some Hindus.

Master Tara Singh called the States Reorganisation Commission's rejection of the demand for a Punjabi-speaking state a 'decree of annihilation'. Before the Commission even submitted its report the Sikh leader launched an agitation for the Punjabi Suba. Every morning *jathas* – the name given to squadrons in the army of Ranjit Singh – would go first to the Akal Takht to say their prayers and receive a blessing. They would then pour out of the Temple shouting slogans, to be arrested by the waiting police. The 4th of July 1955 went down in Sikh history as the day on which the police entered the hostel complex across the road from the Golden Temple itself to raid the offices of the Akali Dal and the SGPC. The Deputy Commissioner of Amritsar told members of the press that the police had raided the offices of the two Sikh organisations in order to arrest 'absconders and proclaimed offenders in connection with the Akali agitation.' That day also went down in history because, according to members of the SGPC, the police had committed sacrilege by firing tear-gas shells to disperse crowds of Akalis, shells which had landed on the sacred marble pavement surrounding the *sarowar* or pool in the centre of the complex. Nearly twenty years later when Bhindranwale and his supporters set up their headquarters in the hostel complex, the government of Mrs Gandhi refused to send in the police on the grounds that it would 'offend Sikh susceptibilities'. But this earlier agitation ended with the Akalis winning a minor victory: the lifting of the ban on shouting slogans in favour of a Punjabi Suba. However, the Prime Minister, Nehru, remained adamant on the basic principle. He maintained the demand for a Punjabi-speaking state was communal.

By 1960 Master Tara Singh felt the Sikhs were ready to support another agitation for the Punjabi Suba. On 24th January, therefore, 132 members of the SGPC took an oath at the Akal Takht. They promised to sacrifice their bodies, souls and

property (*tan, man, dhan*) for the achievement of the Punjabi
Suba. This time the leaders of the agitation went one step
further – they set up their headquarters not in the offices
outside the central part of the Golden Temple complex but in
the Akal Takht itself, as Ajit Singh Sarhadi, a prominent Akali
politician, reported.

> The repressive measures of the Government were such that
> the organisers had to choose Sri Darbar Sahib [the Golden
> Temple] as the centre of the movement from which the
> volunteers came out and courted arrest. The leaders were in
> the Akal Takhat . . . The decision of the organisers to have
> Sri Darbar Sahib as a hide-out and headquarters had become
> the subject of criticism even by well-meaning friends without
> appreciating the theo-political status of the Gurudwaras,
> particularly the Golden Temple, in the religion, history and
> traditions of the Sikhs.[1]

The Punjabi Suba agitation gave Bhindranwale a precedent for
his occupation of the Akal Takht.

After a year Master Tara Singh decided to step up the
pressure. He made a dramatic announcement: 'I do not want to
die but while living I do not want to see the Sikh Panth insulted
and the Sikhs treated as inferior to other communities. I shall
begin my fast unto death from August 15th, and continue it till
the demand for the Punjabi Suba is conceded.'

Unfortunately it was only too true that the Master did not
want to die. Nehru remained resolute in the face of his threat
and after forty-three days Tara Singh gave up his fast. He was
arraigned before the Akal Takht and sentenced to five days'
penance. He was ordered to perform the most menial of tasks,
cleaning the shoes of the pilgrims who came to worship at the
Golden Temple. The schoolmaster from Rawalpindi district
who had guided the Akalis through the freedom movement and
the first fourteen years of independence ended his political
career in ignominy. For the last six years of his life he was
nothing more than the leader of a small breakaway group of
Akalis.

The leadership of the Akali Dal passed to the Master's

lieutenant, Sant Fateh Singh. This was a significant change because Fateh Singh was a Jat, the peasant caste dominant in East Punjab. His succession set the seal on a process which had started at independence – the gradual domination of the Akali leadership by Jats. Large numbers of the Jat peasants of Punjab had been converted to Sikhism in the days of the Gurus. They had formed the backbone of Ranjit Singh's army and later of the Sikh forces within the British Indian army. But until independence they tended to remain subservient to the more sophisticated Sikhs of the trading castes, most of whom were from West Punjab. Under Sant Fateh Singh's leadership the Jats at last came into their own and the Akali Dal became first and foremost a party representing the interests of the peasant farmers of Punjab – the interests, that is, of the Jats.

Nehru remained adamantly opposed to the Punjabi Suba until his death in 1964 but in 1966 his daughter Indira Gandhi agreed to the formation of a Punjabi-speaking state. Fateh Singh helped her by stating unequivocally that his demand was for a linguistic not a Sikh state. Mrs Gandhi was undoubtedly influenced by the gallant role of Sikh troops and the mainly Sikh rural population of the border areas of Punjab in the war with Pakistan in 1965. Addressing the Punjab Assembly after the 1965 ceasefire, the Governor of Punjab, who was the representative of the central government, said:

> Whereas our armed forces personnel enhanced their prestige by their many deeds of daring, courage and sacrifice, our people in the Punjab – cultivators, traders, workmen, and even women everywhere – exhibited rare qualities of resourcefulness, forbearance and fortitude, and gave valuable assistance to the army and the police in many ways, and the public services of all categories played their role magnificently. The zeal, enthusiasm and the daring spirit displayed by the truck drivers, conductors and cleaners in driving their vehicles against all odds to carry supplies to the army, our police and home guards in fighting the enemy and apprehending the paratroopers, were truly commendable.

Almost all the truck drivers were Sikhs.

Shrewd politician that she was, Mrs Gandhi also undoubtedly saw the Akalis as potential allies in the fight she was having with the Congress party bosses her father had left behind. Mrs Gandhi was brought to power in 1966, just twenty months after her father's death. She was brought to power not by popular demand but by a group of elderly politicians known as 'the Syndicate' who had dominated politics in their home states during Pandit Nehru's premiership. When Lal Bahadur Shastri, Nehru's successor, died in Tashkent, where the Soviet Union had successfully mediated between India and Pakistan and persuaded them to sign a treaty formally ending the 1965 war, the Syndicate could not agree on which of its members should become Prime Minister. They fell back on Nehru's daughter because they believed her inexperience would make her their puppet. But they misjudged Indira Gandhi. She very soon realised that if she was to survive she would have to break the Syndicate by wresting control of the party machine in the states from its members. To do that she needed all the friends she could find.

Under the Punjab settlement the Hindi speaking plains became the new state of Haryana with its border running up to Delhi. The foothills of the Himalayas became the new state of Himachal Pradesh, and the rest remained Punjab. Punjab had a narrow Sikh majority of 56 per cent, but language not religion was the basis for the division. Sant Fateh Singh was overjoyed. A bachelor, with typical Sikh rustic humour, he announced, 'A handsome baby has been born into my household.'

However the Punjabi Suba proved a hollow victory for the Akalis. Because the Sikh vote was split they still could not hope to become the natural party of power in the Punjab. The only way they could form a government was in alliance with the Hindu Jan Sangh party. This was tried after the elections in 1967 and 1969 but the coalition governments proved hopelessly unstable. So the Akalis had their homeland but could not govern it. In order to maintain their support while out of office they had to revive a sense of grievance among the Sikhs by returning to agitational politics. In spite of their victory over the Punjabi Suba the Akalis had always kept this option open. Within months of the Punjab settlement Sant Fateh Singh had started a fast unto death to force Mrs Gandhi to concede the city of Chandigarh to the Punjab.

After partition, Nehru, to the chagrin of many Sikhs, had decided that Amritsar, the second city of undivided Punjab, was too near the Pakistan border to be the capital of an Indian state. Pakistan had no such fears about Lahore which was even nearer the border than Amritsar but remained the capital of Pakistani Punjab. Nehru decided that a new city, Chandigarh, should be built well away from the border to be the capital of Indian Punjab. The new city was sited on the banks of an artificial lake within sight of the Simla hills. The architect was Le Corbusier and he laid out the new city on the grid pattern. Its administrative buildings are seen by many as among the best of La Corbusier's work as the American Norma Evenson has written:

> the most successful aspect of the city is to be found in Le Corbusier's monumental government complex, for it would appear that Chandigarh, whatever its faults, has succeeded in giving the modern world its most powerful conception of civil architecture. It is this, of course, which has given the city its international prominence and made it virtually a place of pilgrimage for Le Corbusier's admirers.[2]

Chandigarh was therefore a prized possession and Mrs Gandhi baulked at the difficult decision of allocating it to either Punjab or Haryana. Temporarily, or so it was said, Chandigarh was to be administered by the central government but at the same time it was to house the state assemblies and the secretariats of both Punjab and Haryana — a messy solution if ever there was one.

Sant Fateh Singh called off his first fast without achieving his aim. Then in 1969 the Sant was really put on his mettle by a veteran non-Akali Dal politician, Darshan Singh Pheruman. He actually did fast to death for Chandigarh. To avoid being upstaged the Sant announced that he would sacrifice his life by burning himself to death if Mrs Gandhi did not award Chandigarh to Punjab. A bowl five feet in diameter was set up on the roof of one of the buildings near the Akal Takht, steel chains were provided to bind the Akali Dal leader so that he did not try to escape the flames, and tins of kerosene and petrol were piled up to fuel those flames. But Mrs Gandhi stepped in before the Sant was put to the final test and announced that Chandigarh would go to Punjab. She also insisted that Punjab would have to surrender two *tahsils*, Abohar and Fazilka, to Haryana. This was a messy award too. The only justification for giving the two *tahsils* − the smallest Indian revenue unit − to Haryana was that they were Hindu majority areas. They were Punjabi, not Hindi, speaking. So the award went against the spirit of Pandit Nehru's stand on the alteration of state boundaries on a religious basis. The award was never implemented and Chandigarh became the issue on which negotiations finally broke down just before Operation Blue Star.

The years following the unimplemented Chandigarh agreement were dismal years for the Akali Dal. Mrs Gandhi was at the height of her popularity and power after the defeat of the Pakistan army and the liberation of Bangladesh in 1971. In 1972 she triumphed in the elections to the state assemblies. The party bosses of her father's day were humiliated and opposition parties, including the Akali Dal, were consigned to the wilderness. To make matters worse Mrs Gandhi's Chief Minister in the Punjab, Giani Zail Singh, later to play a prominent role in the Bhindranwale saga and become the first Sikh President of India, was stealing the Akalis' thunder by taking every opportunity to placate Sikh religious sentiments. He went so far that more than one senior member of his own party complained to Mrs Gandhi that the Punjab government was communal.

To protect their position the Akali Dal decided to draw up a list of grievances which they hoped would convince Sikhs that even Zail Singh was not going to meet their 'legitimate' demands. The Akali leaders therefore set up a committee of eminent Sikhs and charged them with 'redrawing the aims and objectives of the Sikh Panth (community) to give a more vigorous lead for their achievement . . . because of the anti-Sikh policies of the Congress government.' In 1973 the Akali Dal Working Committee adopted the eminent Sikhs' proposals at a meeting in Anandpur Sahib, where the last Guru had founded the Khalsa. The committee's report was subsequently

known as the Anandpur Sahib Resolution and became the basis
for the demands that Akalis were to raise in the agitation which
ended with the Indian army storming the Golden Temple. The
Anandpur Sahib Resolution was also to provide Bhindranwale
with a weapon to seize control of the agitation from the Akali
Dal leaders.

Unfortunately for the Akali Dal, the committee which they
set up to write the Resolution was long on politicians and very
short on lawyers; so they made the cardinal mistake of being too
specific when it came to stating their demands for greater
autonomy. They proposed restricting what, in the English
translation of the Resolution, they described as the central
government's 'interference' to 'Defence, Foreign Relations,
Currency, and General Communications'. No Prime Minister,
let alone one with as firm a conviction as Mrs Gandhi that India
needed a strong central government, could ever accept those
terms. To concede that demand would have meant threatening
the unity of India. It could well have destroyed the whole
economy because each state would have been able to set up
tariff barriers impeding the free movement of goods within the
country.

The post-independence economy has been carefully constructed on the basis of self-sufficiency, with imports being
kept to the bare minimum. This has led to the growth of many
industries which are only competitive in the protected but
expanding Indian economy. This avowedly protectionist policy
has isolated India from the storms in the world economy which
have blown other developing countries off course. India has
enjoyed years of steady if unspectacular growth.

The Indian economy has also given Punjab a guaranteed
market for its agricultural produce. More than half the grain
which goes into India's public distribution system comes from
the Punjab. Under the Akali constitution the central government would not have had the powers to set up and regulate a
public distribution system. The more backward states of India
would not have had the resources to buy wheat and rice; other
states might have chosen to buy grain elsewhere. Sikh farmers
did and still do complain about the price the government pays
for their produce. But in the world conditions prevailing in the

1970s and early 1980s they would have found it very difficult to sell their grain on the international market. During the negotiations with Mrs Gandhi between 1982 and 1984 the Akali Dal leaders tacitly agreed not to press the demand to limit the central government's powers to defence, foreign relations, currency and general communications. However Bhindranwale continued to insist on nothing less than the full implementation of the Anandpur Sahib Resolution, undermining the Akali Dal leaders' support among their more simple followers who naturally could not understand why they were surrendering their demands.

In the Anandpur Resolution the Akali Dal baldly stated its claim to be the party of all Sikhs. It said, 'The Shiromani Akali Dal is the very embodiment of the hopes and aspirations of the Sikh nation and as such is fully entitled to its representation.' This claim was of course undemocratic. Indian democracy has given the Sikhs the right to reject it, and many have. In no election so far has the Akali Dal got 50 per cent of the total Sikh vote. In fact only one section of the Sikh community has consistently supported the Akali Dal — the Jat caste of peasant farmers. This is why, in spite of the Akali Dal's claim to be the party of all Sikhs, rural and urban, the Anandpur Sahib Resolution is so heavily biased in favour of the farmers and against the traders and industrialists. It said that the Akali Dal would 'ensure perceptible improvement in the standard of living of all rural classes, more particularly of the poor and middle-class farmers.' The Resolution called for land reforms and for loans to be made available to middle-class and poor farmers. It wanted the prices of agricultural produce to be fixed 'on the basis of the returns of the middle-class farmer.'

The Anandpur Sahib Resolution showed its bias against traders by demanding 'the complete nationalisation of the trade in food grains'. Mrs Gandhi did nationalise the wholesale foodgrain trade briefly, with disastrous results for farmers and consumers. The bias against industrialists was illustrated in the clause saying: 'The Shiromani Akali Dal strongly advocates that all key industries should be brought under the public sector.' In resolutions the party passed five years later the Akali Dal said: 'The historic Anandpur Sahib Resolution has laid particular stress on the need to break the monopolistic hold of the capitalists foisted on the economy by thirty years of Congress rule.' At the same time the resolutions called for the establishment of a stock exchange in the industrial capital of Punjab, Ludhiana. It seems unlikely that the stock exchange would have attracted much capital in the investment climate the Akalis favoured.

For all their bias in favour of agriculture, the result largely of their dependence on the support of Jat peasants, the Akalis consistently maintained that Punjab had been unfairly treated by the central government in the matter of industrial development. It is true that Punjab gained very little from the central government's massive investment in large-scale industry such as steel and heavy electrical plants. But when the Anandpur Sahib Resolution was passed industrial investment in the Punjab was booming, and by the time the army entered the Golden Temple the state's industrial output was growing at 8.4 per cent a year — double the national average. Punjab was also changing from a land of villages to a modern urbanised state. It had become the fifth most urbanised state in India, even overtaking West Bengal which includes the vast city of Calcutta. It is true that the new industries employed a lot of labour from outside the Punjab and so did not solve the state's own problem of unemployment. This appeared to support the Akalis' claim that Punjab was under-industrialised. It was probably more important from the Akali point of view that most of the industry was owned by Hindus.

In spite of the progress Punjab farmers had made, agriculture proved a fertile ground for the nurturing of Sikh grievances too. When the Anandpur Sahib Resolution was drawn up, agricultural production in Punjab was still expanding rapidly in the Green Revolution which made the state the granary of a self-sufficient India. But, by the time the Akali Dal launched its long agitation for the implementation of the Anandpur Sahib Resolution nine years later, the Green Revolution was beginning to run out of steam. Nearly 85 per cent of the Punjab was by then irrigated and there was little room for bringing more land under cultivation. More than 65 per cent of the farms were less than five acres and, with the rising price of fertilisers and other modern inputs, they were not large enough to produce much of a marketable surplus. There was certainly not enough money in the kitty at the end of the year to provide adequately for more than one son to stay back on the farm. So younger sons had to go to the new towns in search of jobs and there they came up against competition from labour which had immigrated from other areas of India. To make matters worse many of the young village men who had been displaced from their family farms were educated, and there is no more fertile ground for revolution than the educated unemployed.

The Akali Dal maintained that the government was even deliberately keeping Sikhs out of their traditional profession – soldiering. The government had adopted a new recruitment policy to give opportunities to communities and areas of India where there was no tradition of joining the army. If rigorously implemented this policy would have cut the Sikhs' share of recruitment down to 2 per cent, as they were only 2 per cent of the total population of India. But the policy never was rigorously implemented and, when the Akali Dal launched its agitation for the Anandpur Sahib Resolution, the Sikhs still formed over 10 per cent of the army. There was also evidence to suggest that Sikhs themselves were no longer so eager to sign on. India's Defence Ministry is very secretive about its recruitment figures but Lt-General Sinha, Vice-Chief of Army Staff at the time of the agitation, maintained that not enough young Sikhs were coming forward to fill the quota. Life in the Indian army has not changed much; a *jawan*, or soldier, still has to live a highly disciplined and restricted life, especially in the 'teeth arms' which are the traditional regiments for Sikhs to join. However, life in Punjab has changed and the cantonment has become a much less attractive place for a young Sikh. This of course has not made an alteration in the recruitment policy any less emotive an issue to Sikhs who support the Akali Dal, especially Jat Sikhs who have a tradition of more than one hundred years of serving in the army and regard recruitment as their right.

The most emotive and misunderstood of all the economic issues raised in the Anandpur Sahib Resolution was water. The waters of three of the united Punjab's five rivers were allocated to India in the post-partition Indus Water Agreement signed

with Pakistan. The rivers are the Sutlej, Ravi and Beas. Sikh
farmers regarded these waters as theirs by right. In a land which
was once near desert that was perhaps not surprising, but it was
hardly a satisfactory basis for distributing something as essen-
tial as water in a modern democracy. Unfortunately the long
and tortuous negotiations which had taken place had been
conducted on that basis too. As the Centre for Research in
Rural and Industrial Development in Chandigarh has pointed
out in the book *Punjab Crisis*, 'the controversy stems from the
principle of considering water to be property . . . the issue
ought to be the optimum harnessing of the existing water
resources.' But to the Sikh farmer 'the optimum harnessing' of
Punjab's three rivers meant stealing his water and giving it to
the new 'Hindu state of Haryana' and to the state of Rajasthan.
There was no immediate shortage. In fact while the arguments
dragged on Indian water was flowing unutilised into Pakistan
because the government could not get on with its planned
irrigation schemes. Sikh farmers were worried about the long-
term implications of these schemes and the central government
made matters worse by basing its case on the legal rights of the
other states instead of trying to persuade Sikhs that there was
enough water to go round.

These were the grievances the Akali Dal highlighted in the
Anandpur Sahib Resolution to convince Sikhs that they were a
deprived minority in India, a minority which must stand up for
itself or sink into a Hindi morass.

On many occasions the government was to refuse to negotiate
on the Anandpur Sahib Resolution, claiming that it was 'a
secessionist' document. The original resolution makes it quite
clear that the Akalis were only demanding greater, admittedly
much greater, autonomy. The Akali Dal President, Harchand
Singh Longowal, himself said: 'Let us make it clear once and
for all that the Sikhs have no designs to get away from India in
any manner. What they simply want is that they should be
allowed to live within India as Sikhs, free from all direct and
indirect interference and tampering with their religious way of
life. Undoubtedly the Sikhs have the same nationality as other
Indians.' After the army had attacked the Golden Temple
complex Longowal still said that the Akali Dal had never

demanded, and was not demanding, secession. That one of the Akali Dal's motives was power within India was shown when the party was a partner in the government of Punjab between 1977 and 1979. The Akalis did nothing about implementing the Anandpur Sahib Resolution beyond 'emphatically urging' the Janata party government at the centre, of which they were also a part, 'to recast the constitutional structure of the country on real and meaningful federation principles'. Once out of power again they launched a full-scale agitation against Mrs Gandhi's government for the implementation of the Resolution, or at least for a long list of demands which enshrined the Resolution. Many Sikhs, particularly the unemployed university graduates and the farmers, did feel that they had genuine economic grievances against the rest of India. The Akali Dal mixed those economic grievances with religious ones and so created a dangerous brand of fundamentalism which the party's leaders eventually could not control. In a pamphlet Harchand Singh Longowal, the leader of the last agitation against Mrs Gandhi, sent to all members of Parliament explaining the Akali stand, he said:

> India is a multi-lingual, multi-religious, and multi-national land. In such a land a microscopic minority like the Sikhs has genuine forebodings that, like Buddhism and Jainism earlier, they may also lose their identity in the vast ocean of the overwhelming Hindu majority.

Bhindranwale fanned the flames of the uprising in Punjab with that foreboding, but it was the Akali Dal which started the fire.

4

The Rise of Sant Jarnail Singh Bhindranwale

Jarnail Singh was born in 1947, the year of Indian Independence, into the family of Joginder Singh, a comparatively poor farmer. But that was no disadvantage to a potential *sant*, or holy man. In fact Bhindranwale could hardly have chosen his family better if he had tried. His father was Jat by caste, the caste which dominates the Sikh community, and his occupation, farming, was the only occupation apart from soldiering considered worthy of a Jat. He had a military connection too. One of Bhindranwale's half-brothers joined the army and by the time of Operation Blue Star he had risen to the rank of subedar-major, the approximate equivalent of sergeant-major in the British army. Bhindranwale's own name Jarnail was the Punjabi transliteration of the English word 'general'. Sikh fathers often call their sons after ranks in the army.

Bhindranwale's family village of Rode was near the town of Moga, which is in the heart of the Jat Sikh country, and the village of Bhindran where the missionary movement the farmer's son was to join as a young schoolboy was founded. Jarnail Singh was helped on his way to becoming a preacher by his father's piety. Joginder Singh went regularly to the *gurudwara* to hear the Guru Granth Sahib recited and he made sure that his son was nurtured in the Sikh scriptures. Joginder Singh described Jarnail Singh, when a young boy, as 'Someone who could fell a tree in a single blow and at the same time memorise whole chapters of the scriptures and recite them a hundred times a day.' Jarnail Singh was also fortunate to be born the last of seven sons. That meant his father had plenty of sons to work his land and to guarantee him a secure old age. The farmer was probably happy to send Jarnail Singh to the Damdami Taksal missionary school to learn the profession of preaching, because his land would certainly not have supported his seventh son.

The word *Taksal* means mint and is used to describe the Sikh schools which preach the pure and unalloyed message of the Gurus. The Damdami Taksal is an influential school founded by one of the great heroes of Sikhism, Baba Deep Singh. He was the leader of one of the bands of warriors who had sworn to defend the Golden Temple during the time the Afghan Ahmad Shah Abdali ruled the Punjab. Baba Deep Singh swore to atone for the Sikhs' failure to defend the Golden Temple after the first desecration by the Afghan army. He collected together a force of some 5,000 villagers armed with the most rustic of weapons. His peasant army was intercepted on its way to the Golden Temple by a hurriedly assembled Afghan army. The Sikhs fought so hard that the Afghan general had to call for reinforcements, but in the end he was able to prevent the army of Baba Deep Singh getting to the Golden Temple. The general desecrated the Temple again as a lesson to the Sikhs. Tradition has it that Baba Singh's head was cut off but that he still managed to fight his way to the Golden Temple with his head in one hand and his sword in the other. Pictures of the decapitated Baba Deep Singh are as common in Sikh households as pictures of the Gurus. The Damdami Taksal he founded had been in the vanguard of the fight against Sikh apostasy for 200 years by the time that Jarnail Singh joined as a young boy.

Most young Sikhs who go to religious schools end their lives in comparative obscurity, reciting the Guru Granth Sahib in *gurudwaras* or travelling around villages preaching. Bhindranwale, however, soon became a dominant figure in the Damdami Taksal. Standing an impressive and lean six feet tall, his looks went with a prophetic role. He had a strong nose and deep-set eyes which almost disappeared when he broke into a toothy grin, and yet had a sinister quality which meant his audiences waited for the Sant to smile first. There were a few white hairs in his thick black beard by the end of his life. Bhindranwale always wore a blue or saffron turban tied in tiers, not in the jaunty fashion of a Sikh layman. He also wore the traditional Sikh loose knee-length shirt, under which were the shorts prescribed by Guru Gobind Singh. As the Guru instructed, he wore a dagger in a belt slung over his shoulder. Whenever I saw him he carried a more modern weapon too, a revolver, in a bandoleer stuffed with live ammunition.

Jarnail Singh became the favourite of the head of the Taksal, Kartar Singh. His break came when Kartar Singh was fatally injured in a road accident. Bhindranwale's teacher was such a fanatical Sikh that he refused to allow doctors to cut his hair so that they could operate on him after the accident. Before Kartar Singh died he made it clear that he wanted Jarnail Singh, not his own son Amrik Singh, to succeed to the leadership of the Taksal. So Jarnail Singh became a Sant or Saint, and head of the Damdami Taksal. He took the name Bhindranwale as many of his predecessors had done, after the village of Bhindran. Amrik Singh was studying at university at the time and wanted to remain there. He later became Bhindranwale's right-hand man and President of the All India Sikh Students Federation, whose members were responsible for many of the atrocities committed in Bhindranwale's name.

The headquarters of the Damdami Taksal are in a comparatively new *gurudwara* in the village of Chowk Mehta, some 25 miles from Amritsar. The *gurudwara* stands apart from the village, like a fortress of the faith. Behind its high walls, young Sikh boys from the age of seven upwards are taught to defend that faith with arms and with words. Many deride the education in Sikh missionary schools as primitive obscurantism, the teaching of blind faith. Much time is certainly devoted to learning the scriptures by heart, but when I visited Chowk Mehta I found myself involved in a deep argument about monotheism with one of the young teachers who had studied theology at university. He had 'read, learnt and inwardly digested' the Bible and the Qur'an as well, of course, as the

Guru Granth Sahib. I was unable to counter his argument that Christianity's doctrines of the incarnation of Christ and the Trinity were not pure monotheism, especially when compared with the Sikhs' doctrine of the one God to whom man cannot ascribe any form.

Bhindranwale's appointment as head of the Damdami Taksal coincided with a change in the political scene in the Punjab. In 1977 Mrs Gandhi surprised India and the world by calling a general election and accepting the electorate's verdict against her Emergency. When Mrs Gandhi took emergency powers eighteen months earlier, arrested opposition leaders and censored the press, it had been interpreted as the end of one of the last surviving democracies in the developing world. Mrs Gandhi's motive in declaring the Emergency had undoubtedly been to protect her own position. The Allahabad High Court had found her guilty of corrupt electoral practices. Although it was generally admitted that the charge against her was a technicality, many of her own colleagues advised that she should resign temporarily until her appeal was heard by the Supreme Court. The opposition, under the leadership of Jayaprakash Narayan, the man many Indians regarded as the inheritor of Mahatma Gandhi's moral authority, had mounted a campaign to highlight government corruption. This campaign seriously damaged Mrs Gandhi and the Congress Party's image. Those of Mrs Gandhi's colleagues who argued that she should step down temporarily said that to do anything less would be playing into the hands of Jayaprakash Narayan's movement. At one stage Mrs Gandhi was swayed by this argument, but her younger son Sanjay dissuaded her from resigning. He told his mother that she could not trust any of her colleagues to hand the job back to her if she was cleared by the Supreme Court, as seemed likely from its interim judgment.

Sanjay had failed to complete an apprenticeship with Rolls-Royce and was in the process of setting up a car manufacturing plant, a scheme which he never got off the ground. Only twenty-eight when the Emergency was declared, he had no political experience and held no party office. However, inexperience did not stop him using the Draconian powers his mother had taken to terrorise the administration, setting up what was in effect a police state. The Indian police needed the restraint of the civil servants, the courts and Parliament to curb their veniality. Without that restraint they ran amok, committing widespread 'excesses'. The worst excesses were committed in the family planning drive, launched by Sanjay Gandhi. In many areas of northern India, government servants, including even school teachers, were forced to collaborate in a programme of compulsory sterilisation.

It is doubtful whether with a censored press and a party silenced by fear of Sanjay, Mrs Gandhi knew the full extent of the Emergency excesses and their effect on the electorate's support for her. The intelligence agencies did not help the Prime Minister. As craven as the Congress Party, they fed Mrs Gandhi with reports that the allegations of excesses were just rumours being put about by opposition workers and picked up by the foreign press and the BBC, which has a very large audience to its services in English and Indian languages beamed to the subcontinent. Had Mrs Gandhi known the true state of public opinion, she might not have called the general election, which had already been postponed by one year. Sanjay in fact advised against it, being more aware of what had happened in the Emergency than his mother because he had been directly involved. But Mrs Gandhi wanted to restore democracy. She was always conscious of her standing in the world and it had been much reduced by the undemocratic Emergency. She maintained that democracy was suspended and not terminated and she was determined to disprove the allegation that she had become a dictator. There is also no doubt that Mrs Gandhi was unhappy about governing India on such a tight rein. She was well aware of the value of elections for letting off the head of steam which builds up against any administration.

The post-Emergency election was an unparalleled disaster for the Congress and Mrs Gandhi. She was heavily defeated in her own home constituency in Uttar Pradesh and her party did not win even a single seat in northern India, the area worst affected by Sanjay's Emergency programmes. In Punjab, the Akali Dal formed a coalition government with the new Janata Party, which found itself in power in Delhi. It was a hurried merger of the non-communist opposition parties which fell apart because of rivalry between the three elderly politicians who vied to be the Prime Minister. In the Punjab the main strength of the Janata Party came from the former Jan Sangh. The Akali Dal had, of course, earlier experience of the difficulties of a coalition with this pro-Hindu party, but they did not hesitate to form a government with Jan Sangh politicians again.

At first, Mrs Gandhi seemed inclined to accept her defeat as the end of her political career. Sanjay certainly was not. He realised how fragile the unity of the new Janata Party was and set out to break it by playing on the rivalries between the leaders of the different parties which had merged so hurriedly and so recently. It took him less than three years to bring down the Janata government and see his mother restored to power.

To achieve the break-up of the Punjab coalition, Sanjay took the advice of the experienced Sikh politician Zail Singh, who had been Chief Minister of the state from 1972 until the Congress Party's electoral defeat in 1977. Zail Singh advised Sanjay to try to break the Akali Dal, not the Jan Sangh. The Akali Dal was dominated by three men – Prakash Singh Badal, a rich farmer and an experienced politician who had succeeded Zail Singh as the Chief Minister; Harchand Singh Longowal, like Bhindranwale a religious teacher who had led an agitation against the Emergency; and Gurcharan Singh Tohra, a cunning but unsophisticated politician with communist connections. He headed the Shiromani Gurudwara Prabandhak Committee. At first, Sanjay thought of playing these three against each other. But Zail Singh, with his deep knowledge of the complexities of Sikh politics, realised that displacing one of the Akali Trinity would only lead to a strong alliance of the other two. He recommended Sanjay to look for a new religious leader to discredit the traditional Akali Dal leadership. Sanjay sent some of the young men, who had been his aides during the Emergency, to search for a *sant* or holy man to do the job. There is no shortage of *sants* in Punjab, and the young men came up with a list of twenty. Some were unwilling, others were unsuitable. The choice eventually fell on Bhindranwale. As head of the historic and widely respected Damdami Taksal, he had a ready-made status in the Sikh community. As a rigid fundamentalist, he could capitalise on the compromises with Sikh religious interests that the Akali Dal leaders were bound to make to stay in power. There was, however, a difficulty. Bhindranwale needed an issue, a cause. When Sanjay's young men found him, he was travelling round Punjab with his followers preaching against the threats to the Sikh religion; but the evils of shaving beards and cutting hair, of drinking and drugs, were hardly political issues. So Sanjay and Zail Singh looked for a cause which was both political and religious.

They found it in the Nirankaris, a heretical sect of Sikhs who are very influential in the Punjabi trading community. The Nirankaris started as a revivalist group in the last century. Their founder, Baba Dayal Das, preached against the growing tendency of Sikhs to revert to Hindu practices like idolatry, Brahmin rituals, and pilgrimages to the Ganges. The Baba stressed the Sikh doctrine that God could not be described because he was formless. *Nirankari* means formless. The movement split and heresies crept in. The larger group of Nirankaris started to revere their founder and his successor as Gurus, in spite of Guru Gobind Singh's pronouncement that he was the last Guru. They forgot their founder's strictures against idols too, and even worshipped his sandals; but most offensive of all to orthodox Sikhs, were the scriptures which the Nirankaris have added to the Sikh canon. Some passages in them are regarded as blasphemy against the Gurus and the Guru Granth Sahib. Faced with the growing popularity of the sect, the Sikh High Priests had issued a religious edict, a *hukmnama*, denouncing the Nirankaris as heretics. Sikhs were told to ostracise Nirankaris and prevent the movement growing. Tension between the Nirankaris and the orthodox Sikhs mounted and there were several riots.

Then in 1978, the Akali Dal government played into the hands of Sanjay Gandhi and Zail Singh. They announced that the Nirankaris would be allowed to hold a convention in the holy city of Amritsar. Raja Harmit Singh Batra, a wealthy young Sikh businessman, was inside the Golden Temple on 13th April 1978, the day of that convention. He heard Jeevan Singh Umranangal, the Revenue Minister in the Akali Dal government, trying to explain to an agitated Sikh congregation that his government could not stop the Nirankari convention taking place. The reason was that the Nirankari traders had links with the Hindu traders supporting the Jan Sangh, the Akalis' coalition partner. But the Revenue Minister could not use that as an explanation to the congregation, consisting mainly of Sikh farmers who, like farmers the world over, regard traders as exploiters. Bhindranwale stood up and shouted, 'We will not allow this Nirankari convention to take place. We are going to march there and cut them to pieces!' This was the first time Batra, and probably many other members of the congregation, had seen Bhindranwale. Batra was not impressed. He said, 'I detested the man's behaviour.'

Bhindranwale, and an agricultural inspector of the Punjab government called Fauja Singh, then marched out of the Temple at the head of a procession shouting slogans against the Nirankaris. Along the two-mile route to the Nihangon ka Bunga or Nihang's shelter, one of the agitated Sikhs cut off the arm of a Hindu sweetshop owner. Still the police made no attempt to stop the procession. When the Sikhs reached the convention, Fauja Singh drew his sword and swiped at the neck of the Nirankari Guru, Baba Gurbachan Singh. One of the Guru's bodyguards shot Fauja Singh dead, and a battle broke out in which twelve Sikhs and three Nirankaris were killed. The twelve Sikhs became martyrs and Sanjay Gandhi and Zail Singh had the issue they needed.

Sanjay Gandhi and the Congress Party used the martyrdom of the twelve Sikhs to whip up the Nirankari agitation. The Akali Dal were in a dilemma which they never resolved so long as they remained in power. As the defenders of Sikh orthodoxy, they could not disassociate themselves from a movement against a heretical sect. As coalition partners in the Punjab government, they could not openly support lawlessness. The Akali Dal leaders did little to encourage the agitation against the Nirankaris so long as they remained in power. Most of the demonstrations took place in Delhi, organised by the local committee in charge of *gurudwaras* which was controlled by the Congress Party.

The Congress publicity machine projected Bhindranwale as the hero of the attack on the Nirankari convention, but there are considerable doubts about this. Fauja Singh's widow, Bibi

Amarjit Kaur, claimed that Bhindranwale slipped away before the procession reached the convention. After her husband's death she retired to the Golden Temple, where she led a small group of extremists called the Akhand Kirtani Jatha, remaining a thorn in Bhindranwale's flesh until his death. She was one of the few people inside the Temple who had the courage to criticise him openly, blaming his 'cowardice' for the death of her husband.

Sanjay Gandhi and Zail Singh also needed a party to promote Bhindranwale and harass the Akalis. So a new party was formed on 13th April 1978, just a week before the attack on the Nirankari convention. The party was called the Dal Khalsa, the party of the pure, the name of the Sikh army in the days before the empire of Ranjit Singh. The inaugural meeting was held in the Aroma Hotel and, according to the staff of the hotel, the bill of 600 rupees was paid by Zail Singh. A stenographer who had been associated with the publication of a recent pamphlet advocating Khalistan was elected president.

The establishment of Khalistan was discussed. Khalistan means 'the land of the Khalsa' and is the name Sikh separatists have given the independent country they are fighting for. The Government White Paper on the army action in the Golden Temple admitted that 'The Dal Khalsa was originally established with the avowed object of demanding an independent sovereign Sikh State.' However, Zail Singh, the man who had been Chief Minister of Punjab and was to go on to become Home Minister in the central Cabinet and then President of India, continued to promote its cause. Journalists in Chandigarh remember how he used to ring them up and ask them to publish news of the Dal Khalsa on the front pages of their newspapers. Bhindranwale was never openly associated with the Dal Khalsa. Until his death he maintained that he was a man of religion, not a politician; but the Dal Khalsa was always known as Bhindranwale's party.

A year later Bhindranwale and the Dal Khalsa were involved in their first elections. The elections were for the influential Shiromani Gurudwara Prabandhak Committee, the SGPC. It was vital for the Akali Dal leaders to retain control over the SGPC because it financed their party and controlled the *gurud-*

waras throughout the Punjab, where the party message was put across. Sanjay Gandhi and Zail Singh had high hopes of Bhindranwale. He had become the most prominent leader of the anti-Nirankari agitation and he had built up a name for his preaching in the villages of the Bhatinda, Faridkot and Ferozepur districts, which were the strongholds of the Akali Dal. They were to be disappointed.

Candidates supported by Bhindranwale only won four out of the 140 seats in the SGPC election. The Akali Dal leaders retained a commanding majority. Sanjay Gandhi and Zail Singh persevered, promoting Bhindranwale's name through the movement against the Nirankaris and through the Dal Khalsa. Fortunately for the two Congressmen, the fighting between the leaders of the Akali Dal became more bitter, giving them another field to operate in. In 1979 the Punjab Chief Minister, Badal, opposed the break-up of the Janata Party, which led to the downfall of the Janata government of the octogenarian Prime Minister, Morarji Desai. Tohra, the President of the SGPC, sided with the breakaway group in the Janata Party.

Although the divisions within the ranks of the Akali Dal and the collapse of the Janata Party drastically weakened the Sikh religious party when it came to fight the general elections in 1980, Zail Singh still thought it worth his while to bring in Bhindranwale on the Congress side. For all his protestations that he was not a politician, Bhindranwale campaigned actively for the Congress in three constituencies. His name was already so influential that two of the candidates printed posters saying 'Bhindranwale supports me.' One of the candidates Bhindranwale supported was the Hindu R.L. Bhatia who was the President of the Punjab Congress Party. Another was the wife of Pritam Singh Bhinder, a senior police officer who played a controversial role in the Emergency. Mrs Gandhi later made Bhinder the police chief of Punjab and gave him the job of eradicating Bhindranwale's terrorists.

The Janata candidate in Mrs Bhinder's constituency of Gurdaspur, Pran Nath Lekhi, alleges that Mrs Gandhi herself actually appeared on the same platform as Bhindranwale in the election campaign. Following an official denial after Bhindranwale's death that Mrs Gandhi or the Congress Party had had any links with the Sant, the Janata candidate wrote a letter to the Prime Minister in which he said: 'Bhindranwale was accompanying you during your election tour of Gurdaspur constituency during the general election to the seventh Lok Sabha [Parliament] held in January 1980.' The nearest Mrs Gandhi ever came to admitting any connection between Bhindranwale and her party was in an interview for the BBC television current affairs programme *Panorama*. In that interview she was asked whether her party had helped the preacher to come to prominence. She replied, 'Certainly not. I didn't know him. I never knew him.' But she did say, 'Mr Bhindranwale did go and speak for one of our candidates in the elections. I don't know which candidate it was. I don't know whether he knew him personally or he was annoyed with the local Akalis.'

5

The Arrest of
Bhindranwale

When Mrs Gandhi returned to power Zail Singh was rewarded with the post of Home Minister in her Cabinet. The man who like Bhindranwale had started off as an obscure preacher but unlike Bhindranwale had never made it to the top of that profession, had now reached the second most important office in the Indian Cabinet. But Zail Singh's happiness was to be short-lived. Later in the year Congress was returned to power in the Punjab State Assembly elections too and Mrs Gandhi chose Zail Singh's arch-rival Darbara Singh as the new Chief Minister. In India all politicians, except members of the Gandhi family, have to protect their base. Only with a strong base in one of the states can politicians hope to command independent influence in Delhi. It was just because Mrs Gandhi did not want politicians to be able to command any independent influence that she did her best to prevent any of her colleagues becoming too powerful in their home states. If Home Minister Zail Singh's nominee had been appointed Chief Minister of Punjab, Zail Singh himself would have been king of Punjab in all but name and that was the last thing Mrs Gandhi wanted. Hence the appointment of his rival Darbara Singh as Chief Minister.

Politically the two men were poles apart. When Zail Singh

was Chief Minister of Punjab from 1972 to 1977 he tried to fight
the Akali Dal with its own weapon, religion. He went out of his
way to show Sikhs that he was as devout as any Akali leader. He
made a point of attending the celebrations of all Sikh festivals,
and of preaching sermons at them. He had developed a flair for
preaching at the Sikh Missionary College at Amritsar where he
was trained to propagate the faith. Zail Singh's deeds matched
his words. He linked all the places where the last Guru had
preached by a road which he called Guru Gobind Singh Marg.
The Chief Minister then set off to drive the 400 miles from
Anandpur in the east, where Guru Gobind Singh had given the
Sikhs his historic charge to defend their faith with arms and to
wear the five emblems of their faith, to the western borders of
Punjab. The cavalcade of tractors and trailers, trucks, buses
and cars took four days to reach its destination, stopping at all
the *gurudwaras* which marked the points where the Guru
himself had stopped. Even the Akali Dal leadership had to
accept that the Guru Gobind Singh Marg had been a stroke of
genius. But Darbara Singh went to Mrs Gandhi and told her
that Zail Singh was risking the Congress Party's reputation for
secularism by 'indulging in communal politics'. Mrs Gandhi,
who was less averse to religion than her father Pandit Nehru,
backed Zail Singh's brand of Sikh politics against Darbara
Singh's secularism. So Zail Singh continued to organise religious congregations and to insist that every public function
start with Sikh prayers. He named a new town after one of the
Guru's sons who had been martyred and even sent a string of
horses said to be related to Guru Gobind Singh's stallion down
the new road he had built. According to one report, 'Villagers
reverently picked up their droppings to take home . . .'[1] Zail
Singh's religious politics took the wind out of the Akalis' sails.
He survived until the Emergency without facing a single significant challenge from them.

When Darbara Singh became Chief Minister in 1980 he
decided to reverse Zail Singh's policies and revert to what he
saw as the orthodox Congress policy of secularism. Darbara
Singh, unlike Zail Singh and most other Congress politicians,
had never been a member of the Akali Dal. He was bitterly
opposed to any compromise with communalism. He once said

to me, 'You can't fight a man with his own weapon.' Although a
Sikh himself, in an interview given while he was Chief Minister,
he candidly stated his opinion that there was no longer such a
thing as Sikh culture: 'There was a Sikh culture before. That
Sikh culture has now reached the limit. Sikh culture is now
dead . . . Now the Sikh culture has been converted into a
composite culture. That is what I am doing.'[2]

Not surprisingly, orthodox Sikhs saw these remarks as proof
of their worst fears that the Congress Party's aim was to absorb
their religion into the Hindu culture of the majority of Indians.

Darbara Singh chose ministers, officials and senior police
officers who were secular and adopted a hard-line policy on
both Sikh and Hindu extremists. That of course only sharpened
his differences with Zail Singh. A study by members of the
Centre for Research in Rural and Industrial Development in
Chandigarh said: 'One faction [in the Congress] though in a
minority with allegiance to Zail Singh kept on advocating the
politics of accommodation [with religious communalism]
rather than confrontation.'[3] These were the battle lines drawn
up between Darbara Singh, the head of the Punjab government, and Zail Singh, the Home Minister in Delhi.

Three murders during Mrs Gandhi's first year back in office
highlighted the tensions within her party and brought the
preacher Sant Jarnail Singh Bhindranwale To the forefront of
Punjab politics. On 24th April 1980 Baba Gurbachan Singh,
the Guru of the Nirankari sect, was shot dead in his house in
New Delhi. Ever since the attack on the Nirankari convention
in Amritsar, Bhindranwale had kept up his campaign against
the sect. He had been infuriated when the Akali Dal government had allowed the case against the Nirankaris who were
accused of killing Sikhs during that attack to be transferred to a
court in the neighbouring state of Haryana, and was even
angrier when the Haryana court found them not guilty. The
Nirankaris had pleaded that they would not get justice from a
Punjab court. So it was no surprise that Bhindranwale's name
figured in the police report on the murder of Baba Gurbachan
Singh.

When Bhindranwale got wind of this he took sanctuary in
one of the hostels of the Golden Temple. He stayed there until

Zail Singh told Parliament that the Sant had nothing to do with the murder. Shortly after that statement, Bhindranwale announced that the killer of the Guru of the Nirankaris deserved to be honoured by the High Priest of the Akal Takht, the most senior priest of Sikhism. Bhindranwale also said that he would weigh the killers in gold if they came to him. These remarks embarrassed Zail Singh but he overlooked them because Bhindranwale was still useful to him in his struggle with Darbara Singh.

The second murder had more serious consequences for Bhindranwale. On 9th September 1981 Lala Jagat Narain, the proprietor of a chain of newspapers published in the Punjab city of Jullundur, was shot dead. His influential daily, the *Punjab Kesari*, was bitterly critical of Bhindranwale and sided with the Nirankaris. In hard-hitting editorials Narain himself had argued that minorities in the Punjab – that is in Punjab terms mainly Hindus – were living in fear of ever getting justice from a government and police force who, he claimed, were siding with Bhindranwale against the Nirankaris in the investigations into the attack on the Nirankari convention. There is no doubt that Lala Jagat Narain's papers played a role in fanning the flames of communal hatred between Hindus and Sikhs. In his editorials his theme was often the support for Khalistan among Sikhs in the Punjab. He gave the impression that this support was far more widespread than it actually was, heightening Hindu suspicions of the Sikh community. Warning that the Khalistan demand was no joke, he urged the government to take drastic action against its supporters. Narain believed that the Anandpur Sahib Resolution of the Akalis was part of the same movement. As he once wrote: 'Sardar Sukhjinder Singh [a Khalistan supporter] has not raised the slogan willy-nilly. He knows very well that the Anandpur Sahib Resolution too is, in a way, making that very same demand for a separate state for the Sikhs.' Narain's partisan attitude was typical. In fact the whole of the Punjab press was divided on communal lines.

Needless to say, Bhindranwale was an outspoken critic of Lala Jagat Narain and once again the police reported that he had conspired to commit a murder. In keeping with his hard-line policy on religious communalism, the Chief Minister of

Punjab, Darbara Singh, decided to arrest Bhindranwale. That was easier said than done.

Four days after the murder of Lala Jaga Narain All India Radio announced that a warrant for Bhindranwale's arrest had been issued. When the police arrived in Chando Kalan, where Bhindranwale had been preaching, they found he had already fled. Despite the fact that the government-controlled radio had announced that Bhindranwale was a wanted man, the police failed to stop him driving some 200 miles back to the security of his own *gurudwara*.

Chando Kalan is in Haryana. The Chief Minister of that state, Bhajan Lal, was at that time very anxious to ingratiate himself with the leaders of the Congress Party. He had been Chief Minister of a Janata Party government when Mrs Gandhi returned to power. She dismissed the Janata-run state governments but the Haryana Chief Minister saved his political neck by coolly transferring his and his government's loyalty to the new party in power in Delhi, the Congress. He was regarded with suspicion by Congress leaders. They justifiably thought that a man who had shown himself to be so fickle would let them down if they ever got into trouble. There was a premium on loyalty in the Congress Party at that time because many politicians, who had deserted Mrs Gandhi when she was in difficulties and the Janata government had set up a commission of inquiry into the Emergency, were now trying to climb on her bandwagon again. Those who had stood by Indira Gandhi resented this and did all they could to keep those Mrs Gandhi did allow back out of office. So Bhajan Lal never missed any opportunity to oblige ministers in the central government. It therefore seems highly unlikely that he would have allowed Bhindranwale to escape unless he had instructions from the central government to do so.

The veteran Indian journalist, Kuldip Nayar, reported that the Home Minister Zail Singh rang Bhajan Lal and told him not to arrest Bhindranwale. A senior police officer told Satish Jacob that the Haryana Chief Minister went so far as to send an official car to Chando Kalan to drive Bhindranwale back to his *gurudwara*. He certainly left in a great hurry because he did not take the vans carrying the copies of his religious discourses with him.

When the Punjab police eventually arrived at Chando Kalan and found that the Haryana police had allowed Bhindranwale to flee, they were furious. According to villagers, they deliberately set his vans on fire. According to the official version: 'The police went to Chando Kalan to arrest Shri Bhindranwale in connection with the case relating to the murder of Lala Jagat Narain but Shri Bhindranwale had already left. There was subsequent violence when some followers of Shri Bhindranwale fired upon the police party. There was an exchange of fire and incidents of arson occurred.' Those incidents of arson were to cost the government dear. Bhindranwale used to have a secretary with him wherever he preached whose job was to copy down every word he said so that it could be recorded for posterity. It was the immortal words of Bhindranwale which went up in flames at Chando Kalan and the preacher never forgave the government for that. In fact it was the burning of his sermons, not his arrest, which turned Bhindranwale against his political godfather, Zail Singh, and against Mrs Gandhi. He used to refer to the incident in all his diatribes against the government. He would ask his audiences, 'What would you do if someone killed your nearest and dearest? They have insulted my Guru by burning my papers.'

When it became public knowledge that Bhindranwale had fled to the *gurudwara* at Mehta Chowk, it was surrounded by police and paramilitary forces. Darbara Singh insisted that Bhindranwale must be arrested, although the central government feared there would be violence because large numbers of Sikhs had gathered at the *gurudwara* to protect him. Three senior police officers were sent to negotiate with Bhindranwale for his surrender and five days after his escape from the police at Chando Kalan he did agree to give himself up. He said that he would surrender to the police at one o'clock in the afternoon on Sunday 20th September. He told police that he and other Sikh leaders would first address a religious congregation. The police meekly accepted his terms. Before his arrest, therefore, Bhindranwale preached a fiery sermon against the Punjab government which was going to arrest him and then, having worked his followers into a frenzy, he told them not to become violent when the police took him away. As soon as Bhindranwale had gone, his supporters opened fire on the police and a battle ensued in which at least eleven people were killed.

The very day Bhindranwale was arrested the violence began which was to bring down Darbara Singh's government and lead eventually to the army action in the Golden Temple. Three Sikhs on motorcycles fired at Hindus in a market in Jullundur, killing four people and injuring twelve. The next day one Hindu was killed and thirteen people injured in a similar incident in the town of Taran Taran near Amritsar. Five days later a goods train was derailed near Amritsar. Two other attempts were made to derail trains by tampering with the track. On 29th September, nine days after Bhindranwale was arrested, Sikhs hijacked an Indian Airlines plane to Lahore just across the Pakistan border. This indicates that Bhindranwale already had an effective organisation behind him. The most significant incident of all was the explosion in the office of the Deputy Inspector-General of Police in Patiala. The Deputy Inspector-General was one of the officers sent to arrest Bhindranwale at Chando Kalan. He escaped unhurt in the bomb explosion but Bhindranwale had started his campaign of vengeance against policemen who took action against him or his supporters — a campaign he pursued with the utmost ruthlessness.

During his brief spell in Ferozepur jail Bhindranwale insisted on being guarded only by Sikhs with flowing beards. He was always obsessive about beards and even objected to the habit adopted by some Sikhs of rolling their beards up into a net. The government gave in to Bhindranwale although his demand had no legal sanction in secular India, where men of all religions are recruited by the police and prison service.

On 14th October, less than a month after the Punjab government had gone to all that trouble to arrest the turbulent preacher, Zail Singh told Parliament in Delhi that there was after all no evidence that Bhindranwale was involved in the murder of the newspaper proprietor, Lala Jagat Narain. The decision to release Bhindranwale was taken by the government. It was not the verdict of a court. It was argued by some that Zail Singh decided to release Bhindranwale in the hope that the violence his arrest had sparked off would stop. If that was so the

Home Ministry's hopes were to be belied. The day after his release a senior civil servant who was a Nirankari was fired on in the Punjab government secretariat in Chandigarh and his brother was killed. That incident was followed by attacks on the police and bomb explosions.

Darbara Singh had a more credible explanation for the strange circumstances surrounding Bhindranwale's arrest when I met him after Mrs Gandhi had dismissed his government. Being a wily politician, he would not mention his rival Zail Singh by name but there was no doubt whom he was referring to in this conversation.

I asked the former Punjab Chief Minister first who had ordered the arrest. He replied, 'I wanted to arrest him at Chando Kalan.'

'Is it true that the Haryana Chief Minister sent an official car to drive Bhindranwale from Chando Kalan before the police could get there?'

'If you know it's true why do you ask me?'

'Why was he released after his arrest?'

'Don't ask me. You know. Why was he allowed to come back to Delhi with his guns. Why was he not arrested then?'

When Bhindranwale came to Delhi to celebrate his release he openly flouted the law. He drove around the capital with eighty of his supporters, many of them sitting on the roofs of their buses brandishing illegal arms. It was Zail Singh's responsibility to arrest him because the Delhi police are controlled by the Home Ministry. During that visit Bhindranwale and his companions, accompanied by thousands of Sikhs drummed up by the Delhi Gurudwara Management Committee, drove in a triumphant procession from a *gurudwara* on the northern outskirts of the capital to Gurudwara Bangla Sahib, Delhi's main Sikh temple situated just behind Parliament. The Delhi Gurudwara Management Committee was controlled by the Congress Party. Its president, Santokh Singh, had close personal links with Mrs Gandhi. The Home Minister also allowed Bhindranwale to go to the Tihar jail to visit a Sikh politician imprisoned there.

There is therefore considerable evidence to suggest that Bhindranwale's release was ordered by the Home Minister. He certainly still enjoyed Zail Singh's patronage. But a senior Congress politician from Punjab told Satish Jacob that it was Mrs Gandhi herself who actually ordered the Sant's release. This is also confirmed by a member of the family of the President of the Delhi Gurudwara Management Committee, Santokh Singh. He told me that Santokh Singh himself went and pleaded with Mrs Gandhi for Bhindranwale's release, threatening that it would not be possible to keep the Delhi Gurudwara Management Committee loyal to the Congress if Bhindranwale was not freed.

Bhindranwale's release was the turning-point in his career. He was now seen as a hero who had challenged and defeated the Indian government. As the preacher himself said after his release, 'The government has done more for me in one week than I could have achieved in years.' Zail Singh wanted Bhindranwale freed because he still believed he could use him to bring about the downfall of his rival, the Punjab Chief Minister. Mrs Gandhi apparently wanted him released so that she could maintain her hold over Delhi's Sikhs. By surrendering justice to petty political gains the government itself created the ogre who was to dominate the last years of Mrs Gandhi and to shadow her until her death.

It took some time for them to realise their mistake. They still thought that they could use Bhindranwale for their own ends, as was shown when the third murder took place, the murder of Santokh Singh — the man who had pleaded for Bhindranwale's release. He was shot dead in his car in Delhi on 21st December 1981 by a rival Sikh politician. When news of his assassination reached the government Mrs Gandhi, her son Rajiv and Zail Singh rushed to the hospital where his body had been taken. Zail Singh insisted that the body be taken back to his house. Santokh Singh was also, of course, a Bhindranwale man. Bhindranwale often said that Santokh Sikh had paid his legal fees when he was accused of complicity in the murder of the Guru of the Nirankari sect and had also paid a monthly sum of 2,000 rupees to Ranjit Singh, one of the others accused in the case. Santokh Singh was present on that Sunday when Bhindranwale agreed to surrender outside his own *gurudwara*. He made a speech in which he said, 'If the government arrests

Bhindranwale they catch at the hearts of the Sikhs. If he is arrested under any false charges the Sikh people will blow up like a volcano and the molten lava will drown this country.'

By the time of Santokh Singh's death Bhindranwale's men were known to have killed two policemen and ten civilians, attempted to murder a senior civil servant and planted a bomb in the office of a deputy inspector-general of police. There had been several other bomb explosions and attempts to derail trains, one successful. An airliner had been hijacked too. Nevertheless Zail Singh, the Home Minister of India, and Rajiv Gandhi, the Prime Minister's son, both agreed to attend memorial ceremonies for Santokh Singh, knowing full well that Bhindranwale would be there. Rajiv Gandhi was already being talked of as the heir apparent to the Nehru/Gandhi dynasty, a position made vacant by his younger brother Sanjay's death in 1980. Sanjay had crashed his light aircraft when he was stunt-flying over central Delhi.

At Santokh Singh's memorial service Zail Singh was even photographed in the company of Bhindranwale. However Bhindranwale was not pleased to see the Home Minister. The wound caused by the burning of his sermons was by now festering in his mind. While preaching to the congregation he made an obvious reference to the fact that Zail Singh dyed his beard, another sin to an orthodox Sikh. The preacher said: 'In a village anyone who has his face blackened and sandals hung round his neck and is made to sit backwards on a donkey is being punished because he has molested someone's sister or someone's mother. I am surprised to see here that some people have blackened their own faces. I do not know whose sisters they have molested.'

Although Bhindranwale had fallen out with the Congress, the Congress had not yet fallen out with him. In spite of Bhindranwale's insulting remarks about his dyed beard Zail Singh still thought that Bhindranwale might be useful to him. But a new bidder for the Sant's support had already entered the ring, the Akali Dal.

6

Mrs Gandhi
Attempts to Negotiate
with the Sikhs

The Akali Dal's decision to adopt Bhindranwale was rank political opportunism. The party leaders paid a heavy price for it. After their defeat in the parliamentary and the state assembly elections, the Akali Dal reviewed their strategy. Kudip Nayar, who is himself a Punjabi, described the Akali Dal's findings. 'They [the Akali Dal leaders] believed their "secular" image during the coalition with [the] Janata had damaged their equation with the Sikhs, who thought that their own [Akali Dal] government did little for them. They came to the conclusion that to get a better image they must woo the Sikhs; they must rely on the traditional stand of combining religion with politics.'[1] No one could be less secular than Bhindranwale and there could be no more effective way of the Akali Dal leaders demonstrating to Sikhs that they had shed their 'secular image' than by enlisting his support. His movement against the Nirankaris which the Akalis had not supported when they were in power had, by the time the Akalis conducted their policy review, demonstrated that Bhindranwale was a force to be reckoned with among the Sikhs. He had also organised a massive demonstration against tobacco in Amritsar, as part of a campaign to get the sale of tobacco banned in their holy city.

Although the Gurus banned all narcotics, for some reason Sikhs are far more obsessed with tobacco than with other narcotics like alcohol and opium. Opium eating is common among the Sikh peasantry. As for alcohol, when India's fervent teetotaller Prime Minister, Morarji Desai, visited Punjab in 1978 the Akali Dal Chief Minister, Badal, announced that in Morarji's honour the Punjab government would introduce a weekly dry day (a day when liquor shops and bars are closed). Morarji Desai replied tartly, 'You need to. Punjab has the highest per capita consumption of alcohol in the country.'

In order to return, yet again, to agitational politics as the champion of Sikh grievances, the Akali Dal leaders had first to define those grievances in the shape of specific demands. They had the Anandpur Sahib Resolution but it was wrapped in too much rhetoric and so they presented Mrs Gandhi with a list of forty-five specific demands based on the Resolution. That list was drawn up in September 1981. It was hurriedly revised when Bhindranwale was arrested and another list, this time of only fifteen demands, was presented to Mrs Gandhi in October 1981. Top of the list, demand number one, was the unconditional release of Sant Jarnail Singh Bhindranwale. This was the first bid that the Akali Dal made for Bhindranwale's support. They were well aware of the sort of man Bhindranwale was but they did not hesitate to enlist him on their side.

Mrs Gandhi was worried by the Akali Dal's threat to launch an agitation against her government. The Akali Dal had shown its muscle during the Emergency. It was the only opposition party courageous enough to defy the Draconian Maintenance of Internal Security Act, which gave the police virtually unlimited powers to arrest and detain without trial. In the tradition of the Gurudwara Reform Movement and all subsequent Akali Dal agitation, every day parties of Sikhs would march out of the Golden Temple complex, shouting slogans against the government, to be arrested by waiting policemen. The cry '*Raj Karega Khalsa*' – 'The Khalsa shall rule' – rang out from the Golden Temple complex to match the Sikh farmers' slogan '*Tanashahi nahin chalegi*' – 'Dictatorship will not last!' Mrs Gandhi regarded the Akali Dal agitation as a serious threat to the Emergency. Fear of the government is the first requirement of any dictator and Mrs Gandhi was a temporary dictator at that time; yet here were the Akalis openly demonstrating that they were not afraid. Mrs Gandhi was so worried that the Akali Dal's example might embolden other opposition parties to defy her and bring down the precarious structure of the Emergency that she sent Amarinder Singh, the wealthy and influential head of the family of the former maharajas of Patiala, and Bhai Ashok Singh, the son of a Sikh priest, to negotiate with them. The two envoys offered the Akali Dal the possibility of forming a coalition government with the Congress but the Akalis rejected the proposal.

Sant Harchand Singh Longowal, the man who organised the campaign against the Emergency, was now the President of the Akali Dal. He was therefore in charge of the party organisation and master-minded the new movement against Mrs Gandhi's government. Longowal was an unlikely person to lead an agitation. Smaller than the other Akali Dal leaders, with a round belly and a straggly beard, he was soft spoken and modest. He came into politics through the religious network. He had originally been the guardian of a *gurudwara* in the village of Longowal in Sangrur district, where he had achieved a reputation for piety. This reputation and links with the left-wing of the Akali Dal got him the party ticket for the state assembly elections in 1969. But until the Emergency he remained a 'hand raiser', which is Indian terminology for lobby fodder. The arrest of the established leadership during the Emergency created a vacuum which Longowal stepped into.

Faced with the prospect of another agitation led by the surprisingly formidable Longowal, Mrs Gandhi hurriedly started talks on the Akali Dal's demands. The demands were for the most part loosely worded and not properly thought out. The Akali Dal's first list submitted in September contained forty-five demands. The list with Bhindranwale's release at the top, which they submitted only one month later, contained only fifteen. They were divided into two categories, religious and political.

The religious demands included the grant of holy city status to Amritsar, on the pattern of Hardwar, Benares and Kurukshetra, three historic Hindu pilgrimage towns. The Akali Dal had not done their homework − no city in India has been given holy city status. The Sikhs also wanted the recitation of the holy scriptures in the Golden Temple to be broadcast; but they could never decide whether they wanted it broadcast by the government on All India Radio or whether they wanted their own radio station. Perhaps the best example of their own confusion was the demand for renaming the 'Flying Mail' from Delhi to Amritsar the Golden Temple Express. In spite of its name and a generous allocation of making-up time provided in its running schedule, the Flying Mail's punctuality record was not good. After putting forward this demand, Sikh leaders began to realise that passengers enraged by the train's 'late-running' might curse the name of the Hari Mandir. They also realised that non-Sikhs might drink and would certainly smoke in the train named after their most sacred shrine, where even the carrying of tobacco is regarded as desecration. The demand for the Hari Mandir Express was quietly dropped. The old demand for Sikhs to be allowed to carry their symbolic daggers on domestic and international flights also came up.

The only religious demand which caused serious difficulties was that for a *gurudwara* act to cover historic Sikh temples throughout the country. The act passed by the British only gave the SGPC control over *gurudwaras* in Punjab. Mrs Gandhi was not at all happy about extending the SGPC's powers any further, especially because with those powers would come even more money. The SGPC's revenue was already reckoned to be over 120 million rupees a year, the equivalent of 8 million pounds sterling, and that money was available to finance activities of the Akali Dal.

The Akalis political demands were more difficult than the religious ones. The three main stumbling blocks were the Punjab river waters, Chandigarh and, of course, the demand for greater autonomy. Three years after the Anandpur Sahib Resolution, Mrs Gandhi had announced an award for sharing the waters of the Rivers Ravi and Beas between Punjab, Haryana and Rajasthan states. When the Akali Dal came to power, they filed a case in the Supreme Court challenging the central government's right to make an award. This case stuck in the Supreme Court, delaying the implementation of the award.

On her return to power Mrs Gandhi got round that one by ordering her Chief Minister, the luckless Darbara Singh, to withdraw the Punjab government's case. At the same time it was announced that work on the canal to carry the water from Punjab's River Sutlej to Haryana's River Jumna would start. There was no way that Mrs Gandhi could go back on her basic commitment to provide adequate water supplies for Haryana and for the £400 million Rajasthan canal project which was under construction.

The status of Chandigarh remained a problem because the Akalis would not agree to cede the two *tahsils* of Abohar and Fazilka, which had been the quid pro quo for getting Chandigarh under Mrs Gandhi's award. Mrs Gandhi insisted that Punjab should cede the two prosperous *tahsils* to satisfy the demands of Haryana, even though neither of them were contiguous to Punjab and the majority of the population were Punjabi not Hindu speakers. If she had changed her view on this there would have been a settlement with the Akali Dal a year before Operation Blue Star. Haryana had a double claim on Mrs Gandhi. Its stand on Chandigarh was represented by a Congress (Indira) state government, while the Punjab demand was represented by the opposition Akali Dal. Haryana was also very much a Hindu majority state and throughout the Akali Dal agitation Mrs Gandhi was making a definite bid for the Hindu vote.

The demand for autonomy was a repetition of the Anandpur Sahib demand to limit the central government's responsibilities to foreign affairs, defence, currency and communication. Once again the Akalis were very unwise to spell out that demand so specifically. They were never to get anywhere near its acceptance and Bhindranwale was to mock them for their failure. This demand also strengthened the hands of Hindu critics of the Akali Dal who had always maintained that the Anandpur Sahib Resolution was in effect a demand for an independent Khalistan.

One of the Akali demands which was dropped in the second list was for the government to stop 'projecting Sikhs in an improper way in films, TV, etc.' This appeared to be a reference to the sense of grievance some Sikhs understandably had about being the butt of the rest of India's humour. Jokes portraying the Sikhs as particularly stupid abound in India, and, in fact, are often told by Sikhs themselves. One story, for instance, concerns a Sikh minister in Nehru's Cabinet who flew with his Prime Minister on an official trip. The cabin was rather cool so the minister asked Pandit Nehru whether he would mind if the pilot turned off the *punkha*, or fan. Nehru replied testily, 'Which fan?' The Sikh minister pointed out of the window to the propeller. In Delhi it is still very common to call twelve midday *sardarji*, or Sikh time. The theory is that the temperature inside a Sikh's turban gets so hot at midday that he goes 'on the boil'. During Bhindranwale's heyday I was often asked, 'Why should India welcome Khalistan or Sikh independence?' The answer was, 'Because India and Pakistan need a duffer state between them.' A poor joke, but typical of those about Sikhs.

Mrs Gandhi first met the Akali Dal leaders in Parliament House on 16th October 1981. That was the day after Bhindranwale was released and so the Akali Dal leaders' first demand had already been met. According to one of the negotiators, Balwant Singh, the former Finance Minister in the Akali Dal government, the Prime Minister was in a very good mood although she did speak sternly about Bhindranwale. The Akali leaders told the Prime Minister that he was her party's creation, not theirs. Another round of talks with the Prime Minister followed the next month. The water issue dominated these two rounds. The talks were broken off temporarily but the Akali Dal leaders were still optimistic. The Prime Minister seemed to be in an understanding frame of mind, according to Balwant Singh. Then, in December, Mrs Gandhi suddenly announced another water award without consulting the Akali Dal. It was an improvement on the 1976 award in that Punjab was now to get more water than the neighbouring state of Haryana. But the lion's share of the water was still to go to the desert state of Rajasthan. It was at this time that Mrs Gandhi ordered the Punjab Chief Minister to withdraw the case the Akali Dal had filed in the Supreme Court.

Mrs Gandhi resumed her talks with the Akali Dal leaders in April 1982. The venue was again Parliament House. But this time Mrs Gandhi was at her most frosty. According to Balwant Singh, all the Prime Minister would offer was 'unspecified alternative ways of making up the loss of water'. This was the last time the Prime Minister played a direct role in negotiations with the Akali Dal. Kuldip Nayar saw the breakdown of those talks as a watershed. He wrote, 'From that day onward the distance between the government and the Akalis began to increase. And like a Greek tragedy both sides relentlessly slipped into a situation that spelt disaster.'[2]

The most obvious explanation for the change in Mrs Gandhi's attitude is that politics came before statesmanship. The following month elections to the state assemblies were due in Haryana and in the Himalayan state of Himachal Pradesh, which also borders on Punjab. Both states had sizeable populations of Punjabi-speaking Hindus who would certainly not have favoured concessions to the party of the Sikhs. Haryana was of course also involved in the water dispute, and that political contortionist, the Haryana Chief Minister, Bhajan Lal, had warned Mrs Gandhi that he already had enough problems on his hands because of her new water award, which had reduced his state's share.

To keep up the pressure, Longowal announced a movement to prevent the digging of the canal to link the Sutlej with the Jumna. He did not remind his followers that when the Akali government was in power it had drawn up plans to start work on this canal. But for once Longowal, the master of *morchas*, or agitations, misjudged the situation. The '*Nahar Roko*', or 'Stop the Canal' agitation, flopped because the Akalis were not strong in the eastern border of Punjab and the issue did not have the religious overtones of other Akali Dal agitations.

Meanwhile Bhindranwale's campaign of violence was continuing and the Akali Dal leaders felt the need to match his extremism with their own. By the end of April 1982, just six months after the campaign of violence associated with the arrest of Bhindranwale started, the situation was so bad that Parliament passed a special resolution expressing 'deep anguish and concern' over the situation in the Punjab. The resolution said: 'The House reiterates that the law shall take its course to bring the culprits to book speedily.' The tragedy of the Punjab was that the law did not 'take its course' and the culprits were not 'brought to book speedily'.

The month in which Parliament passed that resolution was the month in which Bhindranwale was allowed to drive round Delhi with his supporters brandishing automatic weapons. Harkishan Singh Surjeet, a Sikh member of the Upper House of Parliament belonging to the Communist Party (Marxist), accused the Congress Party of actually organising Bhindranwale's visit to Delhi. He said in Parliament, 'I want to tell the House that he [Bhindranwale] gets protection from both the Akali Dal and the Congress (Indira). It is a tragedy that he was in Delhi for ten days last month. Who invited him? Who organised his function? I want to tell you that if political parties for their narrow interests allow these persons to poison the whole atmosphere, you cannot keep communal peace in the state.' Whether the Congress Party was involved or not, there is no doubt that the Congress government's Home Minister, Zail Singh, could have arrested Bhindranwale. The Home Ministry does claim that a warrant was issued for Bhindranwale's arrest when he went on to Bombay but that he escaped before the police could get him. Mrs Amarjit Kaur, a Congress Member of Parliament from Punjab, has claimed that Bhindranwale was tipped off. She said, 'Bhindranwale had planted his own people in government offices, in the police and in the intelligence agencies.'[3] If that was so, it made it all the more urgent for the Home Minister to act swiftly, but he did not.

What should by now have been causing particular concern to the government was a campaign by Bhindranwale to stir up hatred between Hindus and Sikhs. In order to incite Hindus, heads and other parts of the anatomy of cows were thrown into temples — the cow is of course sacred to Hindus — and the Dal Khalsa claimed responsibility. One of the most sinister aspects of Bhindranwale's strategy was his attempt to cause such communal tension that Hindus would leave Punjab in fear. He hoped this would provoke a Hindu backlash elsewhere which would convince many Sikhs that they would only be safe in Punjab. Around 20 per cent of the Sikh population lived outside Punjab. Bhindranwale wanted as many as possible back to weaken the community's links with the rest of India and to increase the Sikh proportion of Punjab's population. To the great credit of Hindu leaders no lasting threat to Sikhs living outside Punjab did develop during Bhindranwale's lifetime.

Although the government made no move against Bhindran-wale himself, his right-hand man and the son of his Guru was arrested on 19th July 1982. According to Sanjeev Gaur of the *Indian Express* who was posted in Amritsar, the Governor of the Punjab personally ordered the arrest because Amrik Singh had insulted him by demanding the release of some members of the All India Sikh Students Federation. Amrik Singh was Presi-dent of this Federation. Although nominally an Akali Dal body, the Federation was by now in Bhindranwale's hands. There were already several charges against Amrik Singh, in-cluding attempting to murder a Nirankari leader near Amrit-sar, but by then in Punjab it needed more than the filing of cases to get the police to arrest a prominent Bhindranwale supporter. Bhindranwale was infuriated by the arrest of his lieutenant, but before challenging the government he took the prudent step of taking up residence again in the hostel complex of the Golden Temple. He moved into Room Number 47 in the Guru Nanak Rest House. The Guru Nanak Rest House is one of a number of offices and hostels which are separated from the main Temple by a public road. The Chief Minister of Punjab always main-tained that the Rest House was not part of the Golden Temple complex and therefore there was nothing to stop the police entering it. They did not because others in the government in Delhi were opposed to it. There is no record of Bhindranwale ever leaving the surroundings of the Golden Temple again until his death.

After securing himself in the Guru Nanak Rest House, Bhindranwale announced a *morcha* or movement to demand the release of Amrik Singh. But to Bhindranwale's chagrin, the *morcha* was not a great success. The response showed that Bhindranwale's following in the villages was not as great as the press had led him to believe. If Bhindranwale's *morcha* had been allowed to flop it would have been a fatal blow to his prestige. But the Akali Dal, cynical as ever, had other ideas. They wanted to relaunch their own *morcha* which had failed in the east. They believed it would succeed if it was relaunched in

Amritsar where Akali support was strong and where, of course, there were the required religious overtones. The way to guarantee success, Longowal thought, would be to take up Bhindranwale's cause too. So on 4th August 1982 in the Golden Temple in Amritsar, Longowal announced a '*Dharam Yudh*' or religious war to fight for the implementation of the Anandpur Sahib Resolution. Bhindranwale announced that his *morcha* for the release of Amrik Singh was merging with the Akali *morcha*.

The new Morcha was a great success. Once again hundreds of Sikhs would gather daily inside the Golden Temple and listen to sermons about the religious duty to fight for the Akalis' demands. Longowal spoke almost every day, Bhindranwale occasionally. The *jathas* (groups) wearing saffron (the colour of martyrdom) bands in their turbans, would then march out of the Temple and down to the police stations, shouting traditional religious slogans like '*Raj Karega Khalsa!*' – 'The Khalsa shall rule!' Many women, with daggers slung over their shoulders, used to take part in these demonstrations too. The whole operation was organised by Longowal who was known as 'Morcha Dictator'. He made sure that a *jatha* from one part or the other of Punjab came to the Golden Temple each day. Within two months the jails were overflowing and special prisons had to be established in schools and other government buildings. On one occasion a thousand Akali prisoners refused to stay in an old fort where the government had set up a temporary jail. They said the fort was infested with snakes. When other Akalis found it was a case of no room at the jail, they made their buses their prisons. The police did not need to guard them because the Akalis had no intention of relieving the government of its embarrassment by escaping.

On 11th September, thirty-four members of a *jatha* were killed when a bus in which they were being taken to jail crashed with a train at an unmanned railway crossing near Amritsar. Bhindranwale and Longowal both alleged that the thirty-four had been deliberately killed by the police, and they were declared martyrs. The Sikhs like to mark every historic occasion with a *gurudwara*, and so now they are building a *gurudwara* at the site of the accident. They are calling it Gurudwara Takkar Sahib (Gurudwara of the Collision). That accident led to a violent demonstration in the heart of Delhi itself.

On 10th October a vast procession wound its way through the streets of Delhi carrying the ashes of the 'martyrs'. That procession passed off peacefully but the next day thousands of Sikhs tried to storm Parliament itself to protest to their MPs about the accident. They set fire to buses, tore down street lighting and uprooted road signs. Police and paramilitary forces battled with them for several hours, firing tear-gas to disperse them.

Mrs Gandhi was worried. It looked as though the Akalis had brought their Morcha to Delhi and if there is one thing which always alarms the Indian government, it is the prospect of prolonged violence and disturbances in the capital. So it was not surprising that, within days of the riot outside Parliament, Mrs Gandhi ordered the release of all the Akali demonstrators and sent a special envoy to Amritsar to re-open negotiations with the Sikh religious party's leaders.

Her envoy was Swaran Singh, who had earlier served for many years in her Cabinet. He came up with a formula which did satisfy the Akali Dal leaders and Mrs Gandhi's Cabinet colleagues. Swaran Singh thought that it had satisfied Mrs Gandhi too. But she turned it down at the last moment. The former Cabinet Minister was bitterly disappointed and never became involved in the negotiations again. However, it would not be long before the talks were resumed. They were resumed because the Akali Dal leaders came up with another highly effective way of keeping the pressure on Mrs Gandhi.

7

The Asian Games
and their Aftermath

On 6th November, the day that the talks with Swaran Singh broke down, Morcha Dictator Longowal announced that the Akali Dal would demonstrate in Delhi during the Asian Games due to start in less than three weeks. Mrs Gandhi's cabinet colleagues and senior officials panicked because the prestige of Rajiv Gandhi was at stake. The Prime Minister's eldest son had entered politics following Sanjay's death and it was already clear that Mrs Gandhi wanted to assure his succession to the dynasty founded by her father. At first politics and Rajiv did not seem to go together. Politicians and journalists were saying that Rajiv was 'too nice' to be an effective politician. He won praise for what he did not do, becoming known as 'Mr Clean' in the international press, but there was no praise for what he did do. Rajiv Gandhi badly needed an achievement to his name and so Mrs Gandhi decided that he should take over the management of the Asian Games.

At that stage Rajiv Gandhi appeared to have more of a flair for management than politics and the Games became his first big test. No effort was spared. Labourers were brought in from the surrounding states to build an Olympic village, with seven new stadiums and a whole crop of five-star hotels. New Delhi

1 *Above*, the Golden Temple in Amritsar, the holiest Sikh shrine

2 *Below*, the Golden Temple, showing the *parikrama*, or pavement, surrounding the holy pool, and the close proximity of the buildings outside the complex, which added to the army's problems

3-4 *Above*, two members of the Akali Trinity: *left*, Gurcharan Singh Tohra, the President of the SGPC; *right*, Harcharan Singh Longowal, the Morcha Dictator

5 *Below*, The Akal Takht in the days before Operation Blue Star. The paved, marble courtyard in front of the shrine became a 'killing ground' during the army action in the Temple complex

underwent a facelift. Seven flyovers were built; *neem*, *jamun* and banyan trees were massacred to widen the leafy avenues the city is justly famous for, and a ring railway was opened.

Much thought was given to the welfare of the athletes and the spectators but none to the labourers building the facilities for them. They were housed in shacks without even adequate water supplies. Contractors took a cut of their meagre wages, and did not bother to provide them with any protective clothing. When the labourers from the neighbouring states, who had some knowledge of their rights under India's elaborate but all too often unimplemented labour laws, became too demanding, contractors went further afield. They scoured the villages of states as remote as Orissa on the east coast and brought in inexperienced manpower which they hoped would be ignorant of their rights. They did all they could to keep the capital's hyper-active voluntary social workers out of the camps but the Supreme Court ordered the government to appoint three ombudsmen to protect the Asian Games workers' rights. The press also highlighted the plight of the workers. A lot of hot air was generated, and not much more. Just before the Games started one of the most active social workers, Inder Mohan, wrote: 'The plight of workers employed in Asian Games construction has to be seen to be believed. Alongside imposing buildings described as visual treats, there are camps where the workers have been living in hovels without any sanitary arrangements. There is no privacy for women. Unlike in their villages they have to squat beside the men. Children squat all over the *jhuggis* [shacks]. The stench can be felt from a distance.' Inder Mohan thought that the hue and cry about these conditions *had* been worth while: 'Certain voluntary workers and organisations have taken it upon themselves to organise the construction workers . . . A process of change has been initiated. It may take some years to achieve substantial results. But they will become a force to reckon with.'[1]

Rajiv Gandhi and his team had troubles with architects too. The badminton and volleyball stadium nearly did not get its roof because the builders said the design was faulty. A British engineer was called in and the stadium eventually got its roof. The swimming pool was not so lucky. It was converted from 'indoor' to 'outdoor' half-way through its construction because the architects and the builders could not agree whether the structure would support the roof or not. A section of one of the flyovers collapsed while it was being built. There was of course trouble with accountants too. The government maintained that it was only spending 700 million rupees, about £46 million, on the Asian Games but independent assessors multiplied that figure by ten. It cost 230,000 rupees, that is £15,000, just to provide a special train, staff and food for thirty-four elephants to travel the length of India to take part in the opening extravaganza.

Opposition politicians inevitably criticised the selection of the Indian athletes, claiming that it was their politics and not their prowess which had counted. It was certainly the politics of Charanjit Singh, a Sikh businessman and Congress Member of Parliament, which counted in the award of a prime site in the middle of New Delhi to build a five-star hotel to house Asian Games guests.

That hotel was not completed in time for the Games but all the most important facilities were. In spite of all the difficulties Delhi was ready for the 9th Asiad. Rajiv Gandhi had bulldozed his way through the Indian bureaucracy and achieved what by the standards of any country was a miracle: starting from nothing he had built all the facilities for the largest ever Asian Games within two years.

When Longowal dropped his bombshell there was consternation at the highest levels of the Indian government. There was widespread resentment in the Hindu community too at the threat to disrupt the greatest sporting spectacle ever seen in India. The police were ordered to throw a cordon round Delhi to prevent any Akali demonstrators reaching the Asian Games. Most roads to the capital pass through Haryana and there the Chief Minister, Bhajan Lal, once again lost no opportunity to demonstrate his loyalty to Mrs Gandhi. No one was spared the attention of the Haryana police. The former head of the Indian Air Force, Air Chief Marshal Arjun Singh, was told to prove that he was not going to demonstrate at the Games. Lieutenant-General Jagjit Singh Aurora, who took the surrender of the Pakistan army after the Bangladesh war, suffered the same indignity. A judge of the High Court was searched so many times that it took him eight hours instead of four to get from Chandigarh to Delhi. A businessman told me he was made to take off his turban so that police could search underneath it. Even Mrs Gandhi's own supporters were not spared. According to Kuldip Nayar, the Congress Member of Parliament, Mrs Amarjit Kaur was in tears in the Central Hall of Parliament when she related to journalists and fellow politicians the way Bhajan Lal's police had treated her and her husband.

The sealing off of Delhi and the arrest of more than 1,500 Sikhs suspected of intending to demonstrate at the Asian Games was grist to Bhindranwale's mill. From then onwards he used to ask those who came to his daily *darshan* or audience: 'You want to know what are the signs that Sikhs are slaves of the Hindus? The first is that Sikhs were prevented from attending the Asian Games in Delhi.' This was to be by no means the last disastrous intervention by Bhajan Lal in the Punjab crisis.

Mrs Gandhi always believed in 'stick and carrot' policies. So she decided to soften the *danda* (stick) of Bhajan Lal's police with another attempt at negotiations. This time she brought in the head of the royal family of Patiala to try to persuade the Akalis to settle. Indian Maharajas lost all their privileges during Mrs Gandhi's first government but the heads of the larger houses, and Patiala is the largest of the Punjab princely states, retained their influence. Amarinder Singh was forty-two. He had served in the Sikh regiment, reaching the rank of Captain. When his father died he retired from the army to manage the family's lands and business. The former army captain entered Parliament as a member of Mrs Gandhi's party. He was an old schoolfriend of Rajiv Gandhi. It was Rajiv who suggested that Amarinder Singh should be involved in the negotiations.

According to Amarinder Singh, agreement was reached between the Akali Dal leaders and Mrs Gandhi's team of negotiators on 18th November 1982 in Delhi. The Akali Dal leaders wanted to fly back to Chandigarh but they were advised to wait until it was confirmed that Mrs Gandhi had approved the agreement. Unfortunately, according to Amarinder Singh, news of the agreement leaked out to Bhajan Lal. He managed to persuade the Prime Minister that settling the water and the

Chandigarh disputes without first being seen to consult his state would be disastrous. The Chief Minister of Rajasthan, the other state affected by the water dispute, also happened to be in Delhi on that night. He was persuaded to support Bhajan Lal's stand and Mrs Gandhi took their point. For the second time that month the Akali Dal leaders were let down at the last moment.

Bhindranwale was delighted because he did not want a settlement at any cost. He had often said that there was no point in dealing with that 'Brahmin woman' or 'Pandit's daughter', as he disparagingly referred to Mrs Gandhi. When he was proved right twice in one month his authority and influence waxed while that of Longowal and the Akali Dal leaders waned. The failure of the Asian Games negotiations marked the start of the split between Bhindranwale and the Akali Dal leaders, a split which was to lead to the total isolation of Longowal and his colleagues, leaving Mrs Gandhi with only two options – to go into the Golden Temple to get Bhindranwale or to negotiate with him. However, the government's immediate problem was solved. The stick worked even if the carrot failed and the Asiad passed off peacefully. Rajiv Gandhi had passed his first test.

The serious consequences of the failure to negotiate a settlement were soon obvious. A month after the Asian Games Longowal called a meeting of Sikh ex-servicemen at the Golden Temple. Sikhs make up at least 10 per cent of the army, including a large number of the officers. There are also Sikhs in the navy, the air force, and in the paramilitary police forces. As many as 170 retired officers above the rank of colonel responded to Longowal's call to rally to the Sikh cause. Many of them fell under the spell of Sant Jarnail Singh Bhindranwale at that meeting in the Golden Temple. Lieutenant-General Aurora, the hero of Dacca, explained this phenomenon of disciplined soldiers falling for a rabble-rousing preacher:

After leaving the army [they] returned to the Punjab to find how values had changed. Their dissatisfaction stemmed from the fact that the retired servicemen were accorded little respect or consideration by the civil administration. To add fuel to the fire, during the Asiad in 1982, when all Sikhs travelling to Delhi from the Punjab were stopped and were searched regardless of convictions, they felt aggrieved and some of them came under Sant Bhindranwale's influence.[2]

Another retired Sikh General, Jaswant Singh Bhullar, also pointed to the Asian Games as a factor which contributed to the success of Longowal's appeal to ex-servicemen. He wrote: 'The treatment meted out to Sikhs by the Haryana government during the days of the Asian Games has badly jolted the Sikh psyche.'[3] Bhullar was to join Bhindranwale, leaving the Golden Temple just before Operation Blue Star. He has since set up an organisation in the United States to propagate Sikh independence.

Among the senior retired officers who attended Longowal's convention was Major-General Shahbeg Singh, a hero of the Bangladesh war who had been dismissed the service on corruption charges the day before he was due to retire and had been nursing a grievance ever since. He was to become Bhindranwale's military adviser and to plan the defence of the Golden Temple. Narinderjit Singh Nanda, the scholarly and gentle public relations officer of the SGPC, was present at the convention. He told Satish Jacob that Longowal was surprised by the turnout of officers and men. Journalists put the figure at 5,000 but Nanda said it was nearer 30,000. Bhindranwale and Shahbeg Singh advocated an armed uprising against the government to force it to grant Sikhs their rights. Other retired officers, however, said that an armed uprising could never succeed on the open plains of Punjab. Nanda suggested that the Sikhs should combat the government with, in his words, 'the power of the pen', by launching a newspaper. Many of the senior officers approved of his suggestion but Bhindranwale shot it down brutally. 'You literate moron,' he snarled, 'do you think this government will give you anything unless you snatch it from them?'

The government was thoroughly alarmed when it received intelligence reports of the convention because many of the ex-servicemen had sons serving in the armed forces. As a result, on 24th January 1983, negotiations with the Akali Dal were hurriedly resumed. It was at this stage that Rajiv Gandhi became a member of the 'Think Tank' which was to end up virtually running Punjab. The irony was that there was not a single Sikh in the Think Tank. At the start of the 1983 negotiations the three most important members were all civil servants. Two of them came from the opposite end of India to Punjab — the south. There was Mrs Gandhi's Principal Secretary P.C. Alexander, a Christian from Kerala at the south-western tip of India. The Cabinet Secretary, Krishnaswamy Rao Sahib, was a Hindu from Andhra Pradesh in the south-east. The third civil servant was the Secretary of the Home Ministry, Mr T.N. Chaturvedi. He was a Brahmin from Uttar Pradesh. Sikhs are deeply suspicious of Brahmins, seeing them as intellectual enemies of their religion. He was replaced in March by M.M.K. Wali, another Brahmin, this time from Kashmir. Longowal and Bhindranwale both used to say in public that Wali had been brought in because Mrs Gandhi was herself a Kashmiri Brahmin.

The opposition parties were also brought into this round of talks. Harkishan Singh Surjeet, the Punjabi Communist Member of Parliament, told me that much progress was made at these talks. He alleged that they would have succeeded if the government had only agreed to allow the Punjab to continue drawing off the amount of river water it was actually using at that time until a tribunal had decided the issue. The government did in fact agree to that in July, but by then it was too late.

The talks involving the opposition leaders broke off in February and Mrs Gandhi announced two unilateral awards. She went to the main *gurudwara* in New Delhi, Bangla Sahib, which is near Parliament, and announced that she had accepted all the Akali Dal's religious demands. The next month she announced the setting up of a one-man commission to study the constitutional arrangements between the central and state governments. Greater powers for the states was of course the main political demand of the Akali Dal. The 'one man' was a retired Sikh judge of the Supreme Court, R.S. Sarkaria. But these two gestures did nothing to help Longowal. If the concessions had emerged from talks with the government, Longowal could have claimed them as a victory for the Morcha, and this would have strengthened his hand against Bhindranwale, who bitterly criticised the Akali Dal leaders for negotiating at all.

The Sikh MP Harkishan Singh Surjeet maintained that another agreement was reached in the negotiations early in 1983 but that Mrs Gandhi reneged on it again. Harkishan Singh Surjeet said to me, 'Three times in six months an agreement was reached and three times the Prime Minister backed out. Each time the interests of the Hindus of Haryana weighed more heavily with her than a settlement with the Sikhs.' Although a communist, Harkishan Singh Surjeet was one of the most trusted advisers of Gurcharan Singh Tohra, the President of the SGPC and of course one of the Akali Trinity. Tohra at this stage was still playing his own game. He was still hoping to use the Akali Morcha and Bhindranwale to discredit the second member of the Akali Trinity, the former Chief Minister Prakash Singh Badal, and take over himself as head of the political wing of the Akali Dal, becoming the party's candidate for the chief-ministership.

The strain these negotiations were putting on the relations between the third member of the Akali Trinity, Longowal, and Bhindranwale was becoming increasingly obvious. Bhindranwale was bitterly critical of Longowal's tactics and he despised the non-violence that Longowal still preached. He used to describe Longowal's office in the Temple complex disparagingly as 'Gandhi Niwas' or Mahatma Gandhi's house. But when pressed Bhindranwale would never say exactly what it was that he wanted.

It was early in 1983 that I first met the Sant. He was sitting on a string bed in his small room at the Guru Nanak hostel surrounded by young men, some armed with automatic weapons, some with old-fashioned Lee-Enfield rifles which are still used by the Indian police, and some with traditional spears. His answers to my questions could at best be described as enigmatic. For instance I asked the preacher to comment on the allegations that he was responsible for the continuing violence in Punjab. He replied, 'It's the government who is doing all the killing. Isn't it the government which killed those martyrs in the bus?' The martyrs he was referring to were of course the Akali demonstrators killed in an accident when a train crashed into their bus at a level crossing. Thinking I might tackle Bhindranwale on a more philosophical level, I asked him whether he thought violence in a good cause was justified. He replied, 'Yes, if to preach Sikhism, and to stop young boys from cutting their hair and shaving, is to believe in violence.' Then I thought I would get him with a specific question and asked, 'Do you or do you not support the demand for Khalistan, Sikh independence from India?' The preacher answered, 'I am neither in favour of it nor against it. If they give it to us, we won't reject it.'

Bhindranwale had by now built up a considerable organisation around himself. Its leading members were to be seen in the Golden Temple on most days. One of them was Harminder Singh Sandhu. He was the General Secretary of the All India Sikh Students Federation. One of the few in Bhindranwale's entourage who spoke English, he used to act as his interpreter. Having studied law he used to inject some coherence into the rambling answers of his leader when interpreting them. Nevertheless when a young Sikh once questioned Sandhu's interpretation Bhindranwale turned on him and said, 'I have implicit faith in him. He can interpret the way he likes. You have no idea what sacrifices he has made. He was hung upside down and he didn't say anything.' In fact Sandhu's loyalty was somewhat suspect. He had, as Bhindranwale said, been arrested, and tortured by the police but his rapid release was never explained. Towards the end of Bhindranwale's time reports based on briefings from Indian intelligence sources started appearing in the press about a double agent called the 'Falcon' who used to cross the border into Pakistan. He was said to be liaising with a Pakistani general and then reporting back to the Indian intelligence agency RAW (Research and Analysis Wing). More details of the alleged activities of the Falcon are contained in the Delhi journalist Chand Joshi's book *Bhindranwale: Myth and Reality*. Sandhu is believed to be the man that Joshi referred to as the Falcon. Whether the Falcon existed or not it is true to say that Sandhu was the only member of the Bhindranwale inner circle to have surrendered to the army during the action in the Golden Temple.

One man whose loyalty to Bhindranwale has never been

questioned was his secretary Rachpal Singh. Like Sandhu he was about thirty years old. Rachpal Singh was a thin-lipped, worried-looking man. He had been a member of Bhindranwale's mission and had been the scribe of some of the preacher's sermons which were burnt by the police when they failed to arrest him at Chando Kalan. Inside the Temple he used to look after Bhindranwale's correspondence and keep a detailed diary of the Sant's visitors.

Bhindranwale's political adviser at this time was Dalbir Singh, a former journalist. He was for many years a member of the Communist Party but had gradually been drifting back towards orthodox Sikhism. He had been in the Golden Temple on the day of the procession which he insisted that Bhindranwale had led against the Nirankaris in 1978. He used to say that the clash that ensued was the turning-point in his life. From that day onward he became a devoted follower of 'Santji'. Dalbir Singh used his contacts with the press to promote Bhindranwale. He also used to advise Bhindranwale on his dealings with the Akali Dal leaders. He was a hawk, strongly opposed to compromising with Longowal or, of course, the government.

The most outstanding of the young Sikh extremists was Amrik Singh, the son of Bhindranwale's Guru, Kartar Singh, who had appointed Bhindranwale to succeed him as head of the Damdami Taksal. Amrik Singh was very quiet, and rarely spoke to journalists, but when decisions had to be made about who should interview Bhindranwale or who should be allowed to film his audiences they were always referred to Amrik Singh. As President of the All India Sikh Students Federation he was responsible for organising many of the murders, robberies and attacks on government property which were almost daily occurrences in Punjab. However at this time, early 1983, he was in jail.

By no means all the young men who had gathered in the Golden Temple were genuine supporters of the Sant or even devout Sikhs. There were many police and army deserters, smugglers and other criminals enjoying the Sant's protection. There were also some Naxalites, left-wing extremists who believe in atheistic communism and violent revolution. Harminder Singh Sandhu once gave Satish Jacob the names of what he called the killer squad. They included four deserters from the Punjab police, Amarjit Singh, Sewa Singh, Kabul Singh and Gurnam Singh, an escaped convict, Talwinder Singh, and Surinder Singh Sodhi.

Sodhi was one of the terrorists who had joined Bhindranwale out of genuine conviction, not because he was fleeing the law. In his late twenties at this time, Sodhi had been a radio mechanic in the town of Hoshiarpur until Bhindranwale and Longowal launched their Morcha. He was a fine marksman and was believed to have been responsible for some of the most audacious terrorist attacks although he liked to be photographed reading the Sikh scriptures. Sodhi was also known as Bhindranwale's transport minister because he claimed that he could drive anything from a scooter to an aeroplane.

Surinder Singh Gill was another devout Sikh who took part in terrorist actions. Aged about twenty-five, he was once an agricultural inspector but as an orthodox Sikh he developed a violent hatred for Nirankaris and left the prized security of government service to join Bhindranwale, the scourge of that 'heretical' sect. He was named as the head of the Dashmesh Regiment, or regiment of the tenth Guru, which claimed responsibility for many of the murders towards the end of Bhindranwale's time. Another man who was inspired by a loathing of the Nirankaris was Ranjit Singh, who was in his mid-thirties. He was notorious for his intolerance and rudeness, and at one stage fell out with Bhindranwale. Singh left the Golden Temple under mysterious circumstances and was arrested by the police in Delhi on the charge of conspiracy to murder the Guru of the Nirankaris in 1980. Bhindranwale accused Longowal and his associates of smuggling Ranjit Singh out of the Temple and surrendering him to Delhi.

All these terrorists were known by name to the shopkeepers and the householders who lived in the narrow alleys surrounding the Golden Temple. They used to join in the conversation at the tea-stalls and wander in and out of shops. The Punjab police must have known who they were also, but they made no attempt to arrest them. By this time Bhindranwale and his men were above the law. It needed sanction from the Prime Minister's Think Tank before they could be arrested and that sanction was not forthcoming.

Nirankaris continued to be the main targets of the terrorists. With the change in Bhindranwale's attitude to the Congress Party, ministers and supporters of the government also came under attack. The Chief Minister himself was attacked, a bomb was thrown into the house of the Punjab Government Education Minister and another into the house of a Congress Member of the Punjab Assembly. Terrorists also attempted to disrupt the celebration of India's national day in January 1983 in Amritsar by throwing bombs. The day after Republic Day Bhindranwale's men robbed their first bank. It was a branch of the Syndicate Bank in Amritsar itself. There was another bank robbery in April. The police believed these robberies showed that Bhindranwale needed money. They suspected that he wanted it to buy arms. Although the violence was alarming, there was little evidence yet of the careful selection of targets which was later to totally demoralise the police and the administration.

After being discredited by the failure of the negotiations in early 1983 Longowal made an attempt to re-establish his control over the agitation which was rapidly moving into Bhindranwale's hands. In April he called for a '*Rasta Roko*'; which means literally 'block the roads'. From the point of view of the Sikhs it was a success. Transport in Punjab was paralysed, and the police suffered 175 casualties. Twenty-one people were killed in the violence. The Sikh response to the *Rasta Roko* gave Longowal the courage to challenge Bhindranwale openly. He ordered the Sant to take an oath of loyalty to him as the 'Dictator' of the Morcha. Dressed in the knee-length blue shirt of a *nihang* or Sikh warrior, Bhindranwale stood with supporters of the Morcha who were going to court arrest, and swore loyalty and obedience to Longowal. That commitment did not last long.

Twelve days later a senior police officer was murdered in broad daylight just as he was coming out of the Golden Temple. The whole of India was outraged and the short-lived treaty between Longowal and Bhindranwale was shattered.

8

Two Brutal Killings – Mrs Gandhi Acts at Last

On the morning of 23rd April 1983 Deputy Inspector-General A.S. Atwal, who was in charge of the police in Amritsar, was among the worshippers thronging the Golden Temple. Like any other believing Sikh he first walked round the *parikrama*, the marble pavement which surrounds the sacred pool in the middle of the complex. He stood and prayed before the Akal Takht, the shrine which symbolises the temporal power of God. He then turned round and joined the queue in front of the Darshani Deorhi, the ornate archway over the entrance to the small viaduct that leads to the sanctum sanctorum – the Hari Mandir itself. He made an offering and took some *prasad*, the sweet wheaten porridge which is the sacrament of the Sikhs, and walked along the viaduct. Inside the shrine the 39-year-old police officer prostrated himself before the Guru Granth Sahib, the Sikh scriptures, stood up and then moved back from the rails so that he could listen to the *granthis*, or priests, chanting hymns to the accompaniment of a harmonium. After a few minutes Atwal left the Hari Mandir and, holding the *prasad* in a leaf so that he could offer it to his family, the Deputy Inspector-General walked towards the main gate. As he was climbing up the marble steps under the ornate clock tower, shots rang out and Atwal collapsed dead. His police bodyguards, who were waiting for him outside, fled. The police post about a hundred yards away did not return fire. Deputy Inspector-General Atwal's body, riddled with bullets, lay in the main entrance to the Sikhs' most sacred shrine for more than two hours before the District Commissioner could persuade the Temple authorities to hand it over.

The Punjab Chief Minister, Darbara Singh, told me later that Atwal had been warned not to enter the Golden Temple. The government had apparently received information that he was a marked man because he had set a trap in which one of Bhindranwale's key men was killed and three others injured. The officer in charge of the CID in Amritsar later told Satish Jacob about that trap. He said that Atwal, who was an unusually active and independent-minded policeman, had planted one of his agents among Bhindranwale's followers. He had told Atwal that on the night of 15th March two of Bhindranwale's most dangerous killers were going out on 'a job'. Atwal had posted a senior superintendent of police with a party of marksmen at the bridge at Manawala, just outside Amritsar on the Grand Trunk Road leading to Delhi. According to the CID officer, at four-thirty in the morning a jeep approached the bridge at speed. It pulled up just in front of the blockade of oil drums the police had put across the road. The Sikhs in the jeep threw a hand-grenade at the police, who returned fire. Senior Superindendent of Police Pandey was injured and one of the Sikhs in the jeep, Hardev Singh, was killed. The driver of the jeep, Gursant Singh, was injured but he managed to get back to the sanctuary of the Golden Temple with the body of Hardev Singh. There Gursant Singh told the press a different version of the incident. He said there was a lorry standing in the middle of the Manawala bridge looking as though it had broken down. When he slowed down to pass it the police who were lying in wait opened fire. They managed to escape but later had to abandon their jeep. Gursant Singh would not say how they managed to get back to the Temple with the body of Hardev Singh. More than twenty-four hours after the incident the Temple authorities rang the District Commissioner and asked him to come to collect the body from the Temple. Bhindranwale issued a statement accusing the police of the cold-blooded murder of one of his followers.

According to the CID officer, Bhindranwale became suspicious of Atwal's agent after the incident. He waited for some time and then tortured and killed him. The police found his mutilated body outside the Guru Nanak Rest House which was Bhindranwale's headquarters. The CID officer suspects that the agent might have revealed the channel he used to communicate with Atwal and that Bhindranwale might have used that channel to lure Atwal into the Temple. So it could be that the Deputy Inspector-General of Police was not quite the innocent worshipper he appeared to be on that morning of 25th April.

The murder of a senior police officer in broad daylight caused a national outcry. Opposition politicians and the press demanded that the police enter the Temple's hostel complex and arrest Bhindranwale and his followers. The *Times of India*, the most influential daily, wrote an editorial bitterly attacking the government, Bhindranwale and the Akali Dal leaders. Longowal had appealed to Sikhs all over the world to resist the entry of the police into the hostel complex. The *Times of India* said, 'Longowal seems hell-bent on worsening an already intensely troubled situation.' It pointed out that the police had already entered the hostel complex when Mrs Gandhi's father was in power. The paper also made the very valid point that the hostel where Bhindranwale had his headquarters was quite separate from the walled complex which housed the actual shrines – the Hari Mandir and the Akal Takht. One of the strangest aspects of the government's handling of this stage of the Punjab crisis was that its information machinery made no effort to bring this point home to the Sikhs. The *Times of India* ended its editorial by saying, 'All this places an awesome burden on the authorities in both New Delhi and Chandigarh, for the laws of the land cannot be allowed to be flouted so flagrantly under cover of religion and natural respect for places of worship.'

According to the Chief Minister of Punjab, his government was anxious to take up that burden but the authorities in Delhi were not. Darbara Singh told me, 'I consistently told the central government that the Guru Nanak Niwas [Rest House] was not part of the Temple complex, that the police should be sent in there, but they told me they were afraid of inflaming Sikh sentiments.' Darbara Singh's old rival Zail Singh had by now been elected President of India, that is to say the constitutional head of state, and so he was no longer directly involved in the government. Still there is no doubt that Mrs Gandhi continued to consult him on Punjab.

The central government made a disastrous mistake by not entering the Guru Nanak Niwas and arresting Bhindranwale after the murder of Deputy Inspector-General of Police Atwal. In the national outcry that followed, very few Sikhs, except those already committed to Bhindranwale, would have raised any objections. In fact many Sikhs, especially those living outside Punjab, would have welcomed it. Sikhs living in the capital, Delhi, and other parts of India were beginning to suffer from the fact that Hindus were now identifying all those who wore Sikh turbans and beards as followers of Bhindranwale.

Longowal and the Akali Dal Trinity must also bear their share of the blame for the failure to arrest Bhindranwale. If, instead of appealing to Sikhs the world over to resist the entry of the police into the Golden Temple, Longowal had told the government that he did not regard the Guru Nanak Niwas as sacred, the government would have had no reason to fear Sikhs reaction to the arrest of Bhindranwale. But Longowal got no support from Gurcharan Singh Tohra, the member of the Akali Dal Trinity who headed the SGPC which controlled the complex. According to Tohra's confidant, Harkishan Singh Surjeet, the SGPC President feared that the other two members of the Akali Dal Trinity were getting together to oust him, and so he still needed Bhindranwale as an ally. Secret negotiations with the government were going on at that time with a view to resolving the Punjab crisis by forming an Akali Dal/Congress coalition government with Badal as Chief Minister. That would have been the end of Tohra's ambitions. So he arranged a meeting between Longowal and Bhindranwale in his office in the Temple complex to scupper the plan for a coalition government. Longowal fell into his trap and the coalition plan was dropped. Once that was achieved Bhindranwale dropped Longowal too.

After that meeting the Sant's close associate Amrik Singh, by now released from jail (by mistake, according to the government), called a meeting of the All India Sikh Students Federation. Although Amrik Singh was the Federation President and Bhindranwale's interpreter, Harminder Singh Sandhu, its General Secretary, the Federation was nominally still an associate body of the Akali Dal. Nevertheless Longowal, the Akali Dal President, was publicly humiliated at the meeting. The journalist Tavleen Singh was there. She said, 'Bhindranwale, dressed in spotless white and carrying a huge sword in a scabbard decorated with gold thread, was the star. Longowal was on the platform but to Bhindranwale went the honour of speaking last. The government was attacked, Hindus were attacked, and Mahatma Gandhi, the father of the nation, was mocked.'[1] According to Tavleen Singh, one of the songs played over the loudspeakers ran: 'Our *bapu* [father] (Guru Gobind Singh) had arms and fine arrows and their [the Hindus'] *bapu* [father] had an old man's stick.' Longowal, sensing the mood of the meeting, felt he had to say, 'It is to rule that we are fighting and it will be a Raj [rule] of the kind that Guru Nanak dreamed of.' He also said, 'Sikhs are involved in a fight for their own freedom.'

Although Longowal meekly towed the Bhindranwale line at that meeting, it did him little good. Bhindranwale was now the hero of the Sikh youth and Longowal was in danger of becoming his prisoner. However he took no initiative to prevent this happening. From then on Longowal rarely emerged from his room in the block next to the Guru Nanak Niwas. He plotted with Badal and with Tohra but he lacked the courage to take the one step which could have saved the situation – to co-operate with the government. In the end it was the Indian army which rescued Longowal from his captivity only to make him a prisoner of Mrs Gandhi.

The row between Bhindranwale and Longowal was causing increasing tension inside the Temple complex where they both spent all their time. This tension was soon to erupt into open violence and to lead to Bhindranwale seeking sanctuary in the Akal Takht. For the present the mounting temperature inside the Temple complex was registered by dead bodies found in the drains outside. The SGPC's Secretary, Bhan Singh, told Satish

Jacob that at least five bodies were found in the sewers in August and September 1983. When Satish Jacob asked him how they had died, he replied, 'Don't ask me. You know.' A police officer told Satish Jacob that the post-mortem reports indicated that the men had been tortured before they were killed. Although the bodies were prima-facie evidence of cases of murder, the police themselves admitted that they made no effort to investigate the deaths.

Bhindranwale was strengthening his grip over the rest of the Punjab too. The murder of Atwal and the failure of the government to do anything about it spread panic throughout the state. Inevitably the public felt that if the government was so weak it could not take action against the murderers of a police officer as senior as Atwal, it certainly would not be able to do anything to protect them. This was the time when stories of Bhindranwale's hit-list started circulating. It was a list of police officers, officials, Hindus and even Sikhs against whom Bhindranwale had a grievance. Much of the legend which grew up around the hit-list was exaggerated. Each name was said to be written on a separate piece of paper and put in a clay pot kept in Bhindranwale's room. Whenever anyone came to Bhindranwale and asked if he could serve the cause, Bhindranwale was said to have asked him to pull a piece of paper out of the pot and read what was written on it. The potential recruit would then read out the name and address on the paper and Bhindranwale would tell him to go and eliminate that person. This seems to be a myth. Neither I, nor Satish Jacob, nor anyone we have talked to, ever saw that pot: but the hit-list did exist. Tavleen Singh, was one of the journalists who did see how a man's name got on that list.

On one occasion Tavleen Singh asked Bhindranwale whether he really believed that the Sikhs were being discriminated against. Bhindranwale became furious and shouted, 'You want to see what they do to Sikhs? Let me show you.' A tall Sikh about thirty years old was brought in front of the preacher. His name was Leher Singh and he was dressed in traditional Sikh clothes, although his beard had been hacked about. Leher Singh said that a police officer called Bichu Ram had slashed off his beard and then told him to go and tell Bhindranwale. When

Tavleen Singh read of Bichu Ram's murder six months later, she realised that she had witnessed the signing of his death warrant.

There was also the much publicised case of Deputy Superintendent of Police Bachan Singh. The All India Sikh Students Federation's President, Amrik Singh, claimed that Bachan Singh had tortured him while he was under arrest. Bhindranwale let it be known that the police officer would have to pay for that with his life. He did, and so did the whole of his family. Bhindranwale and his men also used to send threatening letters to their enemies — for example newspaper editors and journalists who spoke out against him, men such as Khushwant Singh, the Sikh historian and columnist, and Prem Bhatia, the editor of the *Tribune*, the leading English language daily of Punjab and Haryana. Bhatia received so many threats to his life that the police had to camp outside his house in Chandigarh. After the killing of Lala Jagat Narain, one of Bhindranwale's first revenge killings, no journalist could afford to take chances. Bhindranwale himself often said that he saw nothing wrong in killing an enemy of the Sikh 'Panth' (community) and, like every religious fanatic, he saw all his enemies as enemies of the faith.

As the legend of the hit-list grew so did Bhindranwale's influence among the people of Punjab. They came to him to solve their problems instead of going to the courts or to the administration. Satish Jacob once watched a middle-aged woman and her grown-up son pleading their case before Bhindranwale. The woman said that her husband had deserted her and was refusing to support her. She asked Bhindranwale to 'finish' him.

Bhindranwale replied, 'I only finish those who are enemies of the Sikh faith like policemen, government officials and Hindus.'

The son then asked, 'Can you give me a weapon so that I can go and do the job?'

Bhindranwale retorted, 'No. Go and buy a gun yourself.'

'Will I be able to come back here for sanctuary if I do the job?'

'No, we only give sanctuary to those who come back after doing a job in the name of the movement. If you go and eliminate a policeman who has harassed my people or a government official who is against us, then I will not only give you sanctuary, I will welcome you with garlands.'

Eventually the Sant took pity on the young man and his mother. He asked the name of the father's village and said, 'All right. I will tell the *thanedar* [officer in charge of the police station] to break your father's legs.'

When Satish Jacob inquired of Bhindranwale's interpreter how he could do that, the interpreter replied, 'No one can refuse Santji's orders.'

The rich also used to come to Bhindranwale for favours but they had to pay. A Golden Temple priest told Satish Jacob of a wealthy Sikh landlord who wanted to evict the tenant of one of his warehouses. Bhindranwale asked the landlord how much it would be worth to him to get the warehouse vacated. He replied about one million rupees. Bhindranwale told him to put 10,000 rupees at his feet. The next day the tenant was summoned to Bhindranwale's *darshan* or audience and ordered to clear out of the warehouse, and he did. Jagjit Singh Bawa, a Sikh property dealer, said that Bhindranwale used to extort money by threats from his own community too. Bawa once received a letter demanding 20,000 rupees. He paid up at once. Small traders were also harassed, according to Bawa. Young Sikhs would, for instance, go up to cloth dealers and say, 'Santji needs two bales of cloth.' They would then walk off with the cloth of their choice.

The personnel around Bhindranwale changed as his operations spread. The most obvious change was the return of Amrik Singh. After his release it soon became clear to anyone who visited Bhindranwale that Amrik Singh was number two in the hierarchy. General Shahbeg Singh, who was to play such a crucial role in the fortification of the Temple, was also seen in Bhindranwale's company now. People living in the bazaars surrounding the Temple said that they used to hear shots from inside the Temple complex, and had been told that some of the ex-servicemen were giving weapon training to young Sikhs. In June 1983 the government also received reports that Sikhs were being trained to use firearms in camps in Kashmir. The Chief Minister of Kashmir, however, maintained that the camps were merely religious gatherings where young Sikhs brushed up their faith, not their weapon training. The Sikhs, with their martial tradition, are a violent community at the best of times. '*Khun ka badla khun,*' or 'An eye for an eye and a tooth for a tooth,' is the law of the Punjab. So handling guns came naturally to the Sant's young men.

Another new face seen in the Guru Nanak Niwas during the latter half of 1983 was Gurtej Singh. He had been a member of the Indian Administrative Service, the élite body which replaced the Indian Civil Service or ICS of the British. Gurtej Singh had left the service after ten years because of his extreme views on Sikh nationalism. Educated and sophisticated, the former bureaucrat was a sharp contrast to the rustic religious fanatics, deserters and criminals surrounding Bhindranwale. He had invaluable links with the administration and understood how the government worked. Tavleen Singh believes that Gurtej Singh became one of Bhindranwale's 'ideologues'.

After the anti-Hindu slogans, speeches and songs at the students' meeting in the Golden Temple, Bhindranwale concentrated his attention on that community. He had to have enemies to maintain the fervour of his followers and the Hindus were the obvious candidates. Journalists and politicians who tried to prevent relations between the two communities deteriorating by writing and speaking about the close links between Hindus and Sikhs, achieved the very opposite. Bhindranwale told his followers, 'These utterances show that Hindus want to undermine our nation and our faith.' There had been earlier incidents of sacrilege by placing heads and other parts of the anatomy of cows in Hindu temples, but in September 1983 a series of far more savage outrages against the Hindu community began. The first took place in Jagraon, near the industrial city of Ludhiana, on 28th September when young Sikhs fired indiscriminately at Hindus out for their morning walks. A week later came the attack which forced Mrs Gandhi to act. On the night of 5th October Sikhs hijacked a bus in Kapurthala district, separated the Hindu passengers from the Sikhs, and shot the Hindus. Six Hindus died and one was seriously injured. The bus was travelling from Amritsar to Delhi on the Grand Trunk Road, India's National Highway Number One.

The next day Mrs Gandhi suspended the government of Darbara Singh and imposed President's Rule, or central government rule, in Punjab. It was a difficult decision to take because it meant admitting that her own party had failed to rule Punjab. In 1980 Mrs Gandhi had fought her way back to power with the slogan, 'Elect a government that works.' In Punjab it was now clear that her government had not worked.

The Chief Minister, Darbara Singh, thought, with considerable justification, that it was an unfair verdict on him. I met him shortly after President's Rule had been declared. He was still living in the Punjab Chief Minister's house in Chandigarh and was unwell. He had a slight impediment in his speech and one half of his face was bandaged. The former Chief Minister refused to speak on the record, but he made it clear that he blamed the faction in the central government loyal to Zail Singh for his downfall. A senior colleague of Darbara Singh went so far as to claim that President Zail Singh was still in daily contact with Bhindranwale. There is no doubt that Darbara Singh had wanted to take action against Bhindranwale, and that it was the central government which had refused to allow him to send the police into the Temple Rest House which the Sant had made his headquarters. Darbara Singh was also one of the very few Congress leaders who had the courage to attack Bhindranwale by name. As far back as March, speaking about the fact that the terrorists who escaped the police trap set by DI-G Atwal managed to get back to the sanctuary of the Golden Temple, Darbara Singh told the Punjab State Assembly: 'This proves conclusively the oft repeated charge that the extremists are being sheltered and being given active support in religious places in general and in the Guru Nanak Niwas in particular. It can thus be seen that Sant Jarnail Singh Bhindranwale is openly supporting and giving shelter to such desperate people.'

Darbara Singh matched his words with deeds in as far as the central government allowed him. He did order the police to take action against those terrorists they could get hold of, and there was a series of what the Indian police call 'encounters' – a euphemism for cold-blooded murder by the police. Darbara Singh admitted as much to us. On another occasion, when Satish Jacob and I both met him, the former Chief Minister said, 'Encounters did take place, and they were killed. I told my senior police officers, "You kill the killers and I will take the responsibility." ' The trouble was that the police killings sparked off revenge attacks against them by Bhindranwale's men and demoralised the force. The other problem was, of course, that Darbara Singh's police were not allowed to tackle the problem at its roots — the Guru Nanak Niwas.

9

President's Rule Fails

Within hours of the announcement that the central government would now govern Punjab, Mrs Gandhi had the paramilitary police marching through the streets of Amritsar in a show of force. She also promulgated a new ordinance declaring parts of Punjab 'disturbed areas', giving the police almost total freedom from the courts in those areas. They could shoot who they wanted when they wanted and search where they wanted. Mrs Gandhi's government also made it clear that the police did have the power to enter places of worship. Four senior civil servants were sent to run the Punjab government. Mrs Gandhi chose B.D. Pande, one of the most experienced retired civil servants, to head the administration as Governor. During his distinguished career he had held many senior appointments including the top job of all, that of Cabinet Secretary. Pande was a man renowned for his efficiency and incorruptibility, a man with no political ambitions.

Mrs Gandhi wanted to show India that she had not lost the will to act. India was impressed but Bhindranwale was not. Two days after the imposition of President's Rule an assistant superintendent of jails was beaten up by Bhindranwale's young men inside the Golden Temple; a Sikh who was a known opponent of Bhindranwale was shot dead near the industrial city of Jullundur; elsewhere another man was shot and injured; and, in a fourth incident, a Hindu's shop was looted. Two weeks after President's Rule started, the Calcutta to Kashmir Express was derailed while passing through Punjab: nineteen people were killed and 129 injured. The next month Bhindranwale openly defied Mrs Gandhi by repeating the incident which had led her to impose President's Rule. On 18th November 1983 another bus was hijacked and four Hindu passengers were shot in cold blood.

By this time Mrs Gandhi had appointed her trusted lieutenant P.S. Bhinder to head the police in Punjab. Bhinder's wife was a Congress (Indira) Member of Parliament. Bhinder himself, throughout his long and controversial police career, had never wavered in his loyalty to Mrs Gandhi — a quality which the Prime Minister valued above all others. However what was needed in Punjab was efficiency and independence of mind, and Bhinder had not shown those qualities while in charge of the Delhi police.

Shortly after the imposition of President's Rule I met Bhinder in the Punjab capital of Chandigarh. As part of Mrs Gandhi's drive to restore confidence in her government, the press had been fed reports about the police 'combing' the Punjab countryside for terrorists. There were almost daily reports of arrests. Bhinder told me that ten people he described as 'Bhindranwale's do or die men' had been shot by the police and that more than 1,600 people had been arrested. I asked Bhinder where I should go to see the police in action. He suggested the area surrounding Bhindranwale's own village of Rode. But when I reached Bhindranwale's village, I was told by his brother that no one had so much as seen the police. In the neighbouring villages I was told that most of the people arrested were known to the police as '*das namberi*', that is petty criminals such as thieves and opium smugglers, who are always brought in for questioning whenever the police investigate a crime. It appeared that Bhinder's 'combing' was not quite as effective as he had made out to the press. A senior official of the Punjab government admitted as much to me. He said, 'We must appear to be doing something. But the trouble is that the Punjab police are demoralised. So many of their colleagues have been killed by Bhindranwale's men that they have no faith in our ability to protect them.' When I asked about the paramilitary police who had been moved into the state to stiffen the backbone of the Punjab police, he replied, 'What can the paramilitary police do on their own? They do not know the state and have to rely on the local knowledge of the Punjab police.' This was the first time that I came across evidence of a conflict within the police force which was to have disastrous consequences. The paramilitary police never believed that the Punjab police were serious about stamping out terrorism. In fact many paramilitary police officers believed the Punjab police were on Bhindranwale's side. As the months went by evidence grew to suggest that they were right.

Bhinder later admitted to me that his force was demoralised by Bhindranwale's successes in killing policemen who had taken action against his men, especially those involved in Chief Minister Darbara Singh's encounters. However he maintained that he was taking steps to restore the morale of his force. These steps were so ineffective that, within two months of the imposition of President's Rule, even Mrs Gandhi's own members of Parliament were complaining about the government's 'weak-kneed' policy in Punjab. During a debate in Parliament, members on both sides of the House demanded the arrest of Bhindranwale. The Home Minister confirmed that the police had registered cases against Bhindranwale but he gave no assurances that the preacher would be arrested.

Once again Bhindranwale reacted to the threat of arrest by seeking sanctuary. He told Tohra that, after the debate in Parliament, the government would not be able to withstand the political pressure to enter the hostel complex and arrest him. He managed to persuade the SGPC President that the only safe place would be the Akal Takht itself. The shrine, representing the temporal power of God, stands within the walls of the Temple complex, opposite the Golden Temple itself. The last thing Tohra wanted was for Bhindranwale to be arrested; so he agreed to allow him to set up his headquarters in the Akal Takht. But the High Priest of the Shrine, Giani Kirpal Singh, objected. He pointed out that no Guru or later Sikh religious leader had ever been allowed to live in the Akal Takht. The High Priest also said that Bhindranwale would be committing sacrilege because he would be living above the Guru Granth Sahib. No Sikh is allowed to stand above the holy book. Throughout the day *granthis*, or priests, recite the Guru Granth Sahib in the main hall of the Akal Takht and at night the most sacred copy of the holy book, the one which is read in the Golden Temple itself, is laid to rest in a room in the shrine, below where Bhindranwale wanted to live. The Sant's needs were too pressing to allow such theological niceties to stand in his way. Matters were, in any case, taken out of the hands of the High Priest by an outbreak of civil war in the hostel complex.

Longowal, who was still living in another building of the hostel complex, had decided that he needed a private army to defend himself from Bhindranwale. He called in men from the Babbar Khalsa, one of the many splinter groups spawned by the movement against the Nirankaris. They were quite as violent in their hatred of those 'heretics' as Bhindranwale. They took their name from the Babbar Akalis, the group of terrorists who rejected the Akali Dal's non-violent policy during the Gurud-wara Reform Movement in the 1920s and killed many police informers and others they regarded as *dalals*, or touts of the British. Many of them were arrested by the British and sentenced to death or to long terms of imprisonment. The leader of the new Babbar Khalsa was Jathedar Sukhdev Singh. He claimed that his group had killed forty-five Nirankaris. Sukhdev Singh was, however, strongly opposed to the murder of Hindus and to the violence Bhindranwale unleashed in Punjab. In fact he often described Bhindranwale as a coward. He remained inside the hostel complex guarding Longowal, but managed to escape to Britain after the army action.

During the days that Tohra was negotiating with the High Priests for Bhindranwale's move into the Akal Takht, the Babbar Khalsa decided to challenge their enemy openly. They marched into the Guru Nanak Niwas, where Bhindranwale was based, and ordered his men to get out. According to Bhindranwale's men, they moved out voluntarily in order to avoid a fight. According to the Babbar Khalsa, they fled. Where else could the Sant go now except the Akal Takht? So Tohra argued, and his argument was accepted. Bhindranwale claimed that he had to move into the Akal Takht because the Morcha Dictator was negotiating with the government for his arrest.

From the day that the preacher set up his headquarters in the Akal Takht there was open warfare between Bhindranwale and Longowal. Unfortunately, however, Longowal did not have the courage or good sense to call in the government on his side. But the fault did not lie entirely with him. Tohra who, as President of the SGPC, was technically responsible for the Temple complex, refused to lend his support to Longowal which meant that he could not guarantee the full support of the Akali Dal for action against Bhindranwale. Tohra still had his eye on that chief-ministership which for him was the ultimate objective of the Morcha.

The only entrance to the third-floor room Bhindranwale now made his headquarters was a narrow staircase built into the wall. Armed men guarded this entrance day and night. The room itself was dark and low-ceilinged. The Sant used to sit on a mattress in one corner with his legs stretched out in front of him, surrounded by his followers. During the day he usually moved to the roof of the building which housed the Golden Temple's 'Langar', or dining hall, where every day a free lunch was served to all-comers, Sikh or non-Sikh. No one was excluded, demonstrating the Gurus' teaching that all men are equal, no matter what their caste or religion.

Bhindranwale used to hold court sitting on the roof of the Langar. Once again he was surrounded by his armed supporters who lounged around in a thoroughly unprofessional manner. Perhaps they were unprofessional or perhaps they did not fear an attack on the Sant, although he would have been a sitting target for a marksman firing from one of the many buildings surrounding the Langar. At his morning *darbars*, or congregations, on the roof of the Langar, Bhindranwale used to preach hatred against India and against Hindus. By this time his doctrine of hate was also spreading throughout the villages of Punjab by means of tapes that Bhindranwale's followers circulated. The tapes were openly on sale in the shops of the Golden Temple too. The police never attempted to prevent their sale.

A tape recording of one of Bhindranwale's sermons which

was widely circulated started with an allegation against the police: 'The police got hold of Jagdip Singh, son of Thara Singh, made a cut in his thigh and filled it with salt.'

Bhindranwale then moved into his favourite theme, the slavery of the Sikhs. 'I shall tell you how we are slaves in our own country. If a Hindu dies there is an inquiry. If a Sikh dies there is no inquiry. If a Hindu dies the body is handed back to his kith and kin, but if a Sikh dies the body is not given back to his people. If a Hindu is killed it is not excusable but if a Sikh is killed the inquiry is scuttled.'

This was an indirect reference to the outcry over the killing of Hindu bus passengers.

The preacher attacked Mrs Gandhi, calling her disparagingly, 'the Brahmin's daughter'. He compared the Prime Minister's attitude to two young men, who had hijacked an airliner at the time she was arrested by the Janata government, with her attitude to the Sikhs who hijacked an airliner when Bhindranwale was arrested.

He said, 'If the hijacking for the Brahmin's daughter can be done, why not hijacking for the Sikhs' sentiments, for the Sikhs' symbols, for the Sikh beard, for the Harmandir Sahib.'

Not surprisingly the sermon was full of references to the beard, Bhindranwale's favourite symbol of his faith.

The Sant asked members of the congregation to raise their hands if they wanted the Anandpur Sahib Resolution implemented in full. After the congregation had raised their hands, Bhindranwale said: 'You need not say anything more. I am satisfied with your hand-raising only.'

He then went on to encourage all the young men to go to the sacred town of Anandpur Sahib, where the tenth Guru instituted the Khalsa, and to take an oath to implement the Resolution. Bhindranwale was cutting the ground from underneath the feet of Longowal, who wanted a negotiated settlement with the government which would inevitably have fallen short of the Anandpur Sahib Resolution.

He warned the congregation not to be misled by what he called 'sustained propaganda' by the newspapers against the Sikh Morcha [agitation] and against him in particular. He said, 'I plead with you to beware of attempts to malign my *taksal* [school]. They [the newspapers] are bent upon turning the Sikh community against me.'

The Sant also accused the government of spreading propaganda against him. He said, 'The government is trying to paint me as the agent of the Congress Party — a traitor to the cause — to divide the Panth [Sikh community] and weaken the Morcha, so that the government's chair is left intact.' 'Chair' in India is frequently used as a symbol for political power.

The Sant ended this section of his sermon by saying, 'Beware of their propaganda. They want us to fight among ourselves like shrews. Beware!'

This was actually a reference to Bhindranwale's enemies among the Sikhs who tried to discredit him by reminding their community that he was originally a creation of the Congress Party.

Bhindranwale distanced himself from Longowal and the political leaders of the Akali Dal by disowning all political ambition himself.

I have sworn it at the Akal Takht and I repeat the same at your request. I shall never agree to become the President of the Akali Dal, or the Head of the SGPC, or a Minister, or a Member of the Assembly. I swear that I am prepared to receive any punishment from the congregation if I lie. I am only responsible for the cause of Sikhism, preaching the symbols of the faith. My responsibility is to see that your beards remain intact, your hair is uncut, and that you do not go after the evil things in life, like alcohol and drugs.

Indians, disgusted by the blatant misuse of office for personal profit by so many of their politicians, have a special respect for someone who forswears ambition. Mahatma Gandhi did, and so did Jayaprakash Narayan, or J.P., who led the movement against Mrs Gandhi before the Emergency.

Bhindranwale then returned to the theme of the Anandpur Sahib Resolution. Reminding the congregation that Longowal had also sworn to accept nothing less than the fulfilment of all its demands, he warned: 'If any of our leaders accepts anything less than all the Anandpur Sahib demands, I will expose him in front of the *sangat* [congregation].'

Bhindranwale went on to appeal to Sikh villagers to organise and support terrorism. He said, 'For every village you should keep one motorcycle, three young baptised Sikhs and three revolvers. These are not meant for killing innocent people. For a Sikh to have arms and kill an innocent person is a serious sin. But, Khalsaji [members of the Khalsa], to have arms and not to get your legitimate rights is an even bigger sin. It is for you to decide how to use these arms. If you want to remove the shackles of your slavery you must have a plan.'

Bhindranwale also pleaded, 'I once again, with my hands folded at your feet, appeal to you − if you have not entered the Anandpur Sahib House, if you do not have the five 'k's (symbols of Sikhism), if you are not armed with a rifle and a spear, you will be given the beating of your lives by the Hindus.'

The sermon ended with the congregation shouting, '*Wahe Guruji ka Khalsa, Wahe Guruji ki Fateh*' − 'The Khalsa belongs to the Lord − all victory is HIS!'

Bhindranwale's open support for violence eventually led to a protest from Longowal, who was, after all, still meant to be leading a non-violent agitation. He issued a statement to the press criticising Bhindranwale's call to arm young motor-cyclists. But the next day one of the national news agencies carried a denial of Longowal's statement. In order to clarify the situation I asked Sanjeev Gaur, an Amritsar-based journalist, to go to the Morcha Dictator and ask him outright what he had said. Longowal wavered, but eventually he did agree that he had criticised Bhindranwale for encouraging Sikhs to support terrorism. One of Bhindranwale's spies in the Akali Dal camp immediately reported this conversation. Sanjeev Gaur was stabbed and seriously wounded as he left the Temple complex, and Longowal never again publicly criticised his rival.

Another incident which illustrated Longowal's unwilling-ness to exert his authority took place in January 1984 on India's Republic Day. A Khalistan (independent Sikh land) flag was flown from one of the buildings near the Golden Temple itself. To the end Longowal maintained that his Morcha was not an independence movement and that the Anandpur Sahib Resolu-tion was not a demand for independence; but no action was taken about the Khalistan flag.

In fact on the very day that the Khalistan flag was flown the Akali Dal leadership issued a new demand. They told the government that article twenty-five of the Constitution, which according to the Akalis implied that Hindus and Sikhs were one and the same, should be amended. The article guaranteed freedom of religion. In an attempt to break caste barriers, which had kept Untouchables out of Hindu temples, the article said that Hindu religious institutions of a public character must be open to all classes and sections of Hindus. The article explained that the reference to Hindus included 'persons professing the Sikh, Jain or Buddhist religion'. Constitutional lawyers differ on their interpretation of the implications of this explanation, but the Akali Dal leaders had hit on an emotive issue because, of course, of the fears of most orthodox Sikhs that their religion would go the way of Buddhism and Jainism in India, and be virtually swallowed up by Hinduism.

Nevertheless the demand had not been included in the Akalis' original list, and did not appear in the controversial Anandpur Sahib Resolution. This strengthened Mrs Gandhi's position. The Prime Minister always argued that it was not she who had scuppered earlier agreements with the Akalis but the Sikh leaders themselves who, she said, were always changing their minds. M.J. Akbar in his book *India: The Siege Within* said, however, that the new demand was really a desperate search for a victory which would restore the Akali Dal leaders' prestige and enable them to wrest control of the movement from Bhindranwale. As Akbar saw it, 'What the moderate Akalis really wanted was a "victory" over Delhi which would enable them to take the initiative away from the extremists by restoring their credibility as "champions of the Sikhs".' He went on to say, 'Even a blind government in Delhi could have seen that and offered a way out.'[1]

Balwant Singh, the former Finance Minister of Punjab and one of the most moderate of the Akali Dal leaders, was present at the meeting when it was decided to raise this new demand. He and some others opposed it for the very reason that it would be playing into Mrs Gandhi's hands by providing her with evidence that the Akalis did not know what they wanted. But

Balwant Singh was over-ruled because most of the Akali Dal leaders felt the need to raise a new issue, not to wrest control from Bhindranwale, but to prove that they were still keeping up with him. In other words they were not looking for a way of ending the race to extremism but of keeping in it.

This appears to be confirmed by the events which followed. The government unwisely over-reacted when Akali Dal leaders announced that they were going to burn copies of the Constitution, by threatening to charge them with sedition. Badal and other Akali Dal leaders happily went ahead with their protest and were sent to jail, which was exactly where they wanted to go. What better way was there for them to demonstrate to the Sikhs that they were quite as extreme in their demands as Bhindranwale, who was still free inside the Golden Temple? They left Longowal to withstand the heat of the battle.

Before they went to jail the Akali leaders also decided to revive the agitation for their original demands in an attempt to rival Bhindranwale. They called for a general strike in Punjab on 8th February. With the experience of the violence caused the last time the Sikhs called for a *Rasta Roko*, or 'Block the Roads' day, the government decided to limit the damage, cancelling all train and air services. But Sikhs brandishing their traditional swords did march on government offices in many places and forced them to close. The Punjab police also stood by and watched Sikhs make Hindu traders close their shops. Because of the government's refusal to rise to the challenge, the day passed off comparatively peacefully with only one bomb explosion and ten people injured. But the strike did have serious consequences. It gave the Hindus, particularly the Hindu Chief Minister of Haryana, the excuse they needed to scupper the next round of talks due to start the same month. Bhajan Lal wanted to scupper the talks because he was still afraid that any settlement with the Sikhs would be seen as a sell-out by the Hindus of Haryana.

The talks started on 14th February, almost exactly one year after the last round. Once again Mrs Gandhi involved all opposition parties. On that very day an organisation called the Hindu Suraksha Samiti, or Hindu Defence Committee, called for its own general strike in Punjab. Its leader was Pawan

6 *Above left*, Amrik Singh, the President of the All India Sikh Students Federation and Bhindranwale's right-hand man

7 *Above right*, Major-General Shahbeg Singh, who master-minded the fortification of the Akal Takht

8 *Below*, Sant Jarnail Singh Bhindranwale with his disciples

9 *Above left*, Sant Jarnail Singh Bhindranwale speaking in Delhi at the memorial ceremonies for Santokh Singh, the murdered Sikh politician

10 *Above right*, Rajiv Gandhi was present at one of the ceremonies

11 *Below*, Zail Singh (*second from right*) is pictured with Bhindranwale (*far left*) at another of Santokh Singh's memorial ceremonies

Kumar who was a young man with a criminal record brought into politics by a Sikh Congress (Indira) Member of Parliament. Pawan Kumar also had close links with the Haryana Chief Minister. Fourteen people were killed during the Hindu strike in what the *Times of India* described as 'one of the worst outbreaks of rioting and group clashes in the Punjab since partition'. The next day the Akali Dal leaders walked out of the talks, saying that they would only resume negotiations when 'peace' returned to Punjab. They knew that Bhindranwale would discredit them if they continued to negotiate after the violence which the preacher immediately seized upon as yet further evidence of 'Sikh slavery'.

The strike in Punjab was followed by the first serious out-break of anti-Sikh rioting in Haryana – rioting which the Chief Minister provoked by a speech he made in the industrial town of Faridabad warning the Akali leaders that the Hindus' patience was running out and that retaliation was near. Satish Jacob saw police looking on as Hindu mobs burnt down the *gurud-wara* in Panipat; he also saw Sikhs being pulled off buses and forcibly shaved, and Sikh-owned shops being looted. Eight Sikhs were clubbed to death. The situation became so grave that the police had to halt all traffic on the Grand Trunk Road.

Many of the national papers feared that this was the start of the long-awaited Hindu backlash. The *Hindustan Times*, which supported the government, headlined its editorial 'The Caul-dron Boils Over'. It went on to say, 'The eruption of violence in Punjab and Haryana on an unprecedented scale constitutes the most painful phase of the deepening Akali crisis. The repercussions of the agitation are no longer confined to one state or one community.' The *Tribune*, which is published in Chandigarh, the joint capital of Haryana and Punjab, said, 'There is some truth in the explanation that the violence in Haryana is a backlash to the excesses committed by the "extremists" in Punjab.' But the violence died down almost as suddenly as it arose and from that day onwards there was no sign of that backlash, which suggests that it was not quite as spontaneous as it appeared at first sight. Bhajan Lal had shown his strength and Haryana's position was not ignored again.

Why did Mrs Gandhi allow the Haryana Chief Minister to

have his way at the expense of a possible solution to the Punjab crisis which by now was seriously damaging the credibility of her government? Several explanations have been put forward. The most cynical is that Mrs Gandhi did not want to intervene because she herself was going for the Hindu vote. Another is that she was by now committed to a military solution to the Punjab crisis but felt that the situation must be allowed to get worse before she could justify that solution. It is certainly true that about the time of the Hindu violence there was renewed talk of police or even troops entering the Golden Temple. Tohra, the President of the SGPC, said he had received information that commandos, who had been trained to enter the Temple, had arrived in Amritsar. Longowal warned the government against entering the Temple. Rajiv Gandhi, still very much involved in the Punjab negotiations, told me in an interview that he did not agree with the government's policies on Punjab. He indicated that he was in favour of sending police into the Temple.

In public the government still maintained it would not send police into the Golden Temple; but paramilitary police officers in Amritsar told Satish Jacob that commandos were being trained for such a purpose. They said a large model of the Temple complex had been built at a camp of the Special Frontier Force at Chakrata in the foothills of the Himalayas. The government had started preparing for the military option but that does not mean negotiations were ruled out. In fact the government was negotiating right until the bitter end.

One of the reasons the government was now forced to consider the military option was the deterioration of the police force. President's Rule and Bhinder's morale-boosting drive in the Punjab police had made no impact on the terrorists. Throughout February incidents were reported almost daily. There were raids on Hindu temples and attacks on government offices, including a bomb thrown at the Jullundur television station, bank robberies, firings at the police and, of course, at Hindus. One attack not recorded in the Government White Paper on Punjab gives an indication of the state of morale in the police at the time. On the day of the Hindu strike, young men from the Golden Temple attacked a small police post near the

Temple's entrance. Six policemen were dragged inside with their firearms, including three sten guns and a walkie-talkie. The next day the most senior police officer in Amritsar had to go to Bhindranwale's room in the Akal Takht and plead with him to release the policemen and their weapons. Bhindranwale agreed to release the body of one of the policemen who had been killed. He later released the others who were still alive, but he held on to the sten guns and the walkie-talkie.

Mrs Gandhi's problems were compounded by the growing row between the Punjab force and the paramilitary Central Reserve Police (CRP). The CRP wanted to search vehicles and people going into the Golden Temple but they were not even allowed to post pickets within two hundred yards. With such lax security it was like allowing enemy headquarters to operate freely within your own territory. Mrs Gandhi's Think Tank was obsessed by the fear of provoking an uprising by Jat Sikh peasants and so listened to Bhinder's advice that interfering with access to the Golden Temple would start villagers marching on Amritsar to defend their shrine.

The CRP's patience snapped after a bomb was thrown at one of their patrols in the border district of Gurdaspur. The next day there was a row outside the Golden Temple when some paramilitary police did attempt to search young Sikhs and Bhindranwale's men fired on them. The CRP took up positions on the roofs of buildings overlooking the Temple and returned fire. Panic broke out. Longowal telephoned Bhinder and told him to stop the firing. Bhinder said he was unable to get the paramilitary police to withdraw. The Home Minister, who was the minister in charge of the CRP, passed the buck by ringing Longowal and telling him to bring the situation in the Temple under control. Longowal of course had no influence at all with Bhindranwale's young marksmen. The firing only stopped when there was a telephone call from the President's palace to the CRP, ordering them to withdraw. The President is constitutional head of state, so no member of his staff had any right to intervene.

Later in the week the Home Secretary was sent to Amritsar to try to restore relations between the CRP and the local force which had reached near breaking point. There was a patch up, but it did not last long. Home Secretary Chaturvedi was a member of Mrs Gandhi's Think Tank and so he decided to take the opportunity of his visit to Amritsar to call on Longowal. However the Akali Dal leader refused to see him, saying, 'Chaturvedi is responsible for deploying the CRP in Punjab and for killing innocent Sikhs. His hands are choked with the blood of Sikhs. I will not see him.' By now the police had split on communal lines. Sikhs regarded the CRP as hostile and Hindus regarded the Punjab police as hostile. Another row broke out between the two forces two weeks later. A bomb was thrown at a Hindu temple in Amritsar and the CRP arrested a Sikh suspect. They were prevented from taking him away by the Punjab police. Officers of the CRP had to withdraw their men to prevent a clash with the local police. The dispute was officially patched up again, this time by a *burra khana* (great dinner), but the CRP remained deeply suspicious of the Punjab police.

The CRP is far more disciplined than the local police forces. Its companies are recruited from all over India and sent anywhere law and order breaks down. CRP officers are used to opposition from local police forces, but even they were taken aback by the situation in Punjab. A senior CRP officer said to Satish Jacob, 'I usually find that the local force takes sides in communal disputes but I have never known anything as blatant as the partisan behaviour of the Punjab police.'

Another reason for the failure of President's Rule in Punjab was the backseat driving from Delhi. Mrs Gandhi's advisers would not allow the efficient Governor Pande to run his own government. During a discussion with one of Pande's senior officials Satish Jacob said, 'You people in Chandigarh do not seem to know what is happening in Amritsar.' The official replied, 'We know what is happening. Everybody knows that Mr Pande has a good track-record as an administrator. But Punjab is run by Delhi.' By 'Delhi' the official meant Mrs Gandhi's Think Tank which was remarkable for its lack of thinkers with experience of the Punjab. The official quoted the example of some local administrators and police officers who were known to be in the pocket of Bhindranwale. The Governor wanted to transfer them but 'Delhi' over-ruled him.

Governor Pande's patience was further tried by a fault in the hotline between Delhi and Chandigarh. The extension in his bedroom used to ring of its own accord in the middle of the night, but no one would reply when the governor picked up the receiver.

The confusion in the Governor's House in Chandigarh was made worse by Mrs Gandhi's maintaining contact with Bhindranwale. Her go-between was the President of the Punjab Congress Party, Raghunandan Lal Bhatia. He had come close to Bhindranwale during the 1980 general election when the preacher actively supported his candidature in the Amritsar constituency. A member of Bhatia's staff told Satish Jacob that the Punjab Congress President remained in contact with Bhindranwale until within a month of Operation Blue Star, well beyond the point when Mrs Gandhi had any hope of influencing him. In the last days the contact was maintained through Amrik Singh, Bhindranwale's right-hand man. The same member of Mr Bhatia's staff said that a car used to be sent regularly to the Golden Temple to collect Amrik Singh. This link which was well known to officials enhanced Bhindranwale's status and made the administration even more reluctant to grapple with him.

IO

Last Ditch Negotiations

Taunted by the opposition and the press for the failure of President's Rule, all Mrs Gandhi could think of doing was to take more Draconian powers. The whole of Punjab was declared a disturbed area, giving the police even wider powers of arrest. The National Security Act was also amended, allowing police to hold people for a year without bringing them before a court. But of course the problem was not lack of powers, it was the reluctance of the police to use their powers and the inability of the government to sum up the political will to force them to do so.

Once again the new powers made no difference to Bhindranwale. Just before the powers were announced a prominent Sikh, H.S. Manchanda, was shot in broad daylight when his car stopped at traffic lights in the middle of Delhi. Manchanda was the President of the pro-Congress (Indira) Delhi Sikh Temple Management Committee, and an outspoken critic of the Akali Dal Morcha. On the day the new powers were given to the police Hindus were 'taught a lesson' by the killing of the prominent politician Harbans Lal Khanna in Amritsar. He was a leading member of the right-wing Bhartiya Janata Party, the successor to the Jan Sangh. The next day supporters of Mrs

Gandhi were given a 'sharp' warning by the killing of V.N. Tiwari, a professor of Punjabi who was a Congress (Indira) Member of Parliament. He was shot in his house in Chandigarh. On 22nd April an air-force officer was hacked to death in his home. This was the first time that a serving officer of the defence forces had been killed.

On 30th April one of the prime targets on Bhindranwale's hit-list, the former Deputy Superintendent of Police Bachan Singh, was shot dead in Amritsar. He was riding in a cycle rickshaw when two young Sikhs came up and opened fire at his guard. They then snatched away the guard's sten gun and fired on Bachan Singh. After killing the retired police officer the terrorists shot his wife and daughter who were riding in a rickshaw behind him. They died in hospital. Bhindranwale had often challenged the police to save Bachan Singh who, according to the preacher, had tortured his right-hand man, Amrik Singh, when he was in jail. The police had failed. Bachan Singh's murder was another severe blow to their morale. Then came another terrorist attack which showed the whole of India that no special powers could help the government or the police – Bhindranwale was above the law.

On 12th May Romesh Chander, the son and successor of the editor of the Punjab Kesari group of newspapers, Lala Jagat Narain, was shot dead driving through the streets of the industrial city of Jullundur. It was in connection with Lala Jagat Narain's murder that Bhindranwale had been arrested three years earlier, and he had always sworn to avenge his arrest by murdering Romesh Chander. On the eve of his death Romesh Chander had written in a prophetic vein, 'No one knows whose turn will come next. All Punjab has become a slaughter house.' The government's failure to protect a target as prominent as Romesh Chander was a near fatal blow to India's confidence in Mrs Gandhi's ability to control Punjab. The *Times of India*, in its editorial, commented on the freedom with which Bhindranwale could now select his victims. It said, 'Mr Romesh Chander, whether through his editorial columns, through television and radio, or at public gatherings, strove ceaselessly to voice the distress of the common Punjabi today. His was a still powerful voice of reason in the engulfing fog of mindless terror. Eliminating him therefore meant a lot to the terrorists who seem to have become the main arbitrators to decide who opposes the Panth [Sikh community] and should consequently be killed.'

These were the most outrageous murders. During March and April at least eighty other people were killed and 107 injured in terrorist attacks by Bhindranwale's men.

At the end of April a senior official briefing journalists admitted that, in spite of all the special powers, the police had only succeeded in catching very few of the 'hardcore' of Bhindranwale's men. The official estimated the strength of that hardcore at between 400 and 500. He said that only about a quarter of them were students and the rest were Naxalites (communists outside the mainstream of communism who believed in violent revolution), smugglers and other criminals. The official admitted that the government's reputation was at stake but went on to say that the government had to resist pressures to resolve the Punjab crisis by force.

For some time Bhindranwale had been having his doubts about the government's willingness to resist those pressures. He believed that Mrs Gandhi might be forced to overcome her reluctance to enter the Golden Temple and decided to make that decision as difficult as possible by fortifying the Temple complex. The preacher wanted to make sure that the military option really was a military option by making it impossible for the police to raid his headquarters in the Akal Takht.

On 10th March Satish Jacob and I visited the Golden Temple to check reports that Bhindranwale and his men had started fortifying it. As we approached the main entrance we saw sandbag emplacements on either side of the clock tower. To the left was a high water tower. We noticed that young Sikhs with automatic rifles had taken up positions on the top of it because it gave a good view of the low buildings and narrow alleys surrounding the Temple, as well as the open square in front of the main entrance.

We went first to the office of Narinderjit Singh Nanda, the Public Relations Officer, on the outside of the Temple, next door to a shop selling Bhindranwale tapes. Nanda's assistant was a worried man.

'Don't go inside with your camera until you have checked with Bhindranwale's men,' he said.

'But I thought that we had to get permission from you, not them, before we filmed,' I replied.

'Well that, as you say, is the position. But I am not going to say anything until you talk with them. There are very strange things happening inside the Temple now. You don't know the half of it.'

So Nanda's assistant rang Bhindranwale's room in the Akal Takht and asked for someone to be sent down to speak to us. A few minutes later a young Sikh appeared and agreed to take us to see the preacher.

When we walked down the main steps on to the pavement which surrounds the sacred tank, we saw that the buildings inside the complex were being fortified too. Sandbags were being built up on the roof of the Langar or dining hall where Bhindranwale held his congregations. The buildings on either side of the Akal Takht where he had his headquarters were also being prepared for a siege. In spite of armed followers of Bhindranwale strutting officiously around the tank like young turkey cocks, the religious life of the Temple continued. Sikhs, young and old, were standing in their shorts in the pool annointing themselves with the water and saying their prayers. The sound of Gurbani, or the chanting of the holy scriptures, in the Golden Temple itself was being relayed from all four corners of the complex. Bhindranwale and his fortifications had not yet succeeded in destroying the serenity of the Golden Temple − a serenity which those Hindus who find their own temples too noisy and commercial also valued.

After walking all the way round the pavement as tradition demands, with white handkerchiefs on our heads and our cigars safely lodged with the Public Relations Office (it is a sacrilege even to bring tobacco into the Golden Temple), we came to the Akal Takht. We entered the open hall facing the pool and the causeway to the Golden Temple, passed the priests reciting the scriptures, and moved towards the back where it was quite dark. Our guide told the young Sikhs guarding the entrance to the narrow staircase to let us pass, and we climbed up to Bhindranwale's room. He was, as usual, sitting with his legs stretched out in front of him talking to some young Sikhs who included Amrik Singh, the President of the All India Sikh Students Federation, Harminder Singh Sandhu, Bhindranwale's interpreter, and Rachpal Singh, his secretary. Bhindranwale enjoyed the attention that Western journalists were now paying to him; so when he was reminded that it was the BBC *wallahs* again he smiled and invited us to sit beside him.

I explained to the Sant that we would like to film his congregation the next day and interview him. He liked the idea until I told him that the interview would only last about ten minutes. 'Ten minutes,' he replied. 'It should be at least two hours. There are lots of Sikhs in England, you know, who would like to see me for two hours.' I had some difficulty in explaining the limitations of television news bulletins and schedules to Bhindranwale; but eventually he agreed when I suggested that it was better for the Sikhs of England to see a little of him than nothing at all.

The next day we were taken on to the roof of the dining hall by one of Bhindranwale's men. There was a congregation of about 300 people sitting at the feet of the Sant. His armed guards were lounging casually against the parapet. Sitting beside Bhindranwale was an elderly Sikh with a long, white beard and an immaculately tied turban. He had a thin, intelligent face. I took him for a scholar or a priest — he was in fact a soldier. He was Major-General Shahbeg Singh, the man who was responsible for the fortification of the Golden Temple and the man who was to direct the resistance to the army when they entered the complex just three months later.

During the campaign which led up to the Bangladesh war of liberation in 1971, Shahbeg Singh had trained and led the so-called Mukhti Bahini, or Bangladesh freedom fighters. It was a secret role because India never admitted, and in fact still does not admit officially, that it trained the Mukhti Bahini or fought in the guerrilla operations which bogged down the Pakistan army in the damp delta of East Bengal for nine months. But Lieutenant-General Aurora, who took the surrender of Dacca, now admits that Shahbeg Singh played a crucial and courageous role in the Mukhti Bahini operations. According to Aurora, Shahbeg Singh was not so orthodox a Sikh in those days. He was, for instance, prepared to cut his beard and his hair when operational necessities demanded. Lieutenant-General Aurora said, 'When I knew him he was not a very religious Sikh. I think he used to clip his beard, sometimes he cut his hair off, but he always wore a turban. In fact I think he really acted the part which was relevant to the job he had to do during his army career, because he did have a flair for guerrilla type of operations for which I have known him. When he was working in that way I think he also dressed himself in that manner, looking more like a sort of "catch me alive" type of person rather than a regular soldier.' But the war hero's career ended in disgrace.

After Bangladesh, Shahbeg Singh was given two postings as an area commander, which is an administrative job. During his second posting the army brought three charges against him. According to the first charge, he had built a house in the army town of Dehra Dun and was unable to show where he had acquired the resources to do so. The second charge was that he had used his position to acquire an army truck which was being disposed of. The third charge was that he had accepted a silver salver as a memento.

Major-General Shahbeg Singh was dismissed the service without a court-martial on the day before he was due to retire. He lost his pension. This dismissal preyed on Shahbeg Singh's mind and made him bitterly hostile to the government. He did fight, and win, two cases in the civil courts to prove his innocence, but that did not alter his attitude to the government. As he brooded on what he regarded as his unjust fate, the former guerrilla commander turned to religion for solace and inspiration. His son, Prabpal Singh, said he was not very religious until the last two or three years of his life. That was also when he fell under Bhindranwale's spell. Shahbeg Singh first met the preacher when the Akali Morcha started in 1982.

The government already knew that Shahbeg Singh was inside the Temple and that he was masterminding the fortifications and the training of Bhindranwale's terrorists; but Shahbeg Singh himself always denied this up to the very end. In a letter sent to his son from Room Number 8 in the Akal Rest House, ten days before the army action, the General said:

I am all right. The press has tried to run me down by absolutely wrong and blatantly communal reporting. I have absolutely nothing to do with any killings or the Dashmesh Regiment. I have no idea about such a regiment [Dashmesh or 10th Guru Regiment was one of the names adopted by some of Bhindranwale's terrorists when claiming responsibility for assassinations]. It is to my mind government efforts to keep buried deep the gross injustice done to one of their top army war leaders, who had rendered distinguished service of the most exceptional order. The government highups want to hide their sense of shame under such a press offensive. Anyway the more dishonest approach they have towards me, the more my community love and respect me.

His letter does not read like the letter of a man who was about to command a heroic, if foolhardy, resistance to the might of the army he knew so well — a resistance which he must have known would end with his death.

On 26th May he was still concerned with family matters. He also wrote in the letter to his son: 'I learn from your *amman* [mother] that owing to Kabir [his grandson] being also with you there is need to boost your financial side a little bit. Please therefore send/write to me your bank account number etc. so that I can give standing instructions to our bank to divert rupees five hundred to your account every month.' Shahbeg Singh was also concerned about the health of his grandson. He wrote: 'I hope your small room in Delhi is helpful and Kabir is all right. He will need a lot of protection from the current hot weather until it starts raining.' The General's own wife's health was also causing him concern. She was with him in the Temple complex at that time but, according to Shahbeg Singh's son, left before the army action started. In his letter Major-General Shahbeg Singh just said: 'Your *amman* reached here two days ago. She is on medicine but all right.'

Bhindranwale, too, consistently accused the government of maligning him. On that morning in March he told me that it was the government, not he, which was indulging in violence. He repeated his litany of woes to demonstrate that Sikhs had become the slaves of Hindus, starting with the complaint that

Sikhs had not been allowed to watch the Asian Games. He gave his standard reply when I questioned him about Sikh independence: 'I am neither for independence nor against it, but if I am offered it I will not refuse it.' In spite of the steps that his men were taking to fortify the Temple, Bhindranwale did not seem to be unduly worried about the future. He was too busy enjoying all the attention he was attracting in the present.

During that interview I nearly committed a sacrilege. I was sitting uncomfortably on the ground next to the preacher. When I stretched my leg to relieve the cramp, my foot nearly touched the metal arrow, the symbol of the tenth Guru, which Bhindranwale took with him wherever he went. General Shahbeg Singh dug me in the ribs and said angrily, 'Watch your feet. Santji will not be amused if you touch that arrow.'

Satish Jacob and I also saw the sinister side of Bhindranwale's operation that morning. A young boy, who could not have been more than fifteen, was dragged up in front of the preacher by a burly six-foot tall Sikh dressed in the blue robes of a *nihang*, or Sikh warrior. The *nihang* explained that the boy had run away 'on a job'. The congregation started to mutter angrily. Bhindranwale calmed them down by telling the Sikh to 'take the boy away and deal with him'. He did. The young boy was taken round the corner and we saw him being thrashed with the shaft of a spear.

Bhindranwale used these congregations to hear petitions. The replies he gave to these petitions showed that by now he had penetrated deep into the Punjab administration and police. One senior Punjab police officer, Simranjit Singh Mann, used to admit openly that he was a supporter of Bhindranwale. The authorities also had evidence that Mann was helping Bhindranwale's terrorists to smuggle arms across the border when he was in charge of Faridkot district; but all they did was to transfer him to Bombay. No attempt was made to question Mann or discipline him. It was only after Mrs Gandhi's death that the authorities suddenly woke up to his importance, and arrested him as he was trying to escape across the border into Nepal.

Gurdev Singh, the Deputy Commissioner of Amritsar, the man responsible for the entire civil administration of the area, was a supporter of Bhindranwale too. He it was who consistently opposed the attempts by the CRP to tighten up security around the Golden Temple. He also used to criticise the CRP in front of the press. According to a CRP officer, the Deputy Commissioner once ordered him to release a truck which had been searched and found to be carrying arms for the arsenal in the Golden Temple. The arms were hidden under building material intended for the maintenance of the hostel complex, and the driver told the police that he was doing *kar seva*, or religious service. When questioned about his order the Deputy Commissioner replied that it was against his religious feelings to stop a truck on *kar seva*. Even the academic world bowed to Bhindranwale. Two professors from the medical college at Amritsar were summoned to the Golden Temple to discuss one of their students who was having difficulty in passing his exams. Bhindranwale explained very politely that the student was a follower of his and that he thought it might be a good idea if he did a little better in his exams. Next time round the student passed both subjects.

The telephone exchange was also in Bhindranwale's control. After the army had taken over responsibility for security in Punjab, a general was surprised to learn that the Sant's calls always used to get priority. At no time was Bhindranwale's telephone cut off, nor was the telephone of the head office of the All India Sikh Students Federation inside the Golden Temple. The police appeared to make no use of the invaluable intelligence they could have got from the telephones. Satish Jacob once heard the preacher talking to some of his followers who had sought sanctuary inside a *gurudwara* in Ferozepur. The police had surrounded the *gurudwara* and were demanding that the young men surrendered. They rang up the Sant to ask his advice and he told them to stick it out.

By now the terror had spread throughout the countryside. This was largely because of the young men who had taken seriously the Sant's injunction to buy arms and motorcycles and attack the enemies of the Sikhs. On 26th April, for instance, young Sikh motorcyclists shot a Hindu commission agent in the village of Bhikiwind in Amritsar district and a Hindu shopkeeper in the village of Samadh Bhai in Faridkot district. Satish Jacob visited the village of Bhikiwind and found the doors of most of the Hindu shops locked. The owners and their families had fled to the neighbouring state of Haryana. Bhindranwale's plans to alter the population of Punjab in favour of the Sikhs were bearing fruit.

By April 1984 it began to look as though he might succeed in clearing the Hindus out of Punjab. Not only were the small-time traders, money-lenders and shopkeepers in the villages fleeing, confidence among Hindu businessmen in the cities was collapsing too. A bank manager in Amritsar told me that Punjab industry had been badly hit by the violence because customers from other parts of India were not willing to come to towns like Jullundur and Amritsar to do business. He said that many industries were dependent on advances but businessmen were unwilling to pay advances because they feared they would never see their goods. The manager also admitted that the large number of bank raids had affected business confidence. As a result many Hindu industrialists were planning to move their factories to the neighbouring state of Haryana where the Chief Minister, Bhajan Lal, was only too anxious to welcome them. Fear even drove many Hindus to adopt Sikh dress. A retired school teacher in Amritsar told Satish Jacob that he now wore a turban when he went out for a walk. Young Hindus working at petrol stations, which were targets for attack by Bhindranwale's supporters, started growing beards and wearing turbans, so too did Hindus who used to travel regularly by bus. By the end of April Bhindranwale's reign of terror had driven the Akali Dal leaders back into Mrs Gandhi's hands. At last the Sikh political leaders realised the appalling risk they had taken by trying to play Bhindranwale off against the government — but it was too late.

Longowal finally accepted that Bhindranwale would have to be eliminated when civil war broke out inside the Golden Temple and the hostel complexes again. It broke out this time because of the murder of one of Bhindranwale's most trusted assassins, Surinder Singh Sodhi. He was shot on 14th April while drinking tea in a shop just outside the Temple. Men like Sodhi, well known to be murderers, were still able to move freely in the alleys surrounding the Temple because the CRP had been ordered not to come within 200 yards of the complex.

Sodhi, famous for his marksmanship, was said to have been responsible for killing Manchanda, the President of the Delhi Sikh Temple Management Committee; Khanna, the Hindu politician; and Tiwari, the Professor of Punjabi who was also a Member of the Upper House of Parliament belonging to Mrs Gandhi's party. The story told by Bhindranwale's supporters was that Sodhi was shot by a Sikh called Surinder Singh (alias Chinda) and his girlfriend Baljit Kaur. After the murder Baljit Kaur rushed into the Temple and up the stairs of the Akal Takht. There she first tried to convince the Sant that Sodhi had made advances to her. Bhindranwale was known to take a very firm line on offences against the Sikh teachings on chastity. However, after 'interrogation' Baljit Kaur 'admitted' that she and Chinda had been given money by a close associate of Longowal's to kill Sodhi. Baljit Kaur not only implicated her lover but also the Secretary of the Akali Dal, Gurcharan Singh, and one of Bhindranwale's followers, Malik Singh Bhatia. Bhatia appeared before Bhindranwale's congregation on the morning after the murder. He confessed that he had provided a jeep for the assassin Chinda's escape and pleaded for forgiveness. The Sant did forgive him and told him to go and make an offering at the Golden Temple. A much relieved Bhatia went down to the gateway leading to the Temple, made an offering and took some of the sticky sweet porridge, known as *prasad*, inside for blessing. Unaware of what was being plotted, he then returned to the roof of the Langar to ask Bhindranwale to take the *prasad*. Bhindranwale, apparently still in a forgiving mood, accepted it and Bhatia left the congregation. Some of Bhindranwale's young followers were waiting for him on the stairs. As he passed by they slashed at him with their swords. Bhatia ran towards the safety of the hostels controlled by Longowal. Blood was pouring from gashes on both shoulders and his turban had fallen off. He had nearly reached the entrance to the Guru Ram Das Hostel when a shot rang out. The man who Bhindranwale had forgiven crumpled and fell to the ground, dead. Three journalists saw the pardon and the execution. Immediately after killing Bhatia the young Sikhs shot the owner of a teastall on the road between the hostel and the Temple complexes. They then put up a notice on the wall of the Temple complex saying,

'Within twenty-four hours we have eliminated the killers and two of their accomplices.' Longowal, who consistently denied all knowledge of any violence, could see that notice from his office window.

The next evening the police found the body of Chinda on the Grand Trunk Road. They also found a bloodstained sack near by. Inside was the hideously mutilated body of a woman. According to the police it was Baljit Kaur. Her breasts had been cut off and she had been tortured.

Gurcharan Singh, the Akali Dal Secretary, was the only suspect to escape. He locked himself in a room near Longowal's office, and the party President put fifty armed Sikhs on guard outside the door. Bhindranwale continued to threaten revenge. He told Satish Jacob, 'Sodhi was one of my closest associates. He was with me from his childhood. I will never rest until his death is avenged. I am convinced that Gurcharan Singh is the main culprit. I will never forgive him.'

Satish Jacob managed to penetrate the guard standing out-side Gurcharan Singh's room and speak to him. He denied being involved in Sodhi's death, saying: 'The charge is totally cooked up. The sole purpose is to discredit Harchand Singh Longowal and the Akali Dal party. Bhindranwale's mind had been poisoned against me by the All India Sikh Students Federation because I was responsible for raising the youth wing of the Akali Dal, which Bhindranwale's friends who lead the Student Federation regard as a rival.'

Longowal, fearing that Bhindranwale might invade his offices, called for help and two Sikh leaders sent their followers to his rescue. In an attempt to calm the atmosphere he also told Gurcharan Singh to resign, even though a special committee had cleared him. The Morcha Dictator had surrendered his authority again.

In a last minute bid to restore his authority Longowal called a meeting of senior Sikh politicians to confirm his leadership of the Morcha. But events had moved too far for the Morcha Dictator. Sixty of the 140 people present walked out and went to Bhindranwale's room where they swore loyalty to him. The Sant was delighted, but he still maintained that he had no interest in politics, that he was just a preacher. He told the politicians, 'I will not give you tickets for any office.' On the day before that meeting Longowal had a long telephone conversation with Mrs Gandhi during which he admitted that he had lost control of the situation. He beseeched her to make some concession for which he could claim credit so that he could call off the Morcha and isolate Bhindranwale. Unfortunately for Longowal, that phone call was reported in the press. Bhindranwale immediately picked upon it as yet one more justification of his claim that Longowal was selling out the cause.

The Temple clergy too were now becoming thoroughly alarmed. They did not want control of their shrine and their livelihood to fall into the hands of Bhindranwale for good. His young men had scant respect for their grey beards. At the end of April Longowal managed to persuade them to issue an edict ordering an end to the violence inside the Temple. They said that no one should fire a gun in or near the Temple complex and no one should commit murder. They also appealed for Sikhs to unite to make their Morcha successful. Longowal later issued a statement saying that Sikhs could not disobey a *hukmnama*, or edict, issued by the five High Priests. Many people, including some of Mrs Gandhi's advisers, believed that the Sikh High Priests and Longowal were at last screwing up courage to issue a *hukmnama* ordering Bhindranwale to leave the Akal Takht. It would have been very difficult for Bhindranwale to disobey an edict of the five High Priests, which by tradition is binding on all Sikhs. But he had his own answers to the new problem.

The preacher issued a statement threatening that the priests would be forced to resign their offices if they issued an edict against him. He gave a grim meaning to this threat by killing three of his Sikh opponents in one week. One of them, Giani Pratap Singh, was a former High Priest of the Akal Takht, the highest seat of religious and temporal authority of the Sikhs. The eighty-year-old scholar had openly criticised Bhindranwale for storing arms and ammunition in the Akal Takht, and had said that Bhindranwale's presence in the shrine was sacrilege. The *hukmnama* against Bhindranwale was never issued. When the High Priest of the Akal Takht was asked, after the army action, why he had not issued an edict, he replied, 'No one complained to me about this matter.'

Not all the High Priests were opposed to Bhindranwale. Giani Sahib Singh, the High Priest of the Golden Temple, agreed to preside over the wedding of six of Bhindranwale's young men in the Temple complex. The most prominent of them was Harminder Singh Sandhu, the Secretary of the All India Sikh Students Federation and the Sant's interpreter. Invitations were sent out to all and sundry. Sandhu made sure that the international press knew of the event too.

So it came about that one month to the day before the army entered the Golden Temple, six young men who had been openly defying the might of the Indian government, who had brought the country's most prosperous state to a standstill, who had been responsible for murders, bank robberies, extracting money by threat, preaching secession, and almost every other crime in the book, walked four times round the High Priest of the Golden Temple, who was sitting in front of the holy scriptures. Each of the young terrorists was followed by his young bride – Sandhu's was the daughter of a wealthy Bombay transport contractor. The ceremony of the six Sikhs taking their marriage vows was filmed for the world's television. The young bridegrooms wore bandoleers over their shoulders and many in the congregation of over 1,000 carried automatic weapons. I stood next to Bhindranwale's young son, aged, I was told, eleven, who was already armed with a revolver and an ammunition belt.

The Sant himself was among the many leading Sikhs who preached. This time he avoided all politics, restricting himself to instructing his young followers in the Sikh teachings on marriage. After he had preached Bhindranwale retired to the roof of the Langar where I found him counting money. When I asked him whether it was the collection from the wedding service he just smiled.

Mrs Gandhi was not smiling. The credibility of her party was now at stake, as she found out early in May when her party was humiliated in a round of by-elections. The most serious setback from the Prime Minister's point of view was in the constituency of Malihabad near Lucknow, the capital of Uttar Pradesh, where, in spite of every effort that her party could make, her estranged daughter-in-law Maneka Gandhi's party won the

seat. Maneka Gandhi had quarrelled with her mother-in-law
after the death of Sanjay Gandhi, her husband, and walked out
of the family home, taking Mrs Gandhi's grandson with her.
The quarrel was over the succession. After Sanjay's death
Maneka thought that she should become the political member
of the next generation. The Prime Minister, however, chose her
elder son Rajiv. After walking out of the house Maneka
mounted a brash but surprisingly successful campaign against
her late husband's family, portraying herself as the injured
young widow and Mrs Gandhi as the spiteful mother-in-law. To
keep the spotlight on her Maneka announced that she would
fight the next general election from Amethi, which had been
Sanjay's constituency and was now Rajiv's. Amethi is near
Lucknow too and Mrs Gandhi's term of office was coming to an
end in eight months' time. So the defeat at Malihabad was a
threat to Rajiv Gandhi's future. His political career had been
slow to get off the ground, and it was generally accepted that he
would have difficulty in surviving defeat in Amethi. It was
becoming increasingly clear that Mrs Gandhi had to resolve the
Punjab crisis quickly to re-establish her government's credibility before the next general election and save both her and her
son Rajiv's political careers.

The Prime Minister realised this but she was still reluctant to
go for the military solution. She knew, from talks that her team
of negotiators had held with the other two members of the Akali
Dal Trinity while they were in jail for burning copies of the
Constitution, that all they were now demanding was Chandigarh. The two rivals for the leadership of the Akali Dal,
Prakash Singh Badal and Gurcharan Singh Tohra, the President of the SGPC, insisted that they must have this one positive
achievement if they were to wrest control of the Morcha from
Bhindranwale.

Mrs Gandhi had been insisting that Punjab could only have
Chandigarh if the Akalis were prepared to surrender the two
tahsils of Fazilka and Abohar to Haryana in exchange. These
were the terms of her original settlement, which had never been
implemented. She now agreed that only the town of Abohar
need be surrendered but maintained that this award should be
made by a commission so that the Hindus of Haryana would not

see it as a surrender. She promised that the findings of the commission would be guaranteed in advance. This was not good enough for the Akali leaders. They needed an announcement of the settlement by the government, not a commission, if they were to convince their followers that the Morcha had been a success and could be called off. In the end, however, even Tohra, who was of course the hardliner, did agree to a commission provided the terms of reference made it quite clear that Chandigarh would go to Punjab and only Abohar town to Haryana. He accepted that face had to be saved on both sides in the tradition of Indian negotiations.

This last round of negotiations was conducted on Mrs Gandhi's side by her External Affairs Minister, Narasimha Rao, with the team of three administrators who were the members of the Punjab Think Tank – Krishnaswamy Rao Sahib, the Cabinet Secretary, P.C. Alexander, the Prime Minister's Principal Secretary, and M.M.K. Wali, the Home Secretary. The Maharaja of Patiala had dropped out of the picture in February because he no longer believed there was any chance of a settlement. Amarinder Singh was bitterly critical of the way that the negotiations had been conducted. He told me that Mrs Gandhi's Think Tank was far too bureaucratic in its attitude to the demands for river waters and Chandigarh, and did not understand the political pressures on the Akali leaders. It was typical of Mrs Gandhi's disregard for the traditions of ministerial responsibility that the External Affairs Minister, not the Home Minister P.C. Sethi, led the last team of negotiators. Certainly P.C. Sethi's handling of the Punjab crisis in Parliament had shown that he was not exactly the best man for the job; but Mrs Gandhi still kept him as her *nam ke waste*, or nominal Home Minister, until after the army action. It was not important who occupied the Home Minister's seat at Cabinet meetings; what was important was who actually advised Mrs Gandhi, and here, as usual, she relied on trusted bureaucrats, not politicians. Narasimha Rao did of course represent the Cabinet, but he was noted for his loyalty to Mrs Gandhi rather than for his independent stature as a politician.

After reaching this agreement the government announced on 11th May that the charges of sedition against the Akali Dal

leaders for burning copies of the Constitution were being
withdrawn, and they were released. Four days later Badal and
Tohra met the third member of the Akali Dal Trinity, Longowal, in the Golden Temple complex. Bhindranwale was now
the key to the settlement. The government had stipulated that
he must agree before they would announce it, and Tohra was
the only man who could sell it to the Sant. In all earlier rounds
of negotiations he was the only one who had supported Bhindranwale's line that nothing short of the full implementation of
the Anandpur Sahib Resolution would do. Tohra was particularly anxious to push the settlement through. During the last
negotiations the two sides had discussed the possibility of
forming a coalition of the Akali Dal and the Congress (Indira) to
govern Punjab. Tohra believed that Bhindranwale would back
him for the chief-ministership of the coalition. So his life's
ambition seemed within his grasp, if only he could persuade the
preacher to accept the settlement.

At the meeting of the Akali Trinity in the Temple complex
Tohra got an agreement to approach Bhindranwale, and the
next day he went to discuss the settlement with the Sant in the
Akal Takht. Tohra told him that Chandigarh was a major
victory for the Sikh movement and that the other issues would
now be decided in the Sikhs' favour by the commissions the
government was setting up. But Tohra was hoist with his own
petard. Bhindranwale would not accept that the settlement met
the Morcha's demands. He had seen through Tohra's game and
told him that he was betraying the Anandpur Sahib Resolution
in the hope of becoming Chief Minister. The SGPC President
then tried threatening to throw Bhindranwale out of the Akal
Takht. He was the man who had persuaded the High Priest of
the Akal Takht to allow Bhindranwale to move into the shrine.
He had also used his influence to prevent the five High Priests
issuing an edict against the Sant. But threats did not work
either. Bhindranwale knew that the priests were by now more
afraid of him than they were of their patron, Tohra, and so the
whole settlement collapsed.

The following day Tohra went to see the Governor of Punjab
to tell him that he had failed and that there was no hope of
Bhindranwale agreeing to a negotiated settlement. A week later

Longowal announced that the Morcha would be resumed with an agitation to prevent grain movements in the state. That announcement gave the government the excuse it needed for tightening up security around the Golden Temple as a prelude to the army action. Many Sikhs believe that this was Longowal's reason for announcing the renewal of the Morcha. They claim he realised that the military solution was now the only answer to Bhindranwale. A senior Congress Member of Parliament also told Satish Jacob that Longowal started to 'cooperate' with the government after Bhindranwale rejected the settlement. It was certainly a remarkable coincidence that the day after the announcement that the Akali Dal planned to stop the movement of grain in Punjab, the Central Reserve Police took up positions in buildings surrounding the Golden Temple for the first time.

Unfortunately many of the best vantage points had already been occupied by Bhindranwale's men. The government knew they had moved into strategic positions in the houses surrounding the Temple two months before. Inspector-General of Police Bhinder had issued a circular to all officers, including those of the CRP, saying that he had received reports of houses near the Temple being fortified. He ordered officers not to take action beyond observing and reporting. Nothing, Bhinder said, was to be done which might disturb the local population. The army was to pay a heavy price for the Punjab police's failure to prevent the spread of Bhindranwale's fortifications. The White Paper on the Punjab Agitation, published to explain the army action in the Golden Temple, said: 'Seventeen houses in the civilian residential areas had been selected by the terrorists at distances of five hundred to eight hundred metres from the outer periphery of the temple complex and held by approximately ten men each. These lookout and early warning posts were veritable arsenals of light machine guns and other automatic weapons with huge caches of ammunition. The posts had been given common communication equipment to be in instant touch with their command posts.'

More than a month before the CRP took up positions surrounding the Golden Temple, the prelude to Operation Blue Star, the government had experimented with a different type of operation – a siege. The paramilitary Border Security Force in the town of Moga, which is the nearest town to Bhindranwale's own village, was given orders to lay siege to the Sikh temples there and not to lift the siege until the terrorists who had sought sanctuary inside them had surrendered. Five days after the sieges started the Sikh High Priests threatened to lead a march on Moga if they were not lifted. The Home Minister replied by telling the priests to get the terrorists out of the temples themselves if they wanted the sieges to be lifted. All seemed set for the first real confrontation between the government and the High Priests. But then suddenly the government changed tack again and lifted the sieges. The head of the Punjab police, P.S. Bhinder, told journalists who arrived in Moga the next day that sixteen terrorists had surrendered and that was why the siege had been lifted. However I could find no evidence in Moga that anyone had surrendered. Suspicions that it was the government which had unconditionally surrendered were heightened by a series of confusing answers to questions in Parliament by the Home Minister.

Lieutenant-General Sunderji, who commanded the eventual assault, admitted that he had considered laying siege to the Golden Temple to starve out Bhindranwale and his followers, and that one reason he had decided against it was the fear of uprisings in the countryside. That lesson was learnt at Moga. With the settlement rejected by Bhindranwale and a siege ruled out by the army, Mrs Gandhi had no alternative left – she had to raid the Akal Takht.

11

Mrs Gandhi Gives
the Go-ahead

On 2nd June Mrs Gandhi finally decided to press the button. The political risks of sending the army into the Golden Temple complex were enormous. Mrs Gandhi knew the risks to her own family too. Rajiv Gandhi had already been told by the Prime Minister's security advisers to withdraw his son and daughter from their boarding schools. Rahul was at the Doon School, India's Eton, where his father had studied. The advisers said that the children's security could only be guaranteed if they lived in the Prime Minister's house in Delhi.

On that 2nd June Mrs Gandhi's diary included a speech to a conference of leaders of her party from district headquarters throughout India. The conference was one of a series organised by Rajiv Gandhi as part of his drive to revive the Congress Party as a political organisation. He himself admitted that during the long years that his mother had dominated the party its roots had dried up. It had become little more than a bandwagon on which politicians jumped at election time. Mrs Gandhi was very anxious to support Rajiv Gandhi's efforts because the rebuilding of the party was his first political undertaking. Nevertheless she arrived two hours late for this meeting. It was meant to be held behind closed doors but three journalists managed to get in. One of them, Anand Sahay, said: 'When Mrs Gandhi walked up to the platform she appeared to be limping. Her shoulders were hunched. She looked dishevelled. Her face was drawn. She choked as she spoke. I was so surprised that I thought someone in her family must have died.' However by the time he got back to his office Sahay had concluded that the normally immaculate Mrs Gandhi's downtrodden and dishevelled appearance must mean that 'something big had been decided'.

Just before eight o'clock that night the government-controlled radio and television services did interrupt their programmes to announce that the Prime Minister would make a special broadcast at 8.30. When 8.30 came there was a silence on the airwaves. After two minutes announcers apologised for the delay in the Prime Minister's broadcast. Mrs Gandhi eventually came on the air three-quarters of an hour late. She had made several last-minute alterations to the script.

The Prime Minister appealed to the leaders of the Akali Dal to call off the next stage of their Morcha, the attempt to prevent grain movements in Punjab due to start the following day. She said, 'Even at this late hour, I appeal to the Akali leaders to call off their threatened agitation and accept the framework of the peaceful settlement which we have offered.' She also outlined that settlement, confirming that the government had suggested setting up a commission to decide the fate of Chandigarh. Mrs Gandhi said, 'Government has suggested that the whole territorial dispute including Chandigarh, Abohar and Fazilka should be referred to a commission whose decision should be binding on both states. Unfortunately the Akali Dal has not accepted the suggestions regarding the transfer of areas to Haryana in lieu of Chandigarh or of the whole dispute to a commission.' Mrs Gandhi did not however tell the nation that the government had even gone so far as to guarantee to fix the commission so that it decided in the Akalis' favour. She did tell the nation that the real problem was not the terms of the settlement but the fact that the Akali Dal Trinity – Longowal, Badal, and Tohra – had let control of the Morcha fall into the hands of Bhindranwale. She said, 'The reality that has emerged is not the adequacy or otherwise of the terms of the settlement offered by the government on the various demands of the Akali Dal but the fact that the agitation is now in the hands of a few who have scant regard for the unity and integrity of our country or concern for communal peace and harmony or the continued economic progress of the Punjab.'

The Prime Minister offered to renew negotiations but at the same time she warned, 'While the government is committed to solving all pending problems through negotiations, it should be obvious that no government can allow violence and terrorism in the settlement of issues. Those who indulge in such anti-social and anti-national activities should make no mistake about this.'

Mrs Gandhi's own political predicament was clear. The people of India were losing faith in her capacity to act. She virtually admitted this in her broadcast when she said, 'Punjab is uppermost in all our minds. The whole country is deeply concerned. The matter has been discussed and spoken about time and again. Yet an impression has been assiduously created that it is not being dealt with.' The Prime Minister ended her broadcast to the nation with a ringing appeal: 'Let us join hands together to heal wounds. The best memorial to those who have lost their lives is to restore normalcy and harmony in Punjab which they loved and served. To all sections of Punjabis I appeal — don't shed blood, shed hatred.' But the Prime Minister had already decided she would shed blood if necessary.

Shortly after that broadcast All India Radio announced that the army had been called into Punjab 'in aid of the civil authority', the phrase used in the military manual left behind by the British which still regulates most of the activities of the Indian army. The army had been called in to aid the civil authorities many times since independence but this was the first time the government of a major state had handed over total responsibility for security to soldiers. All India Radio announced that Lieutenant-General Ranjit Singh Dayal, Chief of Staff, Western Command, would hold the key post of Adviser (Security) to the Governor of Punjab and that the police who usually work to the government would be under the overall command of the army. What that was to mean became clear the next day when I went to the Golden Temple.

I found that the complex had been encircled by soldiers of the

Bihar regiment who had moved into the area overnight. Curfew had been relaxed and Hindus were chatting happily to the *jawans* (soldiers). The Hindus were delighted to see the army. They were confident that their nightmare was over. A shop-keeper said to me, 'Now at last we will get revenge on those Sikhs.' When I asked him what he thought the army would do he replied, 'Oh surely they will go in now, won't they?' The Hindu shopkeeper proved to be right.

The President of India, Zail Singh, who is by virtue of his office Commander-in-Chief of the armed forces was not informed that the army was going to be sent into the Golden Temple to arrest or kill the man that he had raised from an obscure preacher to a leader who was now threatening the unity of India. The President had cut short a visit to north-eastern India because he was worried about the increasing number of murders in Punjab villages, and on 30th May he did receive Mrs Gandhi at the vast sandstone Presidential Palace in Delhi. However, according to Zail Singh's officials, the Prime Minister did not mention the possibility of sending the army into the Golden Temple. She spent one and three quarter hours discussing a new formula for reaching an agreement with the Akalis.

The day before Mrs Gandhi's broadcast, firing between paramilitary police and Bhindranwale's followers in and around the Golden Temple complex started at twelve-forty and lasted until seven o'clock in the evening. An experienced CRP officer told me that he had never been under such heavy fire before. The next day I saw the marks of the bullets in the Golden Temple and hostel complexes. There were bullet holes in the Langar building where Bhindranwale was holding his usual morning congregation when the firing started and there were bullet holes below the window of Longowal's office. The marble pavement surrounding the sacred tank in the centre of the Golden Temple complex was chipped in many places, and angry Sikhs showed me holes marked with red rings in the Golden Temple itself. Some of the holes however were far too large to have been caused by bullets. They appeared to be the result of gradual wear and tear suffered by the structure long before Bhindranwale was ever heard of although they were dutifully ringed with red paint.

The CRP firing took place four days before the army actually entered the Temple. Military experts believe that it was a deliberate attempt to draw Bhindranwale's fire so that he would reveal his dispositions and his firepower. If that was so the exercise was not a great success. When the army did eventually go into the Temple the Generals were, on their own admission, taken by surprise and forced to fight a battle on a scale they had never imagined. I believe that the Central Reserve Police firing was the start of an attempt to frighten Bhindranwale into surrendering, an attempt which lasted almost to the hour that the army did eventually go in four days later.

I saw Bhindranwale the day after the firing. He was in the Akal Takht and had not been on the roof of the Langar that day although he said he would be resuming his morning congregations. When I asked him about the firing he replied, 'The firing shows that the government wants to insult the Golden Temple and cannot tolerate the faces of Sikhs and their way of life.' He promised that he would give the army a 'fitting reply' if they tried to enter the Temple, and a fitting reply he certainly did give them. But Bhindranwale was not his usual relaxed self. He was obviously tense and did not joke with journalists as he usually did. Normally the Sant liked nothing better than being filmed, but this time he became very impatient when a television team asked him to wait until they managed to get their lights into the room. The preacher said angrily, 'You'll have to hurry up. I have got more important things to do.'

By the following day Bhindranwale had recovered his sang-froid. Subhash Kirpekar was one of the journalists who went to see the Sant after the army had surrounded the Temple complex. Bhindranwale did not believe an attack was imminent. He told Kirpekar, 'The army will hang around this place like the CRP and the BSF [Border Security Force] have been doing for the last two years.' He qualified that remark slightly by saying, 'It is premature to say anything about the timing of the entry of the army and its possible impact. Their behaviour and intention will be known in a few days.' Kirpekar went on to ask Bhindranwale, 'Will you not be outnumbered by the army which has superior weapons too?' The Sant, like a good preacher, replied with a parable: 'Sheep always outnumber lions. But one lion can take care of a thousand sheep. When the lion sleeps the birds chirp. When it awakes the birds fly away. There is silence.' Right to the end he insisted that he was not responsible for the murders which had brought the army to the gates of the Golden Temple. When Kirpekar asked what could be done to stop the violence he replied, 'Ask those who are responsible for it.' When asked whether he feared death the Sant said, 'He is not a Sikh who fears death and he who fears death is not a Sikh.'

Major-General Shahbeg Singh, the man who was master-minding the defence of the Temple, was in the room too. With his long years of experience of the Indian army, the disgraced general did realise what the soldiers were up to. When asked by Kirpekar when he expected the action to start he replied, 'Maybe tonight.'

Major-General Shahbeg Singh was to fight to the bitter end but about 200 young Sikhs escaped from the Golden Temple that morning when the civil authorities lifted the curfew to allow Sikhs to celebrate the martyrdom of Guru Arjun, the builder of the Golden Temple. Giani Bakshish Singh, who lived just behind the Akal Takht, saw them going. To celebrate the martyrdom of the Guru he had set up a stall giving glasses of sherbert to all comers. He says that the young men escaped down the *gali* or alley known as 'Baghwali' or Garden Gali, which leads out of the back of the hostel where Bhindranwale was living before he moved into the Akal Takht. According to the Giani, women living in the nearby alleys took the young men in so that they could change from their traditional Sikh clothes into bush shirts and jeans or trousers. The women burnt the Sikh robes to prevent the police or the army finding them. The young Sikhs stopped at Giani Bakshish Singh's stall where he offered them saffron-coloured sherbert because he could not get the traditional red colouring. They joked with him, saying, 'Gianiji, you have made us drink the colour of martyrs.' The Giani said many of them were carrying wads of banknotes.

When news of the young men's escape reached the army the Generals were livid. They ordered curfew to be reimposed and immediately transferred the District Commissioner, the senior local administrator, who throughout the last months of the crisis had often seemed more loyal to Bhindranwale than to the government. Most of the young men who escaped were either criminals or those left-wing extremists known as Naxalites. It was the members of the Sikh Students Federation, and in particular the members of Bhindranwale's own sect, the Damdami Taksal, who stayed behind to fight. Some Sikhs who were inside the hostel complex at the time say that Bhindranwale deliberately sent the criminals and Naxalites out of the Temple so that they could continue the fight in the countryside. As one of the army's main tasks was to mop up the terrorists operating in Punjab villages, allowing those 200 young men to escape was a serious mistake. According to the government's figures, Bhindranwale's terrorists had already killed 165 Hindus and Nirankaris in the twenty-two months since the launching of the Akali Morcha. They had also killed 39 Sikhs because they had opposed Bhindranwale. The total number of deaths in violent incidents, including so-called 'encounters' between the police and Sikhs, riots, and the accident at the level crossing in which 34 supporters of the Morcha were killed, was 410. The injured numbered 1,180.

Operation Blue Star was conducted by the 9th Division commanded by Major-General Kuldip Singh Brar. No one could have been more offensive to Bhindranwale than the good-looking, grey-haired war hero. He was a Sikh from the same area and the same caste as Bhindranwale, who had committed the cardinal sin in the Sant's book of shaving his beard and cutting his hair. Brar was ordered to move his Division from Meerut, the cantonment where the Indian Mutiny broke out, to Amritsar by 30th May. On the next day, before the firing between the CRP and Bhindranwale's followers broke out, Brar was recognised walking around the *parikrama*, or pavement, surrounding the sacred tank in the Golden Temple complex. He must have seen that the Temple and the hostel complexes were unusually crowded because pilgrims had already arrived to celebrate the martyrdom of Guru Arjun. Sikhs were particularly anxious to attend the festival that year because it was followed by the fifth day of the lunar month, an auspicious day to bathe in the Temple tank. General Brar must also have realised that the unusually large number of pilgrims in

the two complexes would make his task of getting Bhindranwale out of the Temple without killing or injuring innocent
people very much harder. But the operation went ahead.

Two distinguished retired Sikh generals of the Indian army
have criticised the decision to start the operation on Guru
Arjun's martyrdom day. Lieutenant-General Jagjit Singh Aurora, the hero of Dacca, has said quite simply that it was 'a bad
choice', while Lt-General Harbaksh Singh who was Colonel-in-
Chief of the Sikh Regiment for twenty years suggested that the
decision was one of the factors which led some Sikh soldiers to
mutiny after the army action in the Golden Temple. In a
statement to the press he said: 'The martyrdom day of Guru
Arjun, being the epitome of supreme sacrifice in the face of
extreme religious persecution, has a special significance for the
Sikh soldier.'

The government's explanation for starting the operation on a
day so sacred to the Sikhs with all the risks of involving
innocent pilgrims in the battle was that Bhindranwale was
about to start a well-organised campaign to murder Hindus in
villages throughout the Punjab. A senior official of the Home
Ministry told Satish Jacob that intelligence officers had intercepted messages from Bhindranwale and Shahbeg Singh instructing their followers to start killing 'en masse' on 5th June.
He also said Bhindranwale had plans to kill all Punjabi MPs and
Members of the State Assembly. Although the government has
never provided any hard evidence to back up its allegation that
Bhindranwale was planning a massacre of Hindus, it is true to
say that the pace of the killings was accelerating alarmingly.
Twenty-three people were killed in the twenty-four hours
before Mrs Gandhi made her broadcast.

After curfew was reimposed on the night of 3rd June the
army opened fire for the first time. I could hear the firing from
the hotel where I was staying but it was impossible to see
anything because of the buildings surrounding the Temple.
Journalists in another hotel said they could see that the Temple
complex was floodlit. I thought the battle had started but I was
wrong. Next morning the firing stopped. It had been a
softening-up operation. Major-General Brar and his seniors still
hoped they could scare Bhindranwale out of his fortress.

12 *Above*, the Akal Takht on fire after being bombarded with squash-head shells during Operation Blue Star

13 *Below left*, the damage to the gold-plated dome of the Akal Takht was extensive

14 *Below right*, rubble at the foot of the Akal Takht. One of Shahbeg Singh's gun emplacements can be seen cut into the marble wall.

15 *Above left*, Indian troops inside the Golden Temple
complex shortly after the defeat of Bhindranwale and his
followers
16 *Above right*, bodies of Bhindranwale's men laid out
on the *parikrama*, the marble pavement surrounding the Golden
Temple
17 *Above*, the body of Major-General Shahbeg Singh.
The ropes around his feet and the marks on his arms indicate that
he was dragged out of the Akal Takht.

Gurcharan Singh Tohra, Bhindranwale's former mentor, also hoped that the Sant could be persuaded to throw in the towel. When the firing stopped he crossed the road from the hostel complex, walked past the Langar building where Bhindranwale should have been holding his morning congregation and the Gurudwara Manji Sahib where frightened pilgrims were huddled together in small groups, and entered the Golden Temple complex itself. The President of the SGPC walked round the marble pavement and came to the Akal Takht. Its windows and arches were now blocked up with bricks and sandbags. Young Sikhs had taken up firing positions in the shrine itself and in the buildings on all sides of it. The President of the SGPC was taken up to see Bhindranwale. He tried to convince the Sant that resistance would be futile, that the army was determined to capture or kill him if he did not surrender. But Bhindranwale angrily dismissed Tohra, telling him that he was an agent of Mrs Gandhi. Tohra was now no better in Bhindranwale's eyes than the other two members of the Akali Dal Trinity – Morcha Dictator Longowal, who was still in the Temple complex, and the leader of the party in the State Assembly, Badal, who was on his farm miles from Amritsar.

Tohra's final attempt to persuade Bhindranwale to surrender again suggests that both he and Longowal were by now collaborating with the government. They must have been in touch with the army otherwise Tohra would not have had the authority to negotiate a surrender. Tohra also knew that the army would not resume firing when he left the comparative safety of the hostel complex to cross to the Akal Takht. The President of the SGPC was not the man to risk getting caught in the Akal Takht during the final battle.

Bhindranwale must have known that the game was up by now; so why did he insist on fighting to the bitter end? He had to die or face ignominy. If the Sant had surrendered he would have been exposed as a cowardly braggart. He had left himself no honourable retreat. Bhindranwale did have genuine religious motives too. He was, for all his faults, a zealot who believed in a religion with a tradition of martyrdom, a tradition honoured only the day before his last chance to surrender by the celebration of the martyrdom of Guru Arjun. He was being given a chance to die in the most honourable cause of all, the defence of the Golden Temple. The Sant must have thought of the glory that martyrdom would bring to his memory. He knew that if he surrendered he would be forgotten but if he died defending the Temple he would be remembered for ever in the annals of Sikh history. Bhindranwale was also by now a bitter enemy of India. In his last interview with the journalist Subhash Kirpekar he was asked, 'Is it your contention that Sikhs cannot live in India?' The Sant replied, 'Yes. They can neither live in nor with India. If treated as equals it may be possible. But frankly speaking I don't think that is possible.' Bhindranwale knew how fervently Sikhs were devoted to the Golden Temple. He knew what strains on the unity of India an attack on the Golden Temple would impose. He knew that he could force the army to attack. He knew, because Major-General Shahbeg Singh had told him, that he could hold out until the army was forced to do severe damage to the Akal Takht and probably to the Golden Temple too. So Bhindranwale had a cause worth dying for and nothing to live for. That is surely why the Sant refused to surrender.

Why did Longowal and Tohra not surrender before the action started? They were certainly not made of the stuff of martyrs. They showed that when the army entered the hostel complex during the battle itself. The two politicians did not surrender earlier because the army did not give them a chance to do so. The Generals were to say later that they made many appeals for surrender after they had surrounded the Temple. But Bhan Singh, the Secretary of the SGPC, told Satish Jacob that the appeals could not be heard inside the hostel complex. At one stage Longowal and Tohra did hear a broadcast on the radio saying that curfew was to be lifted for two hours to allow people to surrender. They sent Bhan Singh to find the Deputy-Superintendent of Police and negotiate the surrender of the pilgrims and the Akali Dal supporters who had come to take part in the renewed Morcha. Bhan Singh did leave the hostel but by the time he reached the end of the Baghwali Gali heavy firing had broken out again and he ran back. The two leaders could not negotiate a surrender themselves because by now they were only receiving incoming calls.

Ranbir Kaur, a nineteen-year-old woman who was staying in a room of the Guru Ram Das Serai, or hostel, with twelve children from a religious school she helped to run, also told me that she did not hear any appeals by the army to surrender or to come out of the hostel. When I asked her whether she ever thought of making an attempt to get out on her own she replied, 'We thought we were safer inside. We never thought they would attack the Temple.'

The pilgrims were terrified by the firing of rifles, machine guns and mortars. They did not know when the firing would stop and when it would start again. Neither Tohra nor Longowal were providing any leadership. So it was at the least naïve of the Generals to imagine that they would get much response to loudspeaker appeals. The hostel complex was eventually evacuated in the middle of the attack on the Temple itself. During that rescue operation many innocent people were killed, many were injured, and many were wrongly arrested. It was the least creditable part of Operation Blue Star. The tragedy could only have been avoided if the hostels had been evacuated before the attack on the Golden Temple complex started; but that was easier said than done. To evacuate the hostels first would have meant separating the two complexes. But both Bhindranwale's men and his old rivals the Babbar Khalsa had taken up positions overlooking the hostels and indeed inside the hostels themselves. Bhindranwale had also sent his interpreter Harminder Singh Sandhu to Longowal's office to prevent him surrendering. So any attempt to separate the two complexes would almost certainly have led to a battle in the hostels. That battle could easily have spread to the Temple too, forcing the army to enter Bhindranwale's stronghold before it was ready to do so.

A more serious problem was that of time. Separating the two complexes would have delayed the main battle and Lieutenant-General Sunderji who was in overall command felt he could not take the risk. From the moment that the army laid siege to the Golden Temple on 3rd June he was obsessed with speed because he was afraid of that uprising in the countryside. Lieutenant-General Sunderji explained his fears to the press after the operation.

We knew that they had plans to utilise the innocent people, the religious-minded innocent people in the countryside. That plan was to incite these people to come to the Golden Temple in thousands and to literally swamp the surroundings as well as the inside, thereby preventing most effectively any action we could have taken to flush the terrorists out. This was confirmed information. We even intercepted messages going out to the countryside. So any extended cordon or siege would have ended up with this type of mass movement.

The army did have good reason to fear the Sikhs in the countryside. The night after the Golden Temple was surrounded a crowd of angry Sikhs from villages near Amritsar stormed into the Sultanwind area of the city and burned down the shops and small factories of Hindus. The strict curfew imposed by the army had proved ineffective. As tension built up throughout Punjab, army helicopters also spotted groups of angry Sikhs gathering in many different places. Troops were able to disperse them but not without loss of life.

On the night of 3rd June Punjab was cut off from the rest of India and movement inside the state brought to a standstill to prevent an uprising. Rail, bus and air services were stopped, telex and telephone lines cut, and the Pakistan border sealed. The Golden Temple was not the only *gurudwara* to be surrounded. On the same night the army surrounded thirty-seven Sikh temples where they believed Bhindranwale's followers had sought sanctuary. In Patiala the army met with considerable resistance from inside the Gurudwara Dukhniwaran and so they decided to attack it. The operation, like the operation in the Golden Temple, was commanded by a Sikh general who had forsworn his beard, Major-General Gurdial Singh. The army says that twenty people were killed in the Patiala *gurudwara*, but doctors at Patiala hospital say that at least fifty-six people died. The army was disappointed by the number of terrorists they captured and killed in the thirty-seven *gurudwaras*. Either Bhindranwale's men were not as widely spread as the army had been led to believe or most of them fled before the soldiers came.

Because all communications had been cut on the night of 3rd June, no news of what was happening in Punjab was reaching the outside world. Journalists were told to stay in their hotels; so we spent most of the day sitting on the lawn of the Ritz Hotel listening to a joint army/police network on the FM band of our transistor radios. Troops were clearly being deployed for a major operation, but just how major I did not appreciate at the time. I heard an officer reporting that the artillery had reached its position but I could not believe that the army would use heavy guns in an area as congested as the old city of Amritsar. I thought that soldiers of the artillery must be being used as infantry to seal off the Temple. I was to be proved wrong.

That night, the night before the army launched its attack on the Temple itself, Superintendent of Police Sital Das came to the Ritz Hotel to tell us that we were to be driven out of Punjab in a police bus. Most of the other journalists agreed to go but a few of us decided it was worth a fight to see if we could at least stay on until the next morning when we would be able to see what was happening in Amritsar and the rest of Punjab. A blazing row ensued during which some of the journalists sided with Sital Das. I felt sorry for him because I knew that he had been harassed all day by the army who did not try to hide their contempt for the police. When a senior army officer had learnt that there were foreign correspondents still in Amritsar he accused the police of revealing military plans to the press. But I still felt the battle was worth fighting and so I shouted at the police officer, 'I am not going to leave. You can arrest me.' He shouted back, 'Yes, I will arrest you. You British think you can still rule us and tell us what to do.' It was an uncomfortable moment because the last thing I wanted after some sixteen years in independent India was to be accused of being an imperialist. However India is a land where tempers die down as quickly as they flare up. Sital Das said he would consult the army. A brigadier arrived at the Ritz Hotel and it was agreed that we should leave early next morning. There was no skin off anyone's nose and Sital Das and I celebrated this happy compromise together, I with one of the last of the bottles of beer that Tiny Mehra, the vast and genial host of the Ritz Hotel, had in stock, the police officer with a soft drink because he was on duty.

The official ruling was that only foreign correspondents had to go because foreigners had been barred from the Punjab under the new regulations brought in when the army took over responsibility for security. Before we left that rule was stretched to cover Indians working for foreign papers too. However Brahma Chellaney, an Indian working for Associated Press, managed to stay behind. He had only arrived in Amritsar that day so his name was not on the police list of journalists.

Early the next morning we were bundled into a Punjab Government Roadways bus which, judging by its state of dilapidation, was not intended for use beyond Amritsar city limits. We started off on our long drive down the Grand Trunk Road to the border of Haryana. We stopped for about five minutes at a hotel near the Golden Temple where a journalist had left his tape recorder. There we were able to hear intermittent small arms fire and the occasional whoof of a mortar. Every alley had been sealed off by troops and we were stopped three times by army road blocks before we even left the city.

As the sun rose I saw a spectacle I had never expected – the Grand Trunk Road empty. During the five and a half hours it took us to drive to the border I did not see a single civilian vehicle, not even a bullock cart. The shops in the villages we passed through were all closed and most of the villagers were in their homes. The only trains I saw were troop trains. At every important road junction we were stopped by an army checkpost. Our escorting officer was a lowly Sub-Inspector and my friend Sital Das had not given him that most important of all pieces of equipment in India, official papers, and so he had the utmost difficulty in persuading army officers unused to these sort of duties to let us pass. He succeeded in the end and we finally crossed the Punjab/Haryana border just before midday. Punjab was cut off from the rest of the world in preparation for the final assault which was to start that evening.

12

Operation Blue Star

At seven o'clock on the evening of 5th June, tanks of the 16th Cavalry Regiment of the Indian army started moving up to the Golden Temple complex. They passed the Jallianwala Bagh, the enclosed garden where General Dyer massacred nearly 400 people. That massacre dealt a mortal blow to Britain's hopes of continuing to rule India and was one of the most powerful inspirations of the freedom movement. When Mrs Gandhi was told that Operation Blue Star had started, she must have wondered whether it would provide the decisive inspiration for the Sikh independence movement, a movement which at that time had very little support outside Bhindranwale's entourage and small groups of Sikhs living in Britain, Canada and the United States.

Major-General Brar had addressed his men before he ordered them to enter the Golden Temple complex. He was commanding a mixed bag of troops, representative of the widespread recruiting pattern of the modern Indian army, which has broken with the British tradition of limiting recruitment to certain 'martial castes'. There were Dogras and Kumaonis from the foothills of the Himalayas, India's northern border. There were Rajputs, the desert warriors from Rajasthan. There were

Madrasis from Tamil Nadu, one of the most southern states. There were Biharis from the tribes of central India, and there were some Sikhs. Major-General Brar told his men that entering the Golden Temple complex was a 'last resort', that they had to do it to 'stop the country being held to ransom any longer'. Bhindranwale was identified as 'the enemy', and the attacking force was told that he had 'seized control of the Temple'. Every man was told that he must not fire at either of the shrines inside the Temple complex, the Golden Temple and the Akal Takht, without direct orders.

It was almost thirty years to the day since Brar had joined the Maratha Light Infantry as a lieutenant. He had fought in the Bangladesh war under Lieutenant-General Jagjit Singh Aurora, the Sikh general who was to be one of the most outspoken critics of Operation Blue Star. Brar had been decorated for gallantry. He had also held an important staff post in the Defence Ministry, and was now commanding one of the crack Infantry Divisions, the 9th. Brar was a stylish soldier with curly grey hair emerging from under the beret he wore pulled well down over his right ear.

Brar's superior officer was Lt-General Krishnaswamy Sunderji, the General Officer Commanding-in-Chief, Western Command. He had joined the Mahar Regiment, a new regiment designed to bring a 'non-martial' caste into the army. During the 1965 war with Pakistan, Sunderji commanded a battalion and during the Bangladesh war he was a brigadier on the staff in the Eastern Sector. Sunderji had also commanded the College of Combat at Mhow, one of the most important training institutes of the Indian army. He had a reputation as a strategist, and was in the running for the number one job, the Chief of the Army Staff.

Sunderji asked his Chief Staff Officer, Lt-General Ranjit Singh Dayal, to draw up the plans for Operation Blue Star. Dayal, like Brar, was a Sikh, but he had not shaved his beard or cut his hair, and still wore a turban. Dayal was also an infantry soldier, having served in the 1st Battalion, the Parachute Regiment, which was to spearhead the attack on the Golden Temple complex. During the 1965 war with Pakistan, Dayal became a legend by capturing a pass which had previously been thought to be impregnable, and blocking off one of the most important routes from Pakistan-controlled Kashmir into the Indian state of Jammu and Kashmir. A frontal assault was impossible and so Lt-General Dayal climbed up the mountain towering over the Haji Pir Pass and came down on top of the Pakistanis. He described the operation himself:

I then sought permission of my commanding officer to capture the Haji Pir Pass. The permission was granted, and then began the march forward. The enemy fired from two directions. I sent one platoon to silence the enemy guns. I and the rest of my men continued to advance and reached Hyderabad Nullah by 7 p.m.

From then on it was bad going. The pass from there was a 4,000-foot-steep climb. It was raining heavily. The ground was slushy. I left the beaten track and took another route. In fact, it was not a route at all. It was a steep climb. Despite the heavy odds, we reached the road leading to the pass at 4.30 a.m. on August 28. I decided to give my men carrying guns and batteries the much needed rest. After two hours, we again started climbing and at 8 a.m. we reached a bund [embankment] near the pass.

Leaving some men there to keep the enemy engaged, along with the rest of the party, I climbed another hill feature and from there rolled down and stormed the enemy position at the pass. The enemy fled in confusion leaving their guns. By 10.30 a.m. we were in complete control of the pass.[1]

When he briefed the press after Operation Blue Star, Lt-General Sunderji described the orders the government had given him:

I was told to flush out the extremists from the Golden Temple with no damage if possible to the Harmandir Sahib [Golden Temple] and as little as possible damage to the Akal Takht. I was told to use the bare minimum of force required for achieving this object and that I was to minimise casualties to both sides. I was to try to prevent internecine fighting between the two major groups which were lodged inside, the one that of Jarnail Singh Bhindranwale and the second that of Mr Longowal and his followers.

Lieutenant-General Dayal told the press, 'The principle of minimum force was to be applied throughout.' He described Operation Blue Star as 'a typical infantry operation'. Dayal also stressed that all troops were ordered not to damage the Golden Temple. He was a deeply religious man who had been coming to the Golden Temple to pray since he was fourteen years old. The Lieutenant-General told the press that he never doubted that his men would obey their orders not to damage the shrine.

As all of you know, the Indian army is a very religious army. Once the orders are given to them they follow them to the letter and once it was told to them [not to damage the Golden Temple] I was sure they will obey this and I am proud to say they did until the end.

Dayal also gave an example of the piety of Indian army soldiers from his own experience.

In 1965 [the war with Pakistan] we went into an objective. There we saw some cows grazing. Suddenly the shelling started. One cow got hurt by a shell and I saw a *jawan* [soldier] pulling out his field dressing and applying it to the cow.

Lieutenant-General Sunderji also stressed the religious aspect of the operation. He said, 'We went inside with humility in our hearts and prayers on our lips. We in the army hold all places of religion in equal reverence.'

To achieve his objectives of 'flushing out' the extremists from the Golden Temple complex, doing minimum damage to the shrines, and preventing a battle breaking out in the hostel complex, Dayal drew up a twofold plan. The essence of the plan was to separate the hostel complex from the Temple complex, so that the hostels could be evacuated without becoming involved in the main battle. To achieve his prime objective of getting Bhindranwale out of the Temple complex, Dayal had planned commando operations. The commandos were to be supported by infantry. Tanks were only to be used as platforms for machine-guns to neutralise fire on troops approaching the Golden Temple complex, and to cover the Temple exits in case anyone tried to escape. Armoured personnel carriers were to be positioned on the road separating the hostels from the Temple complex to keep the two potential battle fields apart.

The three Generals succeeded in achieving only one of their objectives. The Golden Temple complex was cleared, but to say that Bhindranwale was flushed out would be, to put it mildly, an understatement. He was blasted out of the Akal Takht by the 105 mm. main armament of Indian Vijayanta (Victory) tanks. In the process much of the Akal Takht, the shrine which according to the original orders was to suffer 'as little as possible damage', was reduced to rubble. At the start of the operation troops had even been forbidden to use automatic weapons against the Akal Takht. The evacuation of the hostel complex was completed but not without heavy civilian casualties.

The first task was the destruction of Major-General Shahbeg Singh's outer defences. Much of this had been completed in the preliminary firing when Major-General Brar had hoped to frighten Bhindranwale into surrendering. These defences included the seventeen houses which the police had allowed Bhindranwale's followers to occupy in the alleys surrounding the Golden Temple. Some of them were as far as 800 yards away from the complex. These outposts were all in wireless contact with Shahbeg Singh's command post in the Akal Takht. The Temple View Hotel outside the Temple complex had also been occupied. As its name implies, it gave the Sikhs an excellent vantage point from which to keep watch over the main entrance to the Golden Temple, as well as a clear arc of fire. Next to it was Brahmbuta Akhara, a large building housing the headquarters of a Sikh sect. This building also commanded the approach to the Golden Temple. Then there were three towers which had been fortified to make positions from which Bhindranwale's men could fire into the Golden Temple complex. Because they stood well above the rest of the buildings, the towers were also excellent observation posts for watching the movement of troops in the narrow alleys surrounding the Temple. One of

them was a water tower. The other two were eighteenth-
century brick watch towers which resembled minarets. The old
towers stood eighty feet high and were near the Langar or
dining hall on whose roof Bhindranwale had addressed so many
congregations.

Major-General Brar said that he ordered artillery to blast off
the tops of the three towers. However he decided not to capture
the seventeen houses because he did not have 'the resources to
do so'. Firing continued from these houses for days after the
Golden Temple complex had been captured. The use of artillery in an area as crowded and densely populated as the old city
of Amritsar proved, not surprisingly, to be very costly. Artillery is an 'area weapon', used to kill and suppress fire over a
wide area, and is not commonly used against special targets.
Severe damage was caused to several bazaars, but Brar had to
secure the posts commanding the entrance to the Temple and
the inside of the Temple itself before he could send his soldiers
into the historic headquarters of the Sikh religion.

It was only when he was convinced the approaches to the
Temple complex were clear that Brar ordered the tanks to move
into the square in front of the northern entrance to the Golden
Temple, known as the *ghantaghar*, or clock tower entrance.
One of the tank commanders said, 'As soon as I turned right
from Jallianwala Bagh I heard the tik-tik sound of shells landing
on my tank. Over the headphones I got the order to neutralise
the fire.' According to the Lieutenant of the 16th Cavalry, there
were four tanks and three armoured cars. He said that Shahbeg
Singh appeared to be monitoring their movements because,
once the armour was in position, firing from the walls of the
Temple stopped. The Lieutenant reported back to his commanding officer that the firing had been neutralised. But as
soon as the assault on the Temple started it became clear that
Shahbeg Singh's firepower was far from neutralised.

Meanwhile in the narrow alley behind the Akal Takht, those
paramilitary commandos who had trained on the model of the
Golden Temple complex were trying to get into Bhindranwale's
fortress. This operation was a dismal failure. Some commandos
did get on to the roof of the shrine, but they were caught in the
crossfire and had to withdraw. For some reason this part of the

operation was not mentioned at all by the Generals when they briefed the press after it was all over.

It was between ten and ten-thirty in the evening that Major-General Brar decided he must launch a frontal attack on the Akal Takht. Commandos from the 1st Battalion, the Parachute Regiment, wearing black denims, were ordered to run down the steps under the clock tower on to the *parikrama*, or pavement, turn right and move as quickly as they could round the edge of the sacred tank to the Akal Takht. But as the paratroopers entered the main gateway of the Temple they were mown down. Most of the casualties were caused by Sikhs with light machine-guns who were hiding on either side of the steps leading down to the *parikrama*. The few commandos who did get down the steps were driven back by a barrage of fire from the buildings on the south side of the sacred pool. In the control room, in a house on the opposite side of the clock-tower square, Major-General Brar was waiting anxiously with his two superior officers to hear that the commandos had established positions inside the complex. When no report came through he was heard over the command network saying, 'You bastards, why don't you go in.'

The few commandos who survived regrouped in the square outside the Temple, and reported back to Major-General Brar. He reinforced them and ordered them to make another attempt to go in. The commandos were to be followed by the 10th Battalion of the Guards commanded by a Muslim, Lieutenant-Colonel Israr Khan. This battalion had Sikh soldiers in its ranks. The second commando attack managed to neutralise the machine-gun posts on either side of the steps and get down on to the *parikrama*. They were followed by the Guards who came under withering fire and were not able to make any progress towards their objective, the Akal Takht. Lt-Colonel Israr Khan radioed for permission to fire back at the buildings on the other side of the tank. That would have meant that the Golden Temple itself, which is in the middle of the tank, would have been in the line of fire. Brar refused permission. He still believed it would be possible to achieve all his objectives, including preserving the Golden Temple and the Akal Takht intact. But then he started to get messages from the commander of the Guards reporting heavy casualties. They had suffered almost 20 per cent casualties without managing to turn the corner of the *parikrama* to the western side of the complex where the Akal Takht is situated. The Guards were not only being fired at from the northern and western sides. Sikhs would also suddenly appear from man-holes in the *parikrama* the Guards were fighting from, let off a burst of machine-gun fire or throw lethal grenades, made in the complex itself, and disappear into the passages which run under the Temple. These machine-gunners had been taught to fire at knee-level because Major-General Shahbeg Singh expected the army to crawl towards its objective. But the Guards and commandos were not crawling, and so many of them received severe leg injuries.

Brar then decided on a change of plan. As he said after the battle, 'I realised that it was difficult for this battalion to progress operations any further and there was no point in them remaining at the ground-floor level. Unless you got on to the first floor and to the rooftop, and got it to control the situation, you would continue suffering casualties. So the task given to them was, under all circumstances, to get a lodgement in spite of all the casualties they had suffered and I must give full credit to the battalion commander, a very dashing young soldier, Lt-Colonel Israr Khan, who rallied his boys together and worked his way up and did succeed in getting an allotment in this particular area.' That allotment enabled the Guards to neutralise some of the positions on the south side of the tank, but they were still hampered by the order not to fire in any direction which would endanger either of the historic shrines.

In spite of the very heavy firing, some of the commandos did manage to get round that corner of the *parikrama* and make their way to the courtyard in front of the Akal Takht. But they fought their way into a lethal trap. The Akal Takht itself was heavily fortified; there were sandbag and brick gun emplacements in its windows and arches, and holes had been made in its sacred marble to provide firing positions. On either side of the shrine are buildings which overlook the courtyard. They had been fortified too, as had the Toshakhana or Temple Treasury opposite the Akal Takht and the houses which overlooked the building from behind. So when the commandos got into that courtyard, bullets rained down on them from all sides. They were driven back suffering 30 per cent casualties. The courtyard in front of the Akal Takht had been turned, in Major-General Brar's words, 'into a killing ground'. To make matters worse, there was no sign of the Madrasis who were meant to be entering the Golden Temple complex from the southern side to form the other half of a pincer movement on the Akal Takht. When it became clear that the Madrasis had either got bogged down or lost in the narrow alleys, Brar asked his superiors for permission to use troops from another Division, the 15th. The infantry from his own division was fully deployed. The Guards were inside the Temple on the northern side, the Madrasis were trying to make their way to the eastern entrance, the Kumaons were clearing the hostel complex, and the Bihars had thrown a cordon round the Temple. Their main responsibility was to ensure that neither Bhindranwale nor any of his followers escaped.

Sunderji and Dayal agreed to reinforcing the operation and so two companies of the 7th Garhwal Rifles were put under Brar's command. The Garhwals also come from the foothills of the Himalayas in the state of Uttar Pradesh. Brar ordered them to enter the Temple from the southern side and try to relieve the pressure on the Guards and the commandos on the northern side. As soon as they entered the southern gate they came under heavy fire. An officer of the Garhwals said, 'They seemed to be firing on us from everywhere. It was impossible to know where to fire back.' But the Garhwals did manage to establish a position on the roof of the Temple library. Their commanding officer reported this to his Brigadier, A.K. Dewan.

Dewan was very much a soldier's soldier, always wanting to be in the thick of it. His nickname was, surprisingly, Chicken. Apparently he was called Chicken when he was an officer cadet because he had a very long and thin neck. The Brigadier should have left the fighting inside the complex to the battalion officers, but he could not resist the temptation to join in himself. The Lieutenant-Colonel commanding the Garhwals tried to dissuade him, saying that his men were under very heavy fire, but this was an added attraction for Dewan. When he got into the Temple he reported to Major-General Brar on the wireless. Brar, whose temper was wearing a little thin by this time, could be heard over the whole network shouting at Dewan: 'What the hell are you doing in there? I am in command of this operation. You don't move without my orders.'

Then Brar calmed down and asked Dewan to stay inside and let him have a sitrep as soon as possible. Dewan realised that it was very unlikely that the Guards and the commandos would be able to achieve their objective. But he did reckon that his position on the southern side was fairly secure and that if he could reinforce it, he might be able to storm the shrine. When he reported this back to Brar he was given permission to call up two companies of the 15th Kumaons. By this time the operation had been in progress for about two hours and Brar was nowhere near achieving his objective. His short, sharp commando operation had got bogged down; so he decided to allow Dewan to fight his own battle inside the Temple complex.

Dewan made repeated attempts to storm the Akal Takht but each time the Kumaons or Garhwals turned the corner of the *parikrama* and ran into the courtyard in front of the Akal Takht, they came under withering fire and had to retreat. Dewan himself was striding up and down the southern side of the *parikrama* encouraging his men. But their task was impossible. Although both the northern and southern sides of the *parikrama* were by now in the control of the army, they had not been able to make any impression on the main fortress and the defences surrounding it, and the four companies had suffered 137 casualties. Of course they were still hampered by the order not to fire in any direction which would endanger the Golden Temple.

Dewan decided to wait for the Madrasis who were still trying to get to the Temple complex and then make one last attempt to storm the Akal Takht. The Madrasis eventually made it at about three o'clock in the morning, some five hours late. They came into the Temple complex through the gate on the hostel side. When they entered heavy firing was still going on and it was dark. In the confusion the Madrasis opened fire on Dewan's troops. The Brigadier shouted, 'Don't shoot! I am the deputy GOC!' When that little 'cock-up', as one officer put it, had been sorted out, Dewan launched his final attack.

There was no way anyone could get into that fortress without taking out its defences first. Dewan's repeated charges were as futile as the charge of the Light Brigade, and he now realised it. He got on the wireless and told Brar that he would have to call up tanks to bombard the Akal Takht. He said, 'I can't afford to lose any more men. I can't accept defeat.' Brar later told the press his version of what happened next:

> The infantry was in danger of being massacred . . . Hesitatingly I had to ask my superiors that I must take a tank in. I cannot allow the infantry now to get massacred. The infantry just cannot carry on doing the impossible task. I must say that the reaction was instantaneous and that was due to the fact that both my commanders were sitting barely fifteen metres away as the line of sight is from the scene of action.

Sunderji's reaction was not instantaneous. He first contacted Delhi where a special operations room had been set up to keep track of the battle. The Deputy Defence Minister, K.P. Singh Deo, a former army officer himself, was in charge, assisted by Rajiv Gandhi's most trusted aide, Arun Singh, who, although not a practising Sikh, came from one of the Punjab royal families. The army and the government were now faced with a dilemma. Sunderji had always insisted that the operation must be completed by daybreak, otherwise his men inside the Temple would be sitting ducks for Bhindranwale's snipers. There could be no question of withdrawing and trying again the next night, because the news that Bhindranwale and Shahbeg Singh had forced the Indian army to withdraw would certainly leak out somehow. That would have disastrous consequences in the villages of Punjab and among Sikhs in the army. The only answer seemed to be tanks. They were the only equipment with the firepower and the accuracy to blast a way into Bhindranwale's fortress. But tanks meant that the army would fail in one of its tasks — the preservation of the Akal Takht. They also meant the horrifying prospect of one mistake by a gunner seriously damaging the Golden Temple itself. In the end Delhi agreed that the tanks should be used and a message was sent back to Lieutenant-General Sunderji, nearly two hours after Chicken Dewan had asked for them.

In the meanwhile Major-General Brar had made one more effort to get his men into the Akal Takht. He called up a Skot OT64 armoured personnel carrier. Tanks had to break down the steps leading to the *parikrama* from the hostel side so that the eight-wheeled, Polish-built APC could get in. The aim was to drive the APC right up to the Akal Takht so that the men from the mechanised infantry, one of the newest units of the Indian army, could get into the fortress under the cover of its wall. But as the armoured personnel carrier approached the Akal Takht it came under fire from two Chinese-made, rocket-propelled grenade launchers. One of the grenades found its target and the armoured personnel carrier was knocked out. The Captain commanding the platoon was wounded.

This forced the Generals to rethink their strategy once again. They had no intelligence reports of Shahbeg Singh having armour-piercing weapons at his disposal. Even the tanks, which had by now made their way on to the *parikrama* to await government clearance to open fire, were now at risk, although the maximum armour of the tanks was more than twice as thick as the APC's. The tanks had been trying to blind the marksmen in Bhindranwale's fortress with their searchlights. As soon as Brar realised that the enemy had armour-piercing weapons, he ordered the tank commanders to switch off their searchlights. The tanks had ploughed up the *parikrama*, each of whose marble slabs was inscribed with the name of the devotee who had donated it to the Temple.

The Vijayanta was the army's main battle tank, being an Indian-built version of the Vickers 38-ton tank. When the orders came, they opened up with their main armament. Photographs of the shattered shrine indicate quite clearly that the Vijayantas 105 mm. main armaments pumped high-explosive squash-head shells into the Akal Takht. Those shells were designed for use against 'hard targets' like armour and fortifications. When the shells hit their targets, their heads spread or 'squash' on to the hard surface. Their fuses are arranged to allow a short delay between the impact and the shells igniting, so that a shock-wave passes through the target and a heavy slab of armour or masonry is forced away from the inside of the armoured vehicle or fortification. Lieutenant-

General Jagjit Singh Aurora, who studied the front of the Akal Takht before it was repaired, reckoned that as many as eighty of these lethal shells could have been fired into the shrine. The advantage of a tank's main armament is that it fires with pinpoint accuracy. Indian army officers talk of the Vijayanta's ability to post shells through letter-boxes.

The effect of this barrage on the Akal Takht was devastating. The whole of the front of the sacred shrine was destroyed, leaving hardly a pillar standing. Fires broke out in many of the different rooms blackening the marble walls and wrecking the delicate decorations dating from Maharaja Ranjit Singh's time. They included marble inlay, plaster and mirror work, and filigree partitions. The gold-plated dome of the Akal Takht was also badly damaged by artillery fire. At one stage during the night Major-General Brar had ordered his Colonel (Administration) to mount a 3.7-inch Howell gun on to the roof of a building behind the shrine and fire at the dome in an attempt to frighten the Sikhs into surrender. Brar explained to his Colonel, 'Maybe the noise and the sting will have its effect.'

The artillery did not scare Bhindranwale's men; but the tank barrage was a different matter. The effect it must have had is impossible to imagine. As shockwave after shockwave rocked the building, the gallant, if misguided, defenders must have feared it was going to come down on top of them. Deafened by the explosions, they were driven to the back of the building by the flames and falling masonry. The deadly machine-gun fire which had been raining down on the army stopped.

Still sporadic resistance continued from some of the buildings overlooking the courtyard in front of the Akal Takht. By now it was light and Brar decided it was too dangerous to make the final assault necessary to re-establish control over the shrine from which Bhindranwale and Shahbeg Singh had withstood the Indian infantry attack. So Brigadier Dewan was ordered not to follow up the tank attack until darkness fell again. The three Generals at the command post knew that they had knocked out Bhindranwale's fortress, but they still faced the agonising possibility that the Sant himself might have escaped.

After the battle Brar told the press that only one tank had been driven on to the *parikrama*, and that it had only fired its secondary armament, a 7.62 mm. machine-gun. But the damage to the Akal Takht tells a different story. There was no machine-gun which could have brought down so much masonry, and the shell marks were clearly those of high-explosive squash-heads. As for the number of tanks involved, other officers Satish Jacob talked to said that as many as six were brought into the complex. As one Vijayanta only carries forty-four rounds of main armament ammunition, it is certain that more than one was used. It also seems likely that the gunners fired from more than one position because the Golden Temple itself was in their arc of fire, standing as it does in the middle of the sacred tank.

The battle for the Akal Takht was not the only one raging that night. Across the road running along the eastern side of the Golden Temple complex, another battalion of the Kumaon Regiment was involved in the second operation that Lieutenant-General Sunderji had been ordered to carry out. He had been told by the government to 'prevent internecine fighting between the two major groups lodged in the Temple and the hostel complexes, the one of Jarnail Singh Bhindranwale and the second of Mr Longowal and his followers'. To prevent the two groups fighting each other, the Generals had decided that the hostel complex housing Longowal and his men must be cleared at the same time as the Golden Temple.

The first problem was to get into the complex. The iron gates at the top of the public road between the hostels and the Temple had been barred. A tank had to break them down. Armoured cars were then positioned along that road to separate the two battlefields, and the 9th Kumaons moved in. They came under fire from the roofs on both sides of the road but unlike their colleagues inside the Temple complex, they managed to fight their way into the buildings they had been ordered to clear.

Most of the terrified pilgrims, supporters of the Akali Morcha, and of course the two members of the Akali Trinity with their staff were huddled together in two buildings. They were without water because the water tower had been destroyed during the preliminary operations, and without electricity. Longowal, Tohra, and some of their senior colleagues were in Tohra's office on the ground floor of the Teja Singh Samundari

Hall. The SGPC Secretary, Bhan Singh, later described the situation in that building:

> They cut our electricity and water supplies. It was very hot in the rooms. There was no water. We had only two plastic buckets of water. Longowal had to place two people as guards over the buckets. Many people would squeeze their undershirts to drink their sweat to quench their thirst.

The army entered the Teja Singh Samundari Hall at about one o'clock in the morning. According to one officer, Tohra and Longowal were in their vests and underpants. The army says they surrendered. Bhan Singh did not accept that statement. He said, 'We did not give ourselves up. The army forced its way in and took us prisoners.' That is really just a matter of semantics. What is absolutely clear is that Longowal and Tohra made no attempt to resist the army.

The Akali leaders were kept inside one of their offices. The rest of the people in the building were ordered to come out and sit in a courtyard of the Guru Ram Das Hostel. According to Bhan Singh, there were about 250 of them. Some terrorists, seeing the people pouring out of the offices and surrendering, threw a grenade at them. Bhan Singh explained what happened.

> Suddenly there was a big explosion. All hell broke loose. It was pitch dark. People started running back into the verandah and the rooms. I and Abhinashi Singh were sitting next to Gurcharan Singh, the former Secretary of the Akali Dal whom Bhindranwale accused of murdering Sodhi. Gurcharan was shot as he tried to run inside. We realised that soldiers were shooting at us. They thought someone from among the crowd had exploded the grenade. But it was probably thrown by extremists on the water tank overlooking the Guru Ram Das Serai [Hostel]. We ran to Tohra's room and told Longowal what was happening. Longowal came out and shouted at the Major. He said, 'Don't shoot these people. They are not extremists. They are employees of the SGPC.' The Major then ordered his men to stop shooting. Later in the morning

we counted at least seventy dead bodies in the compound. There were women and children too.

The White Paper admitted that seventy people including thirty women and five children died in that incident; but the government put all the blame on the terrorists, saying nothing about the army firing.

According to Bhan Singh, the survivors were made to sit in the courtyard of the Guru Ram Das Hostel until curfew was lifted the next evening. He said they were not given food, drink or medical aid. Some people, according to the SGPC Secretary, drank water which had poured out of the tank the army had blown up and had formed puddles in the courtyard. Karnail Kaur, a young mother of three children, who had come with sixty-five other people from her village to join in Longowal's agitation, said, 'When people begged for water some *jawans* [soldiers] told them to drink the mixture of blood and urine on the ground.'

Bhan Singh also told the journalist and historian, Khushwant Singh, that the army did shoot some of the young men they had brought out from the Teja Singh Samundari Hall. He said:

> I saw about thirty-five or thirty-six Sikhs lined up with their hands raised above their heads. And the major was about to order them to be shot. When I asked him for medical help, he got into a rage, tore my turban off my head, and ordered his men to shoot me. I turned back and fled, jumping over bodies of the dead and injured, and saved my life crawling along the walls. I got to the room where Tohra and Sant Longowal were sitting and told them what I had seen. Sardar Karnail Singh Nag, who had followed me, also narrated what he had seen, as well as the killing of thirty-five to thirty-six young Sikhs by cannon fire. All of these young men were villagers.[2]

But not everyone the army rounded up in the Teja Singh Samundari Hall was innocent. Among those who surrendered was Bhindranwale's talkative young interpreter, Harminder Singh Sandhu, who was also the General Secretary of the All

India Sikh Students Federation. When I had seen him on the day before the army action started, he had boasted, 'Every one of Santji's followers will lay down their lives to save the Golden Temple.' But when the time came Harminder Singh Sandhu surrendered meekly.

Inside the Guru Ram Das Hostel, where the rooms were crowded with pilgrims, conditions were reminiscent of the Black Hole of Calcutta. The school teacher Ranbir Kaur and her husband had locked themselves into Room 141 with the twelve children they were looking after. Ranbir Kaur said:

We were all huddled together. We didn't know what was happening. The noise was terrifying. We had not been out of the room for more than twenty-four hours and we had no food or water. It was a very hot summer night. I told the children that we must be ready to die. They kept on crying.

The Kumaon Regiment also entered the Hostel at about one o'clock in the morning and ordered everyone to come out; but this was not the end of their ordeal. Ranbir Kaur described what happened next.

Early on the sixth morning the army came into the Guru Ram Das Serai and ordered all those in the rooms to come out. We were taken into the courtyard. The men were separated from the women. We were also divided into old and young women and so I was separated from the children, but I managed to get back to the old women. When we were sitting there the army released 150 people from the basement. They were asked why they had not come out earlier. They said the door had been locked from the outside. They were asked to hold up their hands and then they were shot after fifteen minutes. Other young men were told to untie their turbans. They were used to tie their hands behind their backs. The army hit them on the head with the butts of their rifles.

The people in the basement were Muslims from Bangladesh who had nothing to do with the Akali agitation. They were non-Bengalis known as Biharis, who had sided with the Pakistan army during the liberation struggle in 1971, and had been living in refugee camps in Bangladesh for the last thirteen years. The Pakistan government had refused to accept responsibility for any more Biharis and so Bhindranwale and his followers were operating a profitable sideline smuggling them across the border.

Two young Sikhs, Sardul Singh and Maluk Singh, who had gone to the Golden Temple to celebrate Guru Arjun's martyrdom day, were not released when the army entered the hostel. An elder from their village wrote to the Sikh President of India, Zail Singh, about their experiences. In his letter the elder, Sajjan Singh Margindpuri, said:

> The young men and some other pilgrims were staying in Room Number 61. The army searched all the rooms of the Serai. Nothing objectionable was found from their room. Nor did the army find anything objectionable on their persons. The army locked up sixty pilgrims in that room and shut not only the door but the window also. Electric supply was disconnected. The night between June 5th and June 6th was extremely hot. The locked-in young men felt very thirsty after some time, and loudly knocked on the door from inside to ask the army men on duty for water. They got abuses in return, but no water. The door was not opened. Feeling suffocated and extremely thirsty, the men inside began to faint and otherwise suffer untold misery. The door of the room was opened at 8 a.m. on June 6th. By this time fifty-five out of sixty had died. The remaining five were also semi-dead.[3]

The five survivors of that night of horror were arrested by the army and taken away to interrogation camps. So were Ranbir Kaur, her husband, and the children in their care. Two months later three of the children that Ranbir Kaur had been looking after were released after a well-known social worker had filed a petition in the Supreme Court in Delhi. Ranbir Kaur was released at the end of August. She rejoined the three children who had been released but no one could tell her what had happened to the other nine.

Speaking later of the battle of the hostel complex, Major-General Brar said:

> The terms of reference given to me as far as this side was concerned were to take them to battle only if forced to do so, to protect the maximum number of lives, and to ensure that all innocent people came out alive. I am glad to say that by isolating this area from the main complex we were able to achieve that aim.

That claim is not borne out by eye-witness accounts.

13

The Golden Temple, 6th June

Throughout the battle for the Golden Temple, Sewadar, or temple servant, Hari Singh had been hiding with about thirty other people in the room in the Akal Takht where the Guru Granth Sahib (the Sikh scriptures) is solemnly laid to rest every night. Miraculously, although it is in the front of the shrine, it was not badly damaged. After the tank barrage ended Amrik Singh, who was the son of the Sant's teacher and masterminded so many of the brutal murders committed by Bhindranwale's followers, came into the room and said, 'Now we can't match tanks. You can get out. We will stay here.' Fifteen minutes later the Sant himself came into the room with forty-five of his followers. He went into the main hall where he prayed before the Akal Takht, the throne of the Gurus, and then said to the survivors, 'Those who want to be *shahid* [martyrs] can stay with me. Those who want to surrender can leave now.'

About thirty people followed Bhindranwale as he picked his way through the rubble towards the front of the Akal Takht. They jumped into the courtyard and, according to the *sewadar*, were greeted by a burst of fire. Some of them tried to make a dash for the gateway leading to the Golden Temple, others ran in the direction of the buildings on the northern side of the complex. Amrik Singh fell immediately but some continued running. Then there was another burst of fire and the temple servant saw twelve or thirteen more young men fall. After that he decided that his position was too exposed and moved into the back of the Akal Takht to the room of Ram Singh, one of the priests. The Head Priest Pritam Singh was also hiding there. Soon a group of Bhindranwale's followers came into the room and said, 'Amrik Singh has gained martyrdom.' Asked about the Sant, they replied, 'We did not see him die.' The young Sikhs then took off their traditional clothes, put on bush shirts and trousers, and escaped through the back of the shrine. There was a bamboo ladder connecting the Akal Takht with the buildings outside. Whether any of the young men managed to get through the cordon of the Bihar Regiment is not known.

Tarlochan Singh, a senior official of the President of India, was told by one of the priests of the Akal Takht that Bhindranwale was shot in the thigh when he ran out of the Akal Takht, but was carried back into the building. One of the senior army officers inside the complex confirmed to Satish Jacob that soldiers did fire on a group of young men who ran out of the Akal Takht. He could not say whether Bhindranwale was one of them. He also said that some young men who had been holding out near the Langar, on the opposite side of the complex, jumped into the sacred tank and tried to swim to the Golden Temple itself because they knew the army would not fire on it. But no survivor actually saw Bhindranwale or Shahbeg Singh die. The government says their bodies were recovered from the basement of the Akal Takht when the army entered the shrine on the night of the sixth. Shahbeg Singh was said to be still clutching a walkie-talkie.

Another temple priest, Giani Puran Singh, was told by soldiers that the bodies of Bhindranwale, Amrik Singh and Shahbeg Singh were found in the courtyard in front of the Akal Takht — but that was on the seventh morning. There are photographs showing the three bodies lying in front of the shrine; but the photographs also show that ropes had been tied round the arms of Shahbeg Singh's body. So it is possible that his body had at least been dragged out of the Akal Takht. It could be that the soldiers were simply reporting that they had seen the bodies lying in front of the Akal Takht, and that they did not know where they had been found originally.

One of the most controversial incidents of the whole operation was the burning of the Golden Temple library with its invaluable manuscripts, including copies of the Guru Granth Sahib handwritten by some of the Gurus. According to a senior army officer present at the time, Brigadier Dewan and his men were eating *puris*, fried chapattis, for their breakfast just outside the library gate when a sniper fired at the Brigadier, narrowly missing him. The Lieutenant-Colonel commanding the Madras Battalion grabbed a machine gun and returned the fire. The snipers ran from window to window of the library, taking pot shots at soldiers, and the army did not manage to get the three men until four o'clock in the afternoon. According to the officer, the library caught fire during this operation. However Bhan Singh, the Secretary of the SGPC, said that he saw the library intact the next morning.

Many Sikhs believe that the army deliberately set the library on fire. For instance, Ashok Singh, who runs the Sikh Institute in Chandigarh, said, 'Any army which wants to destroy a nation destroys its culture. That's why the Indian army burnt the library.' According to the Government White Paper, the library caught fire when the army entered the Temple complex through the southern gate, hours before General Dewan and his men had their breakfast. The White Paper said:

> The terrorists were firing from a number of machine-gun positions in the library building and were hurling country-made grenades, lighting them with match sticks. A fire was noticed at this stage in the library. Troop fire-fighting parties were repeatedly rushed to put out the fire but these attempts were foiled by the heavy machine-gun fire from the terrorists. By the time the terrorist positions could be overcome, the library had been gutted.

The conflict between the account given by the officer who witnessed the burning of the library and the White Paper, inevitably casts doubt on the official version. Nevertheless it is very difficult to believe that an army which did obey orders to refrain from firing at the Golden Temple itself would have deliberately set a building as important as the library on fire.

By late afternoon on the sixth, the army was in control of the situation in both complexes and curfew was lifted for two hours. Major-General Brar, who was inside the Temple complex by this time, knew that people were still hiding in the Golden Temple itself and in some of the rooms in the buildings surrounding the *parikrama*. So he sent officers to order them to surrender. One of those inside the Golden Temple was the priest Giani Puran Singh. He gave Satish Jacob this description of what happened in the Golden Temple.

I went to the Harmandir Sahib [Golden Temple] on 5th June around 7.30 in the evening because I had to ensure that religious ceremonies were performed. The moment I stepped on to the *parikrama* I stumbled across a body. Bullets were flying and I had to take shelter behind each and every pillar to reach the Darshani Deorhi [the arch at the entrance of the causeway leading to the Golden Temple]. Another body was lying there. I ran a few yards and reached the Akal Takht. Night prayers start at the Harmandir Sahib five minutes after they start at the Akal Takht. I wanted to find out if the *path* [recitation] had started there. I had a glimpse of Bhindranwale. We did not speak to each other. Around 7.45 I came out of the Akal Takht and ran into the Darshani Deorhi. I ran towards the Harmandir Sahib, unmindful of the bullets flying past my ears. I began night prayers. Soon a colleague of mine, Giani Mohan Singh, joined me. Seeing the intensity of the fire we decided to close all the doors, barring the front door. Soon we completed all religious rites. We then took the Guru Granth Sahib to the top room to prevent any damage to the holy book. The Head Priest, Giani Sahib Singh, had given clear instructions that under no circumstances was the Guru Granth Sahib to be taken to the Akal Takht if the conditions were not right.

Looking through the window-pane from the first floor of the Harmandir Sahib, I saw a tank standing on the *parikrama* with its lights on. I thought for a moment that it was the fire brigade come to collect water from the *sarowar* [holy pool] to put out the fire which was raging in almost every room. A few minutes later my belief was shattered when I saw the vehicle emitting fire instead of putting it out. By 10.30 or so around thirteen tanks had collected on the *parikrama*. They had come after crushing the staircase from the eastern wing where Guru Ram Das Serai, the Langar and the Teja Singh Samundari Hall are situated. One after another the cannon fire lit the sky. When the first shell hit the bottom of the Darshani Deorhi, creating a hole in it, I saw the room with the historic *chandni* [canopy] presented by Maharaja Ranjit Singh catching fire. One after another big bombs hit the Darshani Deorhi in quick succession, and what was once a lovely building was now on fire. The Toshakhana [Treasury] was also on fire. Occasionally a bullet would hit the Harmandir Sahib. We were twenty-seven people inside, mostly *raagis* [those who chant the scriptures] and *sewadars* [Temple servants].

In the early hours of the morning on 6th June we took the holy book down and performed the religious rites that are performed every day, like *maharaj da prakash karna* [unfolding the holy book] and reciting hymns from the scriptures. The two side-doors were closed and the front and the back doors were open. Bullets kept hitting the wall both inside and outside, ripping off the golden surface at various places. Soon after we finished reciting prayers one of our colleagues, Raagi Avtar Singh, was hit. We pulled him into a corner. Another bullet came and hit the holy Granth Sahib. We have preserved this book.

In the meanwhile the pounding of the Akal Takht was continuing. There was no let-up in the fire in other places either. We were thirsty and desperate for water. We crawled to the holy pool to get water for ourselves and for the wounded colleague.

Around 5 p.m. they announced on loudspeakers that those hiding in the Harmandir Sahib should come out and that they would not be shot dead. While myself and Giani Mohan Singh remained inside, others walked out with the arms above their heads. Our colleagues informed Major-General Brar that we were still inside. Brar asked us to come out.

Around 7.30 p.m. an officer and two soldiers came inside to take us.

When we came out Major-General Brar asked us why we did not obey his orders. We told him that we could not have left the costly belongings and Guru Granth Sahib alone. We asked him to let us go to the toilet. He agreed to this. We were then escorted back to the Harmandir Sahib by a Sikh officer and some soldiers. This officer was rude and he told us to walk in front to make sure that if anyone fired from inside, we would get killed. Since no one was hiding within and there was no gun in the Harmandir Sahib, we saw no harm in doing what we were told. It must have been around 8.30 that night. I noticed Avtar Singh had moved out of the Harmandir Sahib and was lying with his head towards the Holy Granth and his legs stretched towards the eastern gate. The officer was ashamed of his behaviour when he could not find any guns inside the Harmandir Sahib. By the time we came down Avtar Singh was dead. Leaving two of us right there, the officer and the soldiers, who had taken off their shoes before coming in, went out.

Next morning the two of us were escorted to Giani Sahib Singh's house [the Head Priest of the Golden Temple] in Atta Mandi. While we were instructed not to move out or to speak to anyone, Giani Sahib Singh was escorted to the Harmandir Sahib.

Giani Puran Singh's story is confirmed by the fact that one of the copies of the Sikh scriptures in the Golden Temple that night did have bullet holes through its pages. But all the evidence goes to suggest that he was confused about the timing of the arrival of the tanks. He said they were on the *parikrama* by 10.30, while all other reports say they arrived later. He is also the only person to put the number of tanks as high as thirteen. Puran Singh insists that there were no arms inside the Golden Temple, while the three Generals commanding the operation maintain that the army was fired on from the shrine. The retired Sikh Lieutenant-General, Jagjit Singh Aurora, said he could find no evidence of prepared positions in the shrine when he visited it, but he accepted that the shrine might have been used 'as an occasional fire post by mobile pickets'.

What is certain is that there were bullet holes in the Golden Temple. Three hundred of them have been counted. Some of those were caused by the firing of the Central Reserve Police before the army operation started. Many others must also have been the result of erratic firing by the defenders of the Golden Temple complex. The most important fact is that the structure of the Golden Temple remained intact, and that the damage it did suffer was minimal compared to the Akal Takht, the library, the Darshani Deorhi and many other buildings of the complex. To that extent the operation was a success and credit must go to the discipline of the army. The 40-foot-square Temple stood in the middle of the battlefield. The army was fired at from all sides. If soldiers had disregarded Major-General Brar's orders, the Harmandir Sahib would certainly have been much more seriously damaged.

When curfew was lifted on the afternoon of 6th June, nearly 250 people who had been trapped in rooms in the Temple complex overlooking the *parikrama* surrendered. One of them was Narinderjit Singh Nanda, the Public Relations Officer of the Temple, who had once been described by Bhindranwale as 'a literate moron' for suggesting that starting a newspaper was a better way to secure the rights of the Sikhs than armed revolution. Nanda related his experience to Satish Jacob.

On the fifth night, the night of the real assault, mortars started throwing up plaster. My wife and I and my two daughters decided to go down from our flat on the first floor to the office, which is on the ground floor. At this point I thought of surrendering but I was told by a Bhindranwale man, 'One more step outside the complex and you are a dead man.' Faced with this threat to my entire family plus the insecurity of the office room, I decided to move down to a small basement where there was a fridge. An exhaust fan outlet in the basement proved a life saver. I could hear soldiers speaking outside and different instructions from their commanders. Next to the basement was another cubicle facing the Temple where a *sewadar* used to sleep. I heard the army drag out this man. He was shot. Since extremists

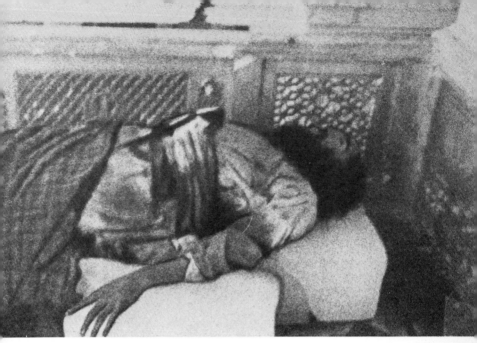

18 *Above*, the body of Bhindranwale laid out on ice within the precincts of the Golden Temple

19 *Below left*, Sikhs taken prisoner by the army during Operation Blue Star were made to sit with their hands tied behind their backs

20 *Below right*, President Zail Singh, accompanied by senior army officers, visiting the Golden Temple shortly after Operation Blue Star, even though snipers were still present

21 *Above*, Rajiv Gandhi in Calcutta on the morning of his mother's
assassination, listening to the news on the BBC

22 *Below*, Mrs Gandhi on her funeral pyre at the cremation site on
the bank of the river Jumna in Delhi

had been using all possible openings as pill boxes and grenade launchers, the *jawans* [soldiers] decided to lob grenades into all such openings, which included my fan outlet. The minute I heard the order we all moved under a staircase. Minutes later two grenades came in. The splinters took three inches away from most of the walls. But luckily we escaped. We spent the night under the staircase. Eventually at about 11 a.m. on the sixth my wife noticed an officer standing outside. She called out to him to attract his attention and requested him to rescue us. She told him she had two young daughters. The officer behaved decently and said, 'Don't worry. I too have two daughters. Nothing will happen to you. Stay put.' He organised chapattis, pickles and drinking water. He eventually let us out when curfew lifted.

We had to step over dead bodies strewn everywhere. We were taken to the square in front of the *ghantaghar* [the main, clock tower entrance]. The minute the soldiers saw me, a male member of the group, they positioned their rifles on their shoulders with the barrels pointing at me. I think they were about to shoot when a brigadier who recognised me intervened. We were then led by soldiers across the *parikrama* to the library side. A lieutenant accompanied us. Upon reaching the other side he asked me to stand against the wall and lined up a firing squad. He asked me to say my prayers. I requested to say goodbye to my wife and the two daughters. At this point the brigadier showed up again and shouted at the young officer, 'What the hell are you doing!' The officer said, 'Sir, I misunderstood your order. I thought this man was to be shot.'

Now we were made to sit on the ground. My hands were tied behind my back. We were about seventy in that lot. All of us were told to keep our heads down. A slight movement of the head resulted in a sharp rifle butt. We spent the whole night sitting there.

After dealing with all the officials of the Temple – the priests, the *raagis*, the *sewadars* and the office workers like Nanda – who had surrendered, the army once again turned its attention to the Akal Takht. The sniping from there had died down but Major-General Brar was still not willing to risk losing any more lives by sending his men into the shrine in daylight. He waited for dusk to fall before giving orders to storm Bhindranwale's fortress and shoot anyone they found inside. The infantry encountered very little resistance and entered the charred Akal Takht. The floors of the shrine were littered with spent cartridges (one officer said they were nine inches deep); bodies lay where they had fallen; the stench of death was in the air. When the officer commanding the party reported that Bhindranwale's fortress had finally fallen, Brar set a guard on it and decided to wait for daylight before starting to search the premises. According to the army, it was during that search on the seventh morning that Bhindranwale, Shahbeg Singh and Amrik Singh's bodies were found in the basement.

Bhindranwale was cremated at seven thirty-nine on the evening of 7th June, according to an army officer who was on duty at the cremation. A crowd of about 10,000 people had gathered near the Temple but the army held them back. The bodies of Bhindranwale, Amrik Singh and Thara Singh, the deputy head of the Damdami Taksal, were brought to the pyre just outside the Temple. Four police officers lifted the body of Bhindranwale from the lorry which had brought it from the mortuary and carried it reverently to the pyre. According to the officer, many of the policemen at the cremation were weeping. One of them objected to Captain Bhardwaj, the officer in charge, smoking. He replied, 'Look up. At least thirty men are covering me.' Bhardwaj insisted on lifting the sheet to make sure it was Bhindranwale. The officer overheard Bhardwaj asking the police why the Sant's body was so badly battered. A police officer replied, 'The extremists broke his bones.' There is however some confusion over the timing of Bhindranwale's cremation because his post-mortem report says that the body was not brought into the mortuary until seven-thirty and was not examined until eight o'clock. The report said Bhindranwale was 'alleged to have died as a result of firearms' injuries'.

There are doubts about the accuracy of the post-mortem reports. According to Major-General Shahbeg Singh's post-mortem, his body was not brought to the mortuary until the ninth. The report says that by then it was not possible to do a full post-mortem because of decomposition and putrifaction. But photographs show that the army discovered Shahbeg Singh's body well before it had started to decompose. It is difficult to understand why the army would want to keep the retired general's body until it had putrified. Both the army and the police had an interest in getting as accurate a post-mortem as possible. It could be that the army wanted to cremate the bodies at the first opportunity to prevent any possibility of their being discovered – there is a no more potent cause of a riot than a dead body – and so dispensed with the formality of the post-mortems. If this was so, the reports which were eventually seen and photocopied must have been convenient afterthoughts.

When Shahbeg Singh's son, Prabpal Singh, rang the Governor of Punjab and asked to be allowed to attend his father's cremation, the Governor said that there were thousands of others who wanted to attend the cremations and if he gave permission to Shahbeg Singh's son to attend, all the others would also have to be given permission, and that was not possible. When Prabpal Singh asked whether he could have his ashes, he was told that the government would 'immerse the ashes in one of India's sacred rivers'.

There is no record of the last rites of Shahbeg Singh. He may well have been cremated with the other bodies found in the Temple and hostel complexes. The municipal sweepers at first refused to clear them away. They were eventually persuaded by offers of rum and by being allowed to strip the bodies of all valuables. They piled the dead into garbage lorries and took them to the cremation ground.

The army, according to the White Paper, lost eighty-three men including four officers. Twelve officers and 237 men were injured. Many people have claimed the army casualties were much higher. The journalist Kuldip Nayar, in his book *Tragedy of the Punjab*, says nearly 700 men and officers died in the operation. He quotes a statement made by Rajiv Gandhi three months after the operation. But Rajiv Gandhi later withdrew that statement which certainly seems far too high.

Estimates that we have made show that the official figure is near the truth. The only units to suffer significant casualties were those which stormed the Akal Takht. The total number of infantry companies involved in that sector of the battle was six on the south side of the *parikrama* and three on the north. The strength of one infantry company is about 200. It is certain that not all the men in the companies would have been on 'bayonet strength'. The number of active infantrymen could well have been just 50 per cent. The Para Commandos, who were the only other troops involved in the entry into the Golden Temple complex, numbered eighty. That means the total number of troops taking part in the attack must have been around 1,000. The Government White Paper admits to 332 casualties. That means, on the government's own admission, the percentage of casualties was about a third. That is well above the limit which is usually regarded as acceptable in any army. Had the casualties been significantly higher it is difficult to see how the units could have continued fighting. As it is the figures indicate gallantry of the highest order.

The Para Commandos, who came from the Parachute Regiment, suffered the most. Their casualties were nearly 50 per cent. The Regiment did not celebrate its Raising Day that year as a mark of respect for the seventeen commandos who died. The Guards also suffered very heavy casualties. Major-General Brar admits that twenty guardsmen were killed and sixty injured in just one assault. A senior officer told Satish Jacob that the six companies with Brigadier Dewan suffered 137 casualties. Those figures indicate that the official toll is about right. All of the officers Satish Jacob talked to also accepted the White Paper's figures.

Unfortunately the same cannot be said for the civilian casualties. The problem here is that the army and the police made no attempt to identify the dead; they were just cremated en masse. Fantastic rumours started circulating about the number of people who died, some putting the figure as high as 3,000. Table 1 shows the figures we have been able to collect for people who were inside the two complexes on 3rd June when they were surrounded by the army.

We know that 200 followers of Bhindranwale escaped on 3rd June when curfew was lifted. Some people also surrendered from the hostel side when the army ceased firing temporarily on

TABLE I

Akali Dal supporters who had come to court arrest and to support the new stage in the Morcha, the attempt to prevent the movement of grain	1,700
Pilgrims who had come to celebrate the martyrdom of Guru Arjun Dev	950
Priests, *sewadars* and other Temple servants	80
Employees of the SGPC, living in rooms in the Golden Temple complex itself, and their families	300
Bhindranwale's followers	500
Babbar Khalsa and other armed groups supporting Longowal	150
	3,680

the fifth just before the operation started. Eye-witnesses put the figure at between 200 and 400. That still means there were more than 3,000 people inside the two complexes during the main battle.

According to eye-witnesses about 250 people surrendered in the Temple complex and 500 in the hostel complex after the two battles were over. The White Paper says that 493 people were killed and eighty-six injured. These figures leave at least 1,600 people unaccounted for. It would obviously be wrong to assume that they were killed in the battle, but there must be a big question mark over the official figures of civilian casualties in the operation, a figure which is appallingly high anyhow for an operation conducted by an army against its own people.

It is very doubtful whether Mrs Gandhi would have ordered the army to enter the Golden Temple if she had known that there would be such high casualties and that tanks would have to be used against the Akal Takht. So what went wrong? The most obvious factor was poor intelligence. The Generals were misled about the arms, the military skill, and, above all else, the will to fight of Sant Jarnail Singh Bhindranwale's followers. Lieutenant-General Sunderji himself admitted to me, 'There was some failure of intelligence.' The army did not even know the layout of the Golden Temple complex. A junior officer told Satish Jacob what that meant:

> Our biggest problem was that we didn't know the layout. We had a general picture of the inside of the Temple complex but we didn't reckon with the myriad of niches, rooms, basements and awnings. We were fired upon from literally every nook and corner.

It is not clear why the army's intelligence about the layout of the Temple was so poor. Right up to the day when the army surrounded the Temple, Bhindranwale never made any attempt to prevent pilgrims entering the Temple. They were expected to walk all the way round the *parikrama*, whether they were Sikhs or non-Sikhs. So trained intelligence men could easily have drawn up reasonably accurate plans of the Temple complex. The army also had the model built by the paramilitary commandos in the hills of Uttar Pradesh to work on. As for the armaments, everyone knew that Bhindranwale and his followers had been smuggling arms into the complex for many months. Two years earlier Darbara Singh, the Chief Minister of Punjab, had said in public that he knew arms were also being manufactured in the Golden Temple. The only weapons the army might not have known about were the Chinese rocket-propelled anti-tank grenade launchers, but they did not intend to use armour anyhow in their original plan.

The failure to estimate Bhindranwale's will to fight is more easy to explain. Bhindranwale himself had a reputation for cowardice. He was reported to have ducked out of the march against the Nirankaris at the start of his rise to fame, and he had three times taken shelter in *gurudwaras* to avoid arrest. If Bhindranwale had confirmed his reputation for cowardice by surrendering, the resistance would have collapsed.

It is also understandable that the army underestimated the training of the terrorists. The young men who used to surround

Bhindranwale when he held his morning congregations were an unimpressive lot. They used to loaf around, leaning against the parapet of the Langar and chatting with each other. They looked more like thugs than skilled fighters prepared to give their lives for their leader. However the Generals should not have underestimated the skill with which the defences were planned, and that they clearly did. They had known for some time that Major-General Shahbeg Singh was fortifying the Temple. They knew he was a brilliant soldier, yet they fell into every trap he laid for them.

What really surprised the officers Satish Jacob spoke to was the courage and commitment of the followers of Sant Jarnail Singh Bhindranwale. One officer said, 'Boy, what a fight they gave us. If I had three Divs like that I would fuck the hell out of Zia [the Pakistan President] any day.' Another told Satish Jacob: 'I have seen a lot of action, but I can tell you I have never seen anything like this. Those extremists were pretty committed. They took a lot of beating from us. They should have realised that they could not win against the army. If one weapon failed we brought another. When that failed we brought another.' A third put it more succinctly: 'The bloody fellows would not let us in.'

Indian and foreign military experts we have talked to believe that the plan as well as the intelligence were at fault. The retired Sikh Lieutenant-General, Jagjit Singh Aurora, for instance, said the plan 'smacked of *ad hocism*'. He told me that the army had been asked to act too quickly without adequate reconnaissance and planning. It seems that the army was only given two weeks' notice. Aurora also criticised the use of commandos. He said, 'The use of commandos in these circumstances was of doubtful value. Unless there is some element of surprise they are no better than ordinary infantry.' The retired General believed that it should have been possible to take the Akal Takht from the narrow alleys running behind it. Lieutenant-General Sunderji's explanation for his failure to do so was that terrorists had occupied houses commanding those alleys.

Retired Lieutenant-General Harbaksh Singh, for twenty years the Honorary Colonel of the Sikh Regiment, criticised the whole concept of an infantry attack: 'You don't send infantry into places where they have no cover.' Retired Major-General S.N. Antia, writing in the *Statesman* newspaper added another criticism. He maintained there had been 'an erroneous civil and military assessment that the terrorists would surrender'.

A military attaché in one of the Western diplomatic missions criticised the repeated attempts to storm the Akal Takht with infantry when it was quite clear that they were not going to be able to get across the courtyard in front of it. He said, 'Reinforcing failure went out with the First World War.' The military attaché also believed it was a mistake to have the three Generals in the command post. He said the operation should have been planned and commanded at brigade level. The Generals put the lower level commanders in a straitjacket. The military attaché did not accept that a 'full frontal attack' was necessary. He believed that the Indian army should have asked for sophisticated modern equipment, including electric sensors, gas, smoke and equipment to jam communications, and should then have mounted a commando operation. The military attaché said the Indian army had been 'arrogant because of its size and fire power.' In the days of Entebbe and the siege of the Iranian Embassy it is certainly very difficult to understand why the Indian army chose such a clumsy and costly way of recapturing the Golden Temple. They might well have done much better if they had gone in for a siege.

Lieutenant-General Sunderji gave a lengthy explanation of his decision to reject that when he met the press after the operation. Because he has been frequently criticised for that decision it is important to give his reasons in full. He asked himself:

Would it be possible to lay siege, as it were, to the buildings and after due warning and, if necessary, starving out, wear them out? Would it be possible to persuade them to come out? It seemed exceedingly attractive on the face of it. But when I analysed further I found that it would be impracticable for the following reasons. First, cordoning off the Golden Temple area sounds very nice on paper, but in practice no amount of troops deployed for effectively cordoning it off will succeed, because those of you who know the area will realise that there are buildings close up all around [the Temple]. Labyrinthine passages underneath, as well as through these buildings, were already in firm control of the extremists. So an effective cordon and siege were exceedingly doubtful. Secondly, they were fairly well stocked as far as food was concerned. Exceedingly well stocked as far as ammunition and warlike material was concerned. And water was there in the *sarowar* [sacred tank]. So any hope of starving them in any of these categories and persuading them to come out would have been virtually impossible. Theoretically it might have been possible at an extended period of a month or more.

Now we also knew that they had plans to utilise the innocent people, the religious-minded, innocent people in the countryside. That plan was to incite these people to come to the Golden Temple in thousands, and to literally swamp the surroundings as well as the inside, thereby preventing most effectively any action we could have taken to flush out the terrorists. This was confirmed information. We even intercepted messages going out to the countryside. So any extended cordon or siege, even if it had been feasible otherwise (which I told you wasn't feasible) would have ended up with this type of mass movement. This would have brought any action to a standstill, quite apart from the enormous amount of any force which would have been used for avoiding innocent casualties. If we wanted to prevent this sort of thing we could have imposed curfew and enforced it strictly, and made sure that such a movement didn't take place. But I'm sure all of you realise that the most practicable proposition for clamping down curfew of this vigour for a period of time which is required to tackle this place [would have been] at the most three, four days. Anything beyond that would have been impossible to enforce and therefore, with great sadness in my heart, I came to the conclusion that there is a mission to be accomplished. There was nothing, but nothing, other than entering the Golden Temple.

Neither of the retired Sikh Generals I spoke to accepted that explanation. Lt-General Aurora felt that the massive deploy-

ment of the army throughout Punjab was quite sufficient to
prevent mobs marching on Amritsar, while Lt-General Harbaksh Singh believed that Bhindranwale could have been
starved out quite quickly by cutting off the water supply to the
sacred tank and by separating the dining hall and kitchens, with
their huge stocks of food, from the Temple complex.

The other question about the army's handling of their mission to 'flush out the terrorists' which has to be asked is whether
their behaviour towards the innocent people in both complexes
was disciplined and humane. Eye-witnesses from both complexes have been quoted as saying that the men who surrendered had their hands tied behind their backs and some of them
were shot. A deputy superintendent of police who saw the dead
bodies, and a doctor who conducted post-mortems told Brahma
Chellaney, the Associated Press correspondent who managed to
stay in Amritsar throughout the operation, that several of the
Sikhs who were killed had their hands tied behind their backs.
We have photographs which show prisoners with their hands
tied behind their backs and a post-mortem report which shows
that at least one of them was shot. Nevertheless the Indian
government has consistently denied those allegations. The
government even went so far as to bring criminal charges
against the Associated Press correspondent for his reporting. It
does not seem surprising to us that the army did tie the hands of
young Sikhs behind their backs. When they surrendered,
soldiers had no way of knowing whether they were Bhindranwale's followers or not. In the tense and ugly atmosphere of the
battles in the two complexes it also seems highly likely that
some 'prisoners' were shot. The senior officer who confirmed to
Satish Jacob that Public Relations Officer Nanda was
threatened, said, 'The soldiers were in a very bad mood because
of the casualties that Bhindranwale's followers had inflicted on
them and it was very difficult to control soldiers in that sort of
mood.'

Subhash Kirpekar, the correspondent for the *Times of India*
who also managed to stay in Amritsar, witnessed an example of
the ugly mood of the army when curfew was relaxed on 6th
June. He saw, 'some *jawans* kicking some of the eleven suspected terrorists as they knelt on their bare knees and crawled

on the red-hot road surface. Among the officers directing this
operation was a Sikh, his face contorted in anger when he lashed
out at his fellow men who he thought were traitors.'[1]

It was not just the casualties they had suffered which en-
flamed the soldiers' tempers. The defenders of the Golden
Temple had also committed atrocities. They threw grenades at
the civilians who surrendered in the hostel complex. They
tortured two junior commissioned officers. One was skinned
alive and then blown up. They hacked to death an army doctor
who went to treat civilian casualties. War is never pretty, and it
was full-scale war which broke out between the Indian army
and the followers of Sant Jarnail Singh Bhindranwale.

14

The Aftermath

Operation Blue Star outraged the Sikhs. The anger spread far beyond the orthodox and the Akalis. Retired senior officers, such as Lieutenant-General Aurora and Lieutenant-General Harbaksh Singh, and the former Chief of Air Staff, Air Marshal Arjun Singh, were shocked. The historian and journalist Khushwant Singh, who had been a courageous and outspoken critic of Bhindranwale and never regarded himself as orthodox, handed back the decoration Mrs Gandhi had awarded him. Among other Sikhs who handed back their decorations was Bhagat Puran Singh, known as 'the bearded Mother Teresa' because of his work among the poor, especially lepers. The Maharaja of Patiala, Amarinder Singh, who had been Mrs Gandhi's go-between in the negotiations with the Akali Dal and whose family still commanded vast influence in Punjab, re-signed from her party and from Parliament, as did another Sikh MP. However one of the few Sikhs who had the courage to accept that her own community must bear a considerable share of the responsibility for the disaster was a Congress (Indira) MP Mrs Amarjit Kaur. She wrote:

Actually the blow to the Sikh community has been quite

profound. We thought we were the cat's whiskers. The saviour of all. But now it was seen that we did not have the guts to face the situation. We the Sikhs should have been the ones to throw Bhindranwale out of the premises of the Golden Temple. We are now finding it difficult to admit our own failure. Our so-called dynamism and bravery has disappeared.[1]

The most crucial Sikh was now President Zail Singh. He let Mrs Gandhi know that he was deeply distressed by the attack on the Golden Temple, and his officials let other Indians know that their first Sikh President was thinking of resigning. That would have caused an unprecedented constitutional crisis which even India's divided and enfeebled opposition might have been able to take advantage of to force the resignation of Mrs Gandhi. Zail Singh insisted on seeing the Golden Temple. Mrs Gandhi reluctantly agreed, although the Generals had told her that even the *parikrama* had not yet been cleaned and that they could not be sure they had recovered all the dead bodies. They also warned that they could not guarantee the President's security. The President took the government-controlled television with him. So three days after the attack, Indians saw on their television screens President Zail Singh, his long, white coat buttoned up to the neck, entering the most sacred shrine of his religion and picking his way gingerly past soldiers scrubbing bloodstains off the marble pavement surrounding the Golden Temple's sacred pool. They also heard the bullets of the snipers still in position in the buildings the army had not yet cleared. Lieutenant-Colonel A.K. Chowdhuri, accompanying President Zail Singh, was shot in the arm. Politically conscious viewers noticed Mrs Gandhi's watchdogs following wherever he went. One was her own Personal Assistant, R.K. Dhawan, a man so close to Mrs Gandhi that he appeared in almost every news photograph of her. He was at her side when she died. The other was Arun Singh, Rajiv Gandhi's closest adviser. He had been one of those monitoring Operation Blue Star on behalf of Mrs Gandhi and her son. The two had been sent to make sure that the President neither said nor did anything untoward. Later Zail Singh admitted that he had hardly been able to control his tears when he saw the Golden Temple. He also delivered a stinging rebuke to the Governor of Punjab when he saw the arsenal recovered from the Temple complex, saying, 'It seems you have given your eyes and ears on loan to somebody.'

When Zail Singh returned to Delhi he cancelled his commitment to present the National Film Awards, one of the great events of the year in India, but he decided against resigning. Instead he insisted on writing his own broadcast to the nation and he told Mrs Gandhi that he would criticise the Congress government and his old enemy Darbara Singh. To Mrs Gandhi that seemed a small price to keep the President in office.

The most serious reaction of all was in the army, where Sikh soldiers mutinied in several different places. The Sikhs, in spite of all their protests about unfair discrimination, still comprise 10 per cent of the army. Sikhs are also the only Indians to have infantry regiments made up entirely of their own community. The Sikh Regiment is manned, although not officered, entirely by Jat Sikhs. The Sikh Light Infantry is manned entirely by Mazhabi or Scheduled Caste Sikhs.

On 7th June, two days after the army entered the Golden Temple complex, there was a mutiny in the 9th Battalion of the Sikh Regiment. Six hundred soldiers, almost the entire other-ranks' strength, broke into the regimental armoury in their cantonment on the outskirts of the town of Ganganagar, near the Pakistan border. They drove through the streets of Ganganagar shouting, 'Long live Sant Jarnail Singh Bhindranwale', and firing indiscriminately. One policeman was killed and one injured. One group then turned towards Delhi and the other towards the Pakistan border. The Rajputana Rifles were sent in pursuit of the Sikh mutineers and managed to round up most of them. They were brought back to their cantonment in open lorries covered with barbed wire. However local residents say that some of the mutineers did manage to escape across the border into Pakistan.

The largest mutiny took place in the Sikh Regimental Centre at Ramgarh in Bihar. The centre is the equivalent of a British infantry regiment's depot where recruits for the battalions of the Sikh Regiment are inducted and trained. According to the report of the court of inquiry presided over by a major-general,

the mutiny was led by Sepoy Gurnam Singh. He was a renowned barrack-room lawyer whose religious fervour had
earned him the nickname of Giani or preacher. Earlier in the
week Gurnam Singh had expressed his concern about events in
the Punjab to the deputy commandant of the Regimental
Centre. Although all the officers knew that Gurnam Singh was
very influential among the other ranks, they made no effort to
set his mind at rest or to explain the situation to the men. The
court of inquiry report said, 'No central *durbar* [meeting between officers and men to discuss regimental morale and
welfare] was held nor were any efforts made to keep all ranks
fully informed of the current position in the Punjab.'

The last straw was, apparently, my report on the BBC about
the mutiny of the 9th Sikhs near Ganganagar. On the night of
that report Gurnam Singh and a few senior NCOs finally
decided to mutiny and make for Amritsar. The next day was a
Sunday. The soldiers assembled in the *gurudwara* as usual. The
Sikh Regimental Centre's Subedar-Major, whose job it is to
provide the same link between the other ranks and the officers
as a regimental sergeant-major in the British army, noticed the
men were restless. He reported this to his fellow junior commissioned officers but did not inform the commandant.

At about ten o'clock in the morning sepoys and NCOs
attacked the armoury and the magazine. There was no resistance from any of the guards on duty. The junior commissioned
officers remained 'silent spectators' as the mutineers loaded
arms and ammunition into regimental lorries.

The Subedar-Major did get in touch with the commandant,
Brigadier S.C. Puri, when the mutiny broke out. The commandant climbed into his car with two other senior officers and
drove towards the magazine. As the car approached, the
mutineers opened fire. The officers drove on towards the gate
of the magazine where more shots were fired, seriously wound-
ing Brigadier Puri and his colleagues. Puri could not get out of
the car but the other two officers managed to scramble clear.
However, seeing that the situation was beyond their control,
they got back into the car and drove to the military hospital
where Brigadier Puri died at 11.15.

Sepoy Gurnam Singh was one of those who opened fire on his

commanding officer. After emptying the armoury and the magazine and looting the station canteen, Sepoy Gurnam Singh led almost the entire other rank strength out of the cantonment in a convoy of army vehicles. When they reached Ramgarh they hijacked civilian vehicles and set off in the direction of Amritsar, which was 840 miles away. Army helicopters failed to spot the convoy but their progress was monitored by the police wireless.

The Ramgarh cantonment appears to have been in a state of panic. The court of inquiry report said: 'There was complete loss of command and control from about ten o'clock until about 16.30 in the Sikh Regimental Centre. Some semblance of authority was regained by about 18.30 hours.' The Sikhs' neighbours were the Punjab Regiment. They were informed about the mutiny at 10.45 but, according to the court of inquiry report, 'They did not start to take effective steps to control the situation until 17.30.'

When news of the mutiny reached army headquarters, units all along the route from Ramgarh to Delhi were ordered to set up roadblocks. The leaders of the mutiny divided the column just before Benares because they had heard that a roadblock had been set there. One half of the column was eventually engaged by the artillery at Shakteshgarh railway station, 190 miles from the Sikh Regimental Centre. A few trucks escaped but they were rounded up by the 21th Mechanised Infantry Regiment.

The other half of the column was halted by the artillery again and by soldiers of the 20th Infantry Brigade. Thirty-five people were killed in battles between the mutineers and the soldiers manning the roadblocks. The total number of soldiers who joined the mutineers was 1,461; 1,050 of them were raw recruits. The court of inquiry found that many of them had been forced to desert at gun-point.

The court of inquiry bluntly rejected efforts by the government to pin the mutiny on 'outside agencies', a phrase which would be taken by most to mean Pakistan. The report said, 'There is no evidence of any attempt to subvert Sikh troops at Ramgarh by outside agencies.' It placed the blame fairly and squarely on the officers and junior commissioned officers of the Sikh Regimental Centre. The report stressed the fact that it is impossible to isolate soldiers from the influences at work in their home villages. It said, 'The emergence of religious fundamentalism and linguistic chauvinism in many states, particularly the Punjab, would no doubt have its effect on troops hailing from that region even when they are emotionally integrated, particularly in an organisation like the army.'

After that comment the future of Sikh soldiers, one of the finest fighting elements in the Indian army, is bound to be questioned. The comment also raises an even more fundamental issue. How many more times can the Indian army be used to put out the fires of religious, communal and caste hatred before it too becomes consumed in their flames?

There was further unrest among Sikhs in the army after Operation Blue Star. There was a mutiny in another battalion of the Sikh Regiment in the Jammu region on the borders of Punjab, and a mutiny of Sikhs serving in the Punjab Regiment at Poona. One party of Punjabis fought a pitched battle just outside Bombay in which at least one of the soldiers sent to arrest them was killed and ten soldiers were injured. There were also three other, smaller mutinies.

This was the most serious crisis of discipline the Indian army had faced since independence. Its soldiers live in cantonments separated from the civilian population. Everything is provided for them in these cantonments so that the indiscipline which is endemic in Indian society does not infect the army. But the decision to send soldiers into the Golden Temple strained the loyalty and discipline of even the Indian army. It is important to remember that only about 3 per cent of the Sikh troops in the army did mutiny, but that was enough in a community which is important to the armed forces. The mutinies strained relations between Sikhs and members of other communities in the army, and raised doubts about the Sikhs' suitability for military service. It was a blow to the pride of the army too.

Retired officers believe that the mutinies could have been avoided if the men had been fully informed about events in Punjab. Lieutenant-General Harbaksh Singh said, 'They thought their villages were being attacked when they heard the announcement that the army was being deployed in the Punjab. Regiments should have sent small parties under the command of officers to the Punjab to see what was happening and report back to their colleagues.'

Retired Lt-General S.K. Sinha, who if luck (or some would say politics) had gone a different way would have been Chief of the Army Staff at the time of Operation Blue Star, was very outspoken in his criticism of the officers. In a newspaper interview he said, 'As far as the mutiny goes, I will squarely blame the officer corps, because they apparently did not know what their men were thinking . . . I am very clear in my mind on this issue. Officers must know their men better than their mothers. In this case they obviously did not.'

Army Headquarters should also accept their share of the blame. The problem of Sikh soldiers' morale should have been anticipated and all officers should have been warned through the normal chain of command to be alert and sensitive. It is surprising that the military police, who have an internal intelligence network, did not warn the Chief of the Army Staff. It is possible, however, that officers did not want to raise the question of Sikh troops' loyalty. Questions of loyalty have to be handled very delicately, otherwise precautions taken can lead to the very thing they are designed to avert — mutinies.

The army then faced the problem of disciplining the mutineers. There were two schools of thought, reflected in conflicting statements put out by the Ministry of Defence and the Officer Commanding, Southern Command. The Defence Ministry indicated that the authorities would take a generous view. A spokesman, who described the Sikhs as deserters not mutineers, said they had been 'misguided'. He went on to say, 'We feel that some people are taking advantage of the emotional state of the *jawans* [men]. He also spoke of 'instigators' narrating 'horror stories' of what had happened in Punjab, and added, 'We understand the feelings of the Sikh *jawans*.' Firmly bolting the stable door after the Sikhs had fled, the spokesman announced that officers were being sent to explain, with the help of photographs, that the Golden Temple itself was unharmed, and that the soldiers who took part in the operation had treated the shrine with the utmost respect. But Lt-General T.S. Oberoi, commanding 80,000 Sikhs in Southern Command, said bluntly, 'The deserters who have surrendered will be court-martialled and punished.'

One month after the mutinies the Chief of the Army Staff, General A.S. Vaidya, took the unprecedented step of broadcasting to the nation. He announced that the conflict between those who feared that severe action would do even more damage to the morale of Sikh troops, and those who feared that leniency would damage discipline throughout the whole army, had been resolved. The 'mutineers' were to suffer the full rigours of Indian military law. General Vaidya said, 'I would like to give an assurance that those who acted in a mutinous manner will be dealt with severely under the law as enacted for the army, so that those who remain with us in the army and have the honour of bearing arms for the country, would be a proud and disciplined body of soldiers.' This was the first time the army admitted that mutinies had taken place; earlier they had used the word 'desertions'.

But retired Sikh officers believed General Vaidya was wrong. Five of them, including Lieutenant-General Aurora and Lieutenant-General Harbaksh Singh, went to see the President, who is Commander-in-Chief of the armed forces, to plead for special treatment for the mutineers. They explained to President Zail Singh that the military authorities were at fault in not telling the men what was going to happen in Amritsar and why. They maintained that even senior officers had not been told. The retired Sikh officers stressed the importance of religion in the army, pointing out that Sikh soldiers swore their oath of allegiance on the Guru Granth Sahib. According to Lieutenant-General Aurora, the President was sympathetic but said he had no direct powers to act. However he did agree to use his influence. When reports started appearing in the press about 'inhuman' treatment of the mutineers, Lieutenant-General Harbaksh Singh issued a statement. He said, 'I have a feeling that this is being done by the army hierarchy to cover up their failure to maintain the discipline and morale of the Sikh soldiers — a very important function of the military command — by forestalling their reaction to the extreme religious provocation caused by wanton (as rumoured) destruction of the Akal Takht, their holiest religious seat.' Rumour was certainly the main cause of the mutinies and Army Headquarters failed in not anticipating rumour-mongering. Lieutenant-General Harbaksh Singh recommended that the Sikhs should not be treated as deserters but be allowed to return to their units. He also recommended that action should be taken against their commanders for dereliction of duty. But his advice was not taken. In fact Defence Headquarters never sought the advice of Lieutenant-General Harbaksh Singh despite his unrivalled experience in handling Sikh soldiers.

Discipline and morale were not the only problems facing the Indian army. Although the battle of the Golden Temple was over, Lt-General Dayal was still the Adviser (Security) to the Governor of Punjab and the army was deployed throughout the state to 'mop up' the terrorists believed to be hiding in the villages. But 'mopping up' proved to be as inappropriate a term for dealing with the terrorists in the countryside as 'flushing out' was for the terrorists in the Golden Temple. The army soon found that terrorists don't just sit around waiting to be 'mopped up'. Military intelligence hoped that they would get information about the identity and whereabouts of the terrorists from the people taken prisoner in the two complexes at the Golden Temple. Although most of them were innocent, the army was not going to let them go without a thorough investigation. Age and sex did not matter, as the teacher Ranbir Kaur found out:

We were taken to an army camp in Amritsar. The children were separated from us. The army interrogated us. They wanted to know who Bhindranwale's associates were. They threatened to shoot us. I only saw Bhindranwale once when he was walking back from his *darshan* [audience]. On 6th July we were taken to Ludhiana jail. Again we were separated. We were interrogated again. I was always questioned by men. We got no letters. Some police people told me I could be bailed out. But I was warned that I would be consistently called back to appear before court if I did that. I had my baby with me because my parents had gone to the army and asked for my release so that I could look after him. When they refused, my parents gave the baby to the army and said, 'You had better give the baby to his mother.'

Even the children Ranbir Kaur had been looking after when she was 'rescued' by the army from the Temple complex were interrogated. Mehrban Singh, aged twelve, said, 'We were repeatedly asked if we were Bhindranwale's men. They hit us at Ludhiana jail, jabbing fingers into our necks, wanting us to confess that we had been filling magazines with bullets for Bhindranwale's men.' Shamsher Singh, aged eleven, said, 'We were given very dirty food in the army camp. The food was better in the jail. We were regularly beaten in the jail. We were told we were Bhindranwale's people and they wanted to know about Bhindranwale's friends. They asked us where Bhindranwale kept his arms.'

Nanda, the Public Relations Officer of the Temple, who the army admitted narrowly missed being shot after he had been 'rescued', escaped interrogation by having a heart attack. But apparently his house was searched, although anyone who knew anything about life in the Temple complex could have told the intelligence officers that he was no friend of Bhindranwale. He described his experience:

We were moved to a camp in the cantonment area the next day (7th June). This camp was originally a military school. The camp was encircled with barbed wire. There were armed guards with dogs patrolling. Massive searchlights lit up the camp. Our room in this camp could be compared to the Black Hole of Calcutta. All seventy of us were put in it. Due to suffocation three elderly men died in the initial hours of imprisonment. We spent about four days there, during which time an agitated soldier kicked my ankle with his boot to near pulp. In the meanwhile I suffered a heart attack. After great efforts medical attention was received. The doctor, after examining me, felt I should immediately be removed to an intensive care unit. I was moved, but to an ordinary hospital ward. Luckily I was noticed by the General Officer commanding Amritsar, Major-General Jamwal, who moved me to an inspection bungalow. At this bungalow I had a brief encounter with General Brar. You see I had accumulated, during my two decades of service with the SGPC, eighty-eight grams of gold in the form of jewellery, two modest diamond necklaces, one Minolta camera, one National Panasonic two-in-one [radio/cassette], and one revolver. Most of this was for my daughter's dowry. My wife, after a trip to the house, reported all this missing. Other household items of furniture, television, fridge etc. were completely destroyed. The blades of the ceiling fans were bent. There was also cash both in my office as well as the flat above it, amounting to rupees 4,500, which was also missing.

I later shifted to a Delhi nursing home for ten days. My bruised ankle was now fully septic. I hated Bhindranwale who had insulted me by getting me frisked and asking his henchmen to remove my trousers. On another occasion Bhindranwale told me that within thirty days he was taking over the SGPC and I would then become his personal servant. Jarnail Singh Bhindranwale was in complete control of the Golden Temple and its management.

When Satish Jacob visited Amritsar after the army action he met many residents of the old city who complained that their homes had been ransacked during army searches for terrorists. One was Surinder Singh, who owns a shop near the Akal Takht. He said to Satish Jacob:

When I returned to my shop on 17th June I found the doors of my apartment above the shop had been forced open. Steel cupboards where clothes, money and jewellery were kept had been broken open. All my money and jewellery was missing. The vegetables I had left in the fridge were stewn all over the floor of the dining room. A small alcove used as a store was also ransacked.

Surinder Singh insisted that it must have been soldiers who broke into his house because the area was under their control. He did not leave his home until curfew was lifted on 6th June.
Members of the Temple staff with rooms inside the complexes also complained that their property had been looted, but a senior officer told Satish Jacob that no formal complaints had been made. He said, 'Some soldiers may have indulged in small-scale pilferage. The army takes a serious view of such conduct. If there had been official complaints and soldiers had

been found guilty, they would have been punished.'

The High Priests complained to Mrs Gandhi and to the Generals about the behaviour of the soldiers occupying the Golden Temple. They maintained that soldiers had used the sacred pool as a bath, and had committed sacrilege by smoking and drinking within the precincts. The army denied these allegations but when Khushwant Singh visited the complex he saw a notice outside the Akal Takht saying 'No smoking or drinking here'. That would seem to indicate that someone had been smoking and drinking there, and the army was in charge of the complex. The army certainly had plenty of drink available. A notification of the Government of Punjab's Department of Excise and Taxation allowed for the provision of 700,000 quart bottles of rum, 30,000 quart bottles of whisky, 60,000 quart bottles of brandy and 160,000 bottles of beer, all free of excise duty. The notification specifically said that the alcohol was 'for consumption by the Armed Forces Personnel deployed in Operation Blue Star'.

There were also allegations of army brutality during their search for terrorists in the rest of Punjab. The journalist Harji Malik wrote in the *Economic and Political Weekly* about a 23-year-old Sikh who was removed by the army from his home in a village near Longowal's home town of Sangrur. The young man's dead body was returned to his family some days later. The official explanation for his death was that he had been killed in an 'encounter'. A local lawyer who had seen the body said that the young man's fingernails had been torn out and there were burn marks on his chest. The lawyer also told Harji Malik of a young, disabled Sikh who was arrested and beaten up by the army.

An incident at Punjabi University, Patiala on 20th July was documented by several journalists. Sixty students returning from complaining to the Vice-Chancellor about a comparatively trivial administrative matter, were stopped by an army party under Major Uppal. Two members of the staff accompanying them told the Major that the students were not terrorists. He ignored the staff members and ordered the students to get down on their knees and crawl. They did so but that didn't satisfy Major Uppal. He then arrested three students and took them away for questioning. One of them alleged that he had been tortured during the interrogation.

Harpal Singh, an executive engineer of an electricity generating plant at Bhatinda, told Satish Jacob that the army had beaten up any young Sikhs they saw on the streets in the immediate aftermath of the attack on the Golden Temple complex. He also said soldiers guarding the plant where he worked treated Sikhs offensively. Gurkhas, for instance, once ordered two young men returning to their quarters to take off their *kirpans*, or daggers, one of the five 'k's of the Sikhs. When they refused, they were made to lie on their bellies. Harpal Singh was asked to intervene. When he arrived he saw the two young men lying on their bellies. Soldiers were standing over them with boots on their backs.

Senior officials and army officers had always accepted that there would be some excesses when the army was deployed throughout Punjab. A senior officer explained to Satish Jacob, 'Very few army officers are trained interrogators, which means inevitably some will resort to unofficial methods of extracting evidence.' That was why many officers were very unhappy about their task. They realised that soldiers acting as policemen could destroy the army's reputation for fairness and integrity, which they valued very highly. They were also afraid that the population of Punjab would turn against them with potentially disastrous consequences. As that senior officer explained, 'Punjab is bound to be a battlefield if Pakistan ever tries it on again and here we will need the civilian population to be on our side.' Army Headquarters were less sensitive. An appeal was published in the July issue of *Batchit*, an official magazine circulated throughout the army to keep officers and men informed of current operations.

> Although [the] majority of the terrorists have been dealt with and [the] bulk of the arms and ammunition recovered, yet a large number of them are still at large. They have to be subdued to achieve the final aim of restoring peace in the country. Any knowledge of the 'Amritdharis' who are dangerous people and pledged to commit murder, arson and acts of terrorism should immediately be brought to the notice

of the authorities. These people may appear harmless from the outside but they are basically committed to terrorism. In the interest of all of us, their identity and whereabouts must always be disclosed.

'Amritdhari' means baptised. So the instruction meant that all orthodox Sikhs were to be treated as suspects – hardly the best way to retain the affection of the people of Punjab.

Lieutenant-General Gauri Shankar, who took over from Lt-General Dayal as Adviser (Security) to the Governor of Punjab, once said, 'They have been making a big noise about the so-called army atrocities but so far they have not been able to point out a single specific case in which the army committed any such atrocities or arrested an innocent person.' That was an exaggeration but when Satish Jacob visited Punjab villages he only heard of isolated incidents of army excesses. There was no widespread repression, no organised brutality.

After two months the army was ordered to pull back. Soldiers were still held in reserve to assist the paramilitary and the Punjab police, but they stopped 'combing' the countryside for terrorists. By then they had arrested nearly 5,000 people. Three thousand of them had been released again. Terrorism had not been eradicated. That, the army realised, was not to be expected, but the terrorists no longer had it all their own way. The law was amended yet again. This time the aim was to make it easier to secure the conviction of those the army was still detaining. The government issued an ordinance which made further inroads into India's tradition of respect for liberty, and turned on its head the fundamental principle that a man must be presumed innocent until proven guilty. Under the Terrorist Affected Areas (Special Courts) Act, in areas like Punjab which were declared 'disturbed', anyone found at places where firearms were used to attack or resist members of the law-enforcing agencies was presumed to have committed an offence unless the contrary was shown. Under the Act special courts were set up in Punjab to try offenders.

It was a sullen Punjab the army ruled. Many Sikhs refused to believe Bhindranwale was dead. Rumours circulated that he would appear on Pakistan television. In spite of the government's propaganda barrage, to many people Bhindranwale remained a *sant*, or holy man, not a terrorist. The attack on the Temple had deeply wounded the pride of the Sikhs. Senior officials of the Punjab government knew that the wound had to be healed if Sikhs were to be reconciled with the rest of India. They also knew that there could be no long-term peace in Punjab, or indeed in the rest of India, until that reconciliation took place.

The press was clamouring for reconciliation. Immediately after Operation Blue Star the *Indian Express* wrote: 'It is imperative that a salve be applied to the hurt collective psyche of this proud and valiant community before any lasting damage is done. What started as a Punjab question and then got enmeshed in terrorist violence cannot be allowed to fester and become a Sikh problem.' The paper went on to make some practical suggestions for preventing damage to what it had quaintly called 'the hurt collective psyche' of the Sikhs. The first was to allow free reporting on Punjab. Papers published in Punjab had been censored and those coming from other parts of India had been banned from the state. The *Indian Express* wisely pointed out that rumour was an enemy, a lesson the army learnt from the Sikh mutineers. The second suggestion was the immediate withdrawal of the army from the Golden Temple complex. The third was entrusting the repair of the Akal Takht and other damaged buildings to the Temple authorities. The fourth was restricting the army's involvement in the search for terrorists in the villages. The fifth was releasing the Akali Dal leaders. The sixth was a broadcast by Mrs Gandhi. The paper said, 'She needs to go on the air and by her words and the measures she proposes impart a healing touch to a wounded nation.'

Mrs Gandhi chose to reject the advice of the *Indian Express* in its entirety. The first time she said anything to Indians about Operation Blue Star, three days after the assault on the Akal Takht, she spoke through the mouth of an official spokesman reporting a speech she had made to officers of the paramilitary Central Reserve Police. There could hardly have been a more inappropriate audience from the Sikhs' point of view. In that speech she was reported to have appealed for 'a healing touch to be given to the wounds inflicted on the hearts of the people by the recent Punjab incidents'. There was apparently no direct reference to the hurt inflicted on the Sikhs. She went out of her way to praise the army and the CRP. Mrs Gandhi followed that speech by rubbing salt not balm into the wounds of the Sikhs.

The Akali Dal Trinity were the only representatives of the Sikh community she could have discussed the healing process with. Longowal and Tohra were arrested when the Kumaon Regiment cleared the hostel complex. Badal was arrested as soon as he emerged from his farm. More than thirty people were killed in protests in Punjab and the neighbouring state of Kashmir in the first three days after Operation Blue Star; so it was perhaps a sensible decision to lock them up for the moment. But the Akali Dal Trinity were still under arrest when Mrs Gandhi was assassinated. They were given no chance to assess the mood of their followers so that they could find ways of restoring the traditional harmony between Sikhs and Hindus, and preventing Operation Blue Star leading to a full-blooded separatist movement. There was never any suggestion that either Badal or Longowal wanted that, and by then even Tohra must have realised the dangers of the path he had so unwisely trodden. After all Tohra did try to persuade Bhindranwale to surrender at the last moment.

Matters were made worse by the cackhanded performance of the government-controlled media, especially the television service, Doordarshan. Under the guidance of a special committee, dominated by a close friend of Rajiv Gandhi, Doordarshan mounted a series of programmes to justify the action in the Golden Temple. Major-General Brar was seen standing outside the Harmandir Sahib itself, describing Operation Blue Star like a victorious conqueror. Other programmes concentrated on proving the guilt of the Sikhs. Pictures of naval divers recovering arms were shown and allegations that drugs had been discovered were also made. They had to be withdrawn later because they could not be substantiated. A visibly unhappy Head Priest of the Akal Takht was forced to read out a statement saying that the Golden Temple was undamaged, when he knew there were bullet holes in the Sikh's most sacred shrine. The leader of a comparatively obscure Sikh sect was produced before television viewers to justify the army action. Within days he was arrested when arms were discovered near his *gurudwara*. Even moderate Sikhs were outraged. They complained that the government was portraying the whole Sikh community as enemies of India. However the Information and Broadcasting Minister, H.K.L. Bhagat, insisted that the television programmes were intended to promote harmony between Sikhs and Hindus. In an interview for the *Calcutta Telegraph*, he said, 'So far as our television programmes on Punjab have been concerned, the programmes were mounted with a view to promoting communal harmony . . . broadly the purpose was communal harmony.' Strangely, Mrs Gandhi herself did not use Doordarshan to appeal to the people of her own country. She did, however, give interviews to several international broadcasting organisations, including the BBC, to justify her action to the world.

After the heavy-booted officials of Doordarshan had trampled Sikh sentiments into the mud came the Government White Paper. Its publication was postponed several times because the mandarins of the External Affairs Ministry insisted that diplomatic considerations were more important than domestic. Officials of the Home Ministry wanted a large share of the blame for all that had gone wrong in Punjab to be laid at the feet of Pakistan. This, they believed, would convince many Sikhs that the government had rescued them from a plot which would have delivered them back to the Muslim domination they had rejected at the time of partition. The Home Secretary issued a statement after Operation Blue Star, in which he said, 'The obvious direction and thrust of the Movement [of Bhindranwale] was towards an independent Khalistan fully supported by neighbouring and foreign powers.' But the External Affairs Ministry warned that mentioning Pakistan would complicate India's relations with the United States. President Reagan saw Pakistan's autocratic military ruler, General Zia-ul-Haq, as a gallant fighter for freedom, threatened by the Soviet Union's invasion of neighbouring Afghanistan.

After lengthy deliberations the White Paper was published without mentioning Pakistan. The writer A.G. Noorani described the White Paper as 'an abject climbdown'. It identified four factors which had 'threatened to undermine the social, political, and economic stability not only of Punjab but the whole country'.[2] The factors were:

The agitations sponsored by the Akali Dal in support of certain demands which had been submitted to the government and on which negotiations were in progress.

A stridently communal and extremist movement which degenerated into open advocacy of violence and sanction for the most heinous crimes against innocent and helpless citizens and against the state.

Secessionist and anti-national activities with the declared objective of establishing an independent State for the Sikhs with external support.

Involvement of criminals, smugglers, other anti-social elements, and Naxalites, who took advantage of the situation for their own ends.

The White Paper, in its anxiety to highlight the threat which had forced the government to take such drastic action, came near to describing the Akali Dal as separatists too, which once again outraged the moderate majority of the Sikh community.

When the White Paper was written off by the press and the Sikhs as an inadequate justification of Operation Blue Star, diplomatic niceties were thrown to the wind and an all-out effort was made to blame Pakistan and other 'foreign hands'. The only foreign arms listed in the White Paper were fifty-seven 7.62 mm. Chinese rifles, but by the time the Congress Party itself came to produce its own explanation of Operation Blue Star, a pamphlet called 'Conspiracy Exposed', the foreign arms discovered by the Indian army had risen dramatically to 'Chinese-made AK–47 gas-operated assault rifles capable of firing 600 rounds a minute at a range of 300 metres; the Chinese-made RPG–7 anti-tank grenade launchers capable of penetrating armour up to a thickness of 320 mm.; the German G–2 automatic rifles generally used by NATO countries; Israeli-manufactured bullet-proof vests; anti-tank weapons of Pakistani origin'.

In all their speeches, both Mrs Gandhi and Rajiv Gandhi highlighted the foreign hand in Punjab, but the effect was often marred by their reluctance to identify that hand. Sometimes it appeared to be the CIA, sometimes Pakistan, and sometimes even Britain. The Prime Minister told Parliament that the Punjab crisis was the result of 'the de-stabilising efforts of foreign powers'. She said direct evidence was hard to find but then continued, 'We know that foreign powers instigate communal riots for their own ends. When I went to London to attend the coronation of Queen Elizabeth II, a former British officer in India told me about his role in instigating communal riots.'

These allegations did not convince the press. The *Indian Express* wrote, 'Bhindranwale has now been assigned a secondary role in the Punjab drama with Mrs Gandhi's reassertion of an international conspiracy to do Indian down with neo-colonialism working to achieve its dirty aims through religious fundamentalism. St Joan had obviously donned her shining armour and one is expected to be duly awed by what the voices told her.'

Sikhs also wrote off the foreign hand. They knew that Mrs Gandhi had a habit of blaming India's problems on foreigners. Between 1972 and 1975, when Mrs Gandhi was getting deeper and deeper into trouble, she and her colleagues dragged the CIA into almost every speech they made. The trouble was that Mrs Gandhi had very little evidence to offer for blaming the 'foreign hand'. There certainly were Sikh groups abroad who welcomed the turmoil in Punjab and supported Bhindranwale, but there is nothing to suggest that they wielded great influence in Punjab itself.

The White Paper mentioned four Sikh groups operating overseas. Only two of those were significant. The first was the National Council of Khalistan led by Dr Jagjit Singh Chauhan, a resident of Great Britain and the self-styled President of the land of the Khalsa. The second was the Dal Khalsa. The White Paper said it was established in India with the avowed object of demanding the creation of an independent, sovereign Sikh state. The White Paper did not mention the connection between Zail Singh and the Dal Khalsa in its early days. The

White Paper also failed to produce any evidence to suggest that these groups were directly involved in terrorism, except for one report in the *Vancouver Sun* about attempts to recruit Sikhs in British Columbia and train them under a mercenary who had fought in Rhodesia. The advocates of Khalistan living abroad certainly did have contact with Bhindranwale. His interpreter, Harminder Singh Sandhu, once wrote to the self-styled President of Khalistan, Dr Jagjit Singh Chauhan, appealing for help from abroad:

> Doctor Sahib you are a very wise and far-thinking person and now utilising those energies of yours, please try to get maximum support and help from the friendly nations and international community in general.[3]

That letter may have produced some money, but not much else. It was Operation Blue Star which brought Jagjit Singh Chauhan to prominence. After the assault on the Akal Takht he threatened Mrs Gandhi and her family a number of times. In a broadcast by the BBC's Radio 4 he 'prophesied' that she would be killed, a prophesy which was seen as a threat. Although Radio 4 cannot be heard in India, the government sponsored a series of demonstrations against our office in Delhi, and showed the demonstrations on Doordarshan television. This brought Chauhan and his activities to the notice of millions of Sikhs who had never heard of him before.

Did Pakistan play a role in the Punjab crisis as Mrs Gandhi so often implied? In a minor way the answer is almost certainly 'yes'. Smuggling is a well-established practice in the border areas of Punjab. Many Sikhs go to extraordinary lengths to equip themselves for that profession as we found once when we met a police officer who had killed a Sikh 'extremist' on the Grand Trunk Road the day before. The papers had reported that the Sikh was a Pakistani in disguise, but the Inspector laughed when we suggested that. He said, 'Oh no, Sahib. He was a smuggler, I have been to his village and they have identified him. He was not circumcised because he was a Muslim but because he wanted to pee in Pakistan.'

Arms were regularly smuggled across the border, and it is

more than likely that President Zia turned a blinder eye than usual. It is certain that he did not object to Bhindranwale's terrorists crossing the border to seek temporary refuge from the police, although most of them had a safe sanctuary in the Golden Temple complex or some other *gurudwara*. But Zia adopted a very cautious attitude to the Punjab crisis. His advisers told him that Mrs Gandhi was spoiling for a fight because she saw a war with Pakistan as a way of diverting her people's attention from Punjab and other difficulties they were facing. War was the last thing General Zia wanted. He knew there was no guarantee that he would be the first Pakistani ruler to defeat the Indian army and remembered the fate of Field Marshal Ayub Khan and General Yahya Khan, who had both tried and failed. So although he would dearly have liked to avenge the Pakistan army's surrender at Dacca in 1971, he did nothing which could give Mrs Gandhi an excuse for going to war. He did not openly support the Sikhs and we have found no evidence he gave them covert help. In fact he did the very reverse; he set out on what he called a 'peace offensive'. Winning almost every diplomatic trick, General Zia convinced the United States and the Western world that he genuinely wanted good relations with India. Whether Mrs Gandhi ever seriously contemplated war or not, General Zia's peace offensive blocked that option.

Although the allegations of foreign involvement and so much of the other government publicity had the effect of identifying the whole of the Sikh community with Bhindranwale and his terrorists, the White Paper itself did give the Sikhs a clean chit. It said:

The action which the government has had to take in the Punjab was neither against the Sikhs nor the Sikh religion; it was against terrorism and insurgency. The Sikhs are a well-integrated part of the Indian nation. They were second to none in their contribution in achieving and defending the country's freedom and the building of the economic strength of free India. The Sikh community stands firm along with the rest of the nation in its resolve to preserve and strengthen the unity and integrity of the country.

Instead of redoubling her efforts to strengthen that resolve, Mrs Gandhi continued her battle with the leaders of the Jats, the most powerful group of the Sikhs, till the day she died. She was at her most aggressive over the repairing of the Akal Takht. Sikhs believe the maintenance and repairing of their shrines is a sacred duty. They call it *kar sewa*, or the service of work. The work must be carried out by pious Sikhs under the leadership of a recognised holy man. The Sikh High Priests therefore demanded that the army should be withdrawn from the Temple complex and that they should be allowed to repair the Akal Takht and other buildings which had been damaged.

Mrs Gandhi refused to withdraw the army until the repairs were complete. She said she could not trust the Sikhs to repair their shrines because of the suggestion by some eminent Sikhs that the Akal Takht should be left in ruins as a permanent reminder of its desecration. She had appointed the only Sikh member of her Cabinet, Buta Singh, the Works Minister, to negotiate with the High Priests. It was not a happy choice. He was a Mazhabi Sikh regarded by most Jats as a Harijan, or Untouchable. He had also been a member of the Akali Dal; so he was regarded by Akali leaders as a traitor. Nevertheless Buta Singh did eventually succeed in reaching an agreement with the High Priests on repairing the Akal Takht. He announced this in Amritsar, but within hours the agreement had been denied by the government in Delhi. A group of senior army officers also managed to reach an agreement with the High Priests. It satisfied their security concerns but it did not apparently satisfy Mrs Gandhi's political aims. So the army officers were ordered to renege on their agreement.

Mrs Gandhi's political considerations were far from clear. Many Sikhs agreed with Balwant Singh, the only senior member of the original Akali Dal negotiating team not under arrest, who said to me, 'She wants to rub our noses in it.' Many newspaper commentators thought Mrs Gandhi was humiliating the Sikhs because she calculated that Hindu voters wanted that humiliation. The truth seems to be that Mrs Gandhi believed she could use this opportunity to break the Akali Dal once and for all. She ordered her officials to draw up a plan for taking the management and money of the *gurudwaras* out of the hands of the SGPC, which was of course the Akali Dal's financier.

When it became clear that Mrs Gandhi was not going to allow the SGPC and the High Priests to repair their shrines, Buta Singh turned to the leader of a sect of *nihangs* or Sikh warriors, Baba Santa Singh. He was an elderly and extremely portly Sikh whose followers were distinguished for their ruggedness rather than their piety. Many of them were fond of taking opium. Santa Singh had never supervised *kar sewa* under the auspices of the High Priests or the SGPC. They inevitably rejected his claim to be entitled to lead the *kar sewa*.

Santa Singh and his followers would also appear to have been disqualified from such a sacred task by their addiction to cannabis. Sikhism forbids all intoxicants but when Satish Jacob went to visit Santa Singh's camp one morning he found four of his young followers grinding cannabis seeds, almonds, sugar and black pepper into a light-green paste. Two elderly Sikhs were stirring a vast cauldron of boiling milk. The paste and milk were combined to make *bhang*. Santa Singh's followers had no inhibitions about starting their day with a strong draught of this intoxicant. One of the Sikhs stirring the milk said, 'We are making *mahaprasad* [great offering to God]. It is almost ready; come and join us; you will feel good.' Another disciple told Satish Jacob that daily *bhang* brewing was one of their most important rituals.

The repairs started without any of the traditional rituals. The High Priests should have dug up the first of the rubble with golden trowels and carried it away in silver baskets, but the trowels and baskets remained locked in the Temple Treasury. Santa Singh and his wild-looking warriors were shown on television entering the Temple before daylight and saying their prayers hurriedly before the shrine to launch the *kar sewa*. They then moved to the *gurudwara* in Amritsar which had been handed over to them and let the government get on with the work. The *nihangs* put in ritual appearances in front of the television cameras throughout the *kar sewa* but all the work was carried out by contractors under the supervision of the Public Works Department. K. D. Bali, a retired chief engineer of the PWD, was put in charge. Most of the hard work of clearing away the rubble was done by Harijan labourers. Muslim and other craftsmen skilled in marble work were brought from Rajasthan. Goldsmiths were brought from Uttar Pradesh. A senior engineer working on the project said that between nine and ten kilograms of gold were used. The engineer said the repairs cost between 30 to 40 million rupees – two to three million pounds.

The High Priests excommunicated Santa Singh. He brushed his sentence aside haughtily, saying, 'Who are these High Priests but the paid employees of the Temple Management Committee?' The work went on. Santa Singh was well paid for his defiance. The senior engineer told Satish Jacob that the *nihang* was given 100,000 rupees (over £6,500) every day to keep his 300 followers happy. Buta Singh flew in from Delhi regularly to make sure that the work was proceeding rapidly and to sort out any political problems which arose. By the end of September the shrine was repaired. The balconies at the front of the building, which had been reduced to rubble by the tanks, were restored; the gaping hole in the gold-covered dome was covered up; the top of the tower shot away in the battle was replaced. Sikhs admitted to Satish Jacob that the exterior of the shrine had been restored with sensitivity and respect for the original design. But no one had been able to restore the decorations inside.

As the repairs approached completion, the question of managing the Temple arose again. Mrs Gandhi was still reluctant to hand back the shrine to the SGPC. She organised an assembly of Sikhs to endorse the *kar sewa* and outflank resistance by the High Priests and the SGPC. As it was the *kar sewa* was put in the shade by the World Conference of Sikhs the High Priests called on 2nd September. In spite of government attempts to prevent Sikhs getting to the assembly, large numbers did turn up and passed a series of damaging resolutions. One declared the President and Buta Singh *tankaiya* or religious offenders. That is in effect a sentence of excommunication which enjoins Sikhs to avoid all contact with the offenders. The High Priests then called for a peaceful march to Amritsar on 1st October to 'liberate' the Golden Temple.

By now the pressure was becoming too strong for Mrs Gandhi to resist. Even her own usually docile party members

belonging to the Sikh community were urging her to break the
deadlock. President Zail Singh was also exerting pressure again
because he wanted his sentence to be lifted. There had been
another terrorist attack on a bus on 7th September in which
seven passengers had been killed. It had revived unhappy
memories of the days when Bhindranwale had virtually ruled
Punjab, and reminded Hindus of the dangers of Mrs Gandhi's
continuing policy of confrontation with the Akalis. So on 25th
September, just six days before the march on the Temple, Mrs
Gandhi announced that the army would be withdrawn from the
Temple and the SGPC would resume control over it. This was a
setback for Mrs Gandhi because at the same time she had to
drop her plans to amend the Gurudwara Act and remove
control of the temples from the SGPC. Mrs Gandhi did not
accept her defeat with good grace. In an abrupt broadcast to the
nation she said, 'The government does not want to retain
control of the Temple. We are willing to hand it over soon to
legitimate religious authorities. But it is certainly government's
concern that whoever looks after its management should ensure
that it would not be misused.'

A pardon for the President was part of the deal which had
been negotiated in secret. He attended the ceremony in the
Golden Temple when the army handed it back to the High
Priests, and was reported to have said, 'I ask sincere forgiveness
from the Gurus for the unfortunate incidents which have
occurred.' His spokesman later denied that the President had
apologised for Operation Blue Star. The President is also
reported to have said that all outstanding problems between the
High Priests and the government would be sorted out. His was
a visit of goodwill if not of penitence. But the goodwill was not
reciprocated by the High Priest of the Akal Takht. Giani Kirpal
Singh told the President that the government must give up its
anti-Sikh attitude and stop treating believers in his faith like
'second-class citizens'. He called for the ban on the All India
Sikh Students Federation, which had been the backbone of
Bhindranwale's movement, to be lifted and all its members
released from jail. He also demanded the release of the Akali
Dal leaders. The Prime Minister clearly still had a lot of
negotiating to do before Sikhs would accept that her offer of the

healing touch was sincere. But the Akali Trinity, the only people with whom she could have negotiated, were still under arrest when Mrs Gandhi was shot one month later.

15

Conclusion

Who killed Indira Gandhi? 'I,' said Sub-Inspector Beant Singh when he surrendered to the commandos in Mrs Gandhi's garden. But he was a victim himself, carried away by the anger which swept through the Sikh community after Operation Blue Star – anger he had done nothing to create. It was the creation of those who had taken on the responsibility for leading the Sikh community, of those who had taken on the responsibility of governing India, and of the times in which they were living. It is very tempting simply to blame Sant Jarnail Singh Bhindranwale and his brand of Sikh fundamentalism which was nurtured by hatred of Hindus, but fundamentalism does not exist in a vacuum. No Shah, no Khomeini; no Indira and no Bhindranwale. That may seem to be a very harsh judgment, and it is in that Mrs Gandhi was in no way a tyrant or an autocrat. However she *was* responsible for the political atmosphere which made the fundamentalism of Bhindranwale relevant. The Akali Dal Trinity must also bear their share of the responsibility. Badal and Longowal lacked the courage to stand out against a force they knew was evil. Tohra tried to use it for his own ends.

It was Indira Gandhi's Congress Party which launched Bhindranwale, and it was Indira Gandhi's government which allowed him to usurp its role in Punjab. If she had arrested Bhindranwale after the assassination of Deputy Inspector-General of Police Atwal, there would have been no assault on the Akal Takht. Even if Indira Gandhi had acted when she first got reports that Bhindranwale was fortifying the Golden Temple complex, it would still not have been too late. When she did eventually act, it certainly was.

We have already pointed to Mrs Gandhi's indecisiveness as one of the causes of the tragedy of Amritsar. We have also drawn attention to the *darbar*, or court, surrounding her. This *darbar* had a stultifying effect on the institutions and administration of India. All power derived from the court in Delhi, but the courtiers often exercised their power independently. The second most powerful man in India was not Mrs Gandhi's heir Rajiv; it was her personal assistant, R.K. Dhawan. Inevitably the fawners and flatterers rose to the top and the independent-minded sank to the bottom. It is significant that Amarinder Singh withdrew from his role as an intermediary in the negotiations with the Akali Dal because the bureaucrats surrounding Mrs Gandhi obfuscated every issue. It is significant that her coterie prevented B.D. Pande from functioning independently as governor. It is most significant of all that Rajiv Gandhi did manage to reach a settlement with the Akali Dal within seven months of coming to power by dismissing, transferring or by-passing all those who advised his mother.

At first Rajiv Gandhi highlighted the threat to the nation's unity posed by Sikh extremism and the Akali Dal's demands, the Anandpur Sahib Resolution in particular. In his campaign for the general election he called immediately after succeeding his mother, the only issue he put to the electorate was the threat to India's unity. He sold himself as the one leader who could withstand that threat. His triumph in the general election established the young heir to the Nehru/Indira Gandhi heritage as Prime Minister in his own right. He then went on to fight elections to state assemblies where his party did adequately, but less well than in the general election. With these two hurdles behind him, Rajiv did a U-turn on the Punjab. Conveniently forgetting his electoral rhetoric, he started the search for a way to negotiate with the Akali Dal.

Unlike his mother, Rajiv Gandhi realised that Punjab was a political problem which should be handled by politicians and not by courtiers, bureaucrats, the police or the army. His first, and as it proved wisest, step was the appointment of one of India's most astute politicians, Arjun Singh, to take over from the bureaucrat who had succeeded Pande as Governor of Punjab. For the past five years Arjun Singh had ruled India's largest state of Madhya Pradesh as Congress (Indira) Chief Minister. He had reduced the right-wing Hindu Bharatiya Janata Party or BJP to a minor irritant in a state which had once been its bastion. He had also neutralised the powerful sons of Ravi Shankar Shukla, Pandit Nehru's Chief Minister of Madhya Pradesh. The Shuklas had regarded the Madhya Pradesh Congress Party as their own personal feudal estates. One of Rajiv Gandhi's aides said to Satish Jacob, 'Anyone who could cope with the BJP on one side and the Shuklas on the other ought to be able to cope with the Akalis too.' He was proved right.

The Akali Trinity now came up against a powerful well-knit trinity on the government side – Rajiv Gandhi, Arjun Singh and Arun Singh. Arun Singh was a former multinational executive and had been a friend of Rajiv Gandhi since his schooldays. Rajiv Gandhi brought him into politics when he first stepped into Sanjay's shoes. By this time Arun Singh had become the Prime Minister's parliamentary secretary and his right-hand man. He was modern, straightforward and efficient, in sharp contrast to the former stenographer, R.K. Dhawan, who had used his understanding of the devious ways of Indian bureaucracy and politics to control access to Mrs Gandhi.

The new trinity came up with a strategy which differed from Mrs Gandhi's in three crucial aspects. Rajiv Gandhi did not allow any bureaucrat, courtier or politician to come between him and the new Governor of Punjab. He granted Arjun Singh direct access. Mrs Gandhi never allowed a chief minister or a governor to come so close to her. She operated a system of checks and balances on all her colleagues. The trinity also decided that those who had a vested interest in Punjab should be kept out of the search for a settlement. They were the

President, Zail Singh, the former Chief Minister of Punjab, Darbara Singh and the Chief Minister of Haryana, Bhajan Lal. Mrs Gandhi had been only too happy to see Darbara Singh and Zail Singh fighting over Punjab because it prevented either of them dominating the Congress Party in the state. She found Bhajan Lal a convenient pawn to play when she wanted to drag out negotiations.

The most difficult part of the new strategy was to isolate Longowal from the other two members of the Akali Trinity. Mrs Gandhi believed in dividing and ruling her opponents just as much as she believed in dividing and ruling her own party. She had always seen the tension in the Akali leadership as a factor in her favour. After studying the situation Arjun Singh realised that the Akali leaders would never take a united stand on a settlement. Their rivalries and vested interests would prevent them. He persuaded Rajiv Gandhi to deal with Longowal for two reasons. As the 'Morcha Dictator' Longowal was the man who had the authority to accept the settlement and call off the agitation. His verdict would be accepted by the grass roots leaders of the party. Longowal had also shown himself in the earlier negotiations to be the most straightforward and least ambitious of the Akali Trinity.

By the end of April Arjun Singh was already optimistic. He told me he believed the Akali Dal was genuinely anxious for a settlement. The Sikh extremists, sensing the optimism in the air, reacted once again with violence. On 10th and 11th May twenty bombs exploded in the capital, Delhi, and eighteen bombs exploded in other parts of northern India. Eighty-two people were killed. Hindus were obviously the targets. The bureaucrats' response was Pavlovian. They recommended that the Akali leaders should be arrested again and that all efforts to reach a settlement should be dropped. Members of the Congress Party also warned the Prime Minister that the Hindus would not tolerate any concessions to the Sikhs after the explosions. But Rajiv Gandhi and Arjun Singh refused to be deflected from their course. Just over two months later, on 21st July, they took India by surprise in announcing that Sant Harchand Singh Longowal was coming to Delhi to meet the Prime Minister.

The ground had been meticulously prepared in a series of secret talks through intermediaries. Arjun Singh himself met Longowal just before the announcement of the meeting to assure him the settlement would go through. The talks were conducted with determination, speed and efficiency which was in sharp contrast to the dilatory tactics adopted by both sides when they met under Mrs Gandhi. In less than forty-eight hours a settlement was announced. Mrs Gandhi could have resolved the main issues on the same terms three years earlier. Then there would have been no Operation Blue Star, no Sikh mutinies and no assassination.

Rajiv Gandhi's settlement covered eleven points. Many of them referred to incidents which took place after Operation Blue Star – the mutinies, the anti-Sikh violence and the security forces' drive against terrorists. The three major issues which remained unresolved in June 1984 were Chandigarh, the river waters and the Anandpur Sahib Resolution. Rajiv Gandhi gave Chandigarh to Punjab and set up a commission to give a ruling on the border disputes. The commission's terms made it virtually impossible for Abohar and Fazilka to go to Haryana. That had in fact been Mrs Gandhi's final offer, but by then it was too late to reach a settlement because Bhindranwale was insisting that the Anandpur Sahib Resolution should be implemented in full. Rajiv Gandhi only agreed to send the Resolution to the one-man commission on centre-state relations set up by his mother. The Akalis would have accepted that, if Mrs Gandhi had conceded their demands on Chandigarh and the river waters. The river waters issue was also resolved on terms the Akalis had accepted under Mrs Gandhi. Punjab retained its share of water until a commission presided over by a judge decided on a permanent allocation. So in the end it all came down to the one issue – Chandigarh. The others were, as an Akali leader said to me three months before Operation Blue Star, 'Just a matter of commissions.' It was Mrs Gandhi's tragedy to be guided by bureaucrats to whom nothing could ever be as simple as that.

One of the most remarkable achievements of the new government trinity was secrecy. Mrs Gandhi could not even keep a telephone call to Longowal a secret. In her days there would have been a run of speculative stories based on leaks by bureaucrats or politicians using the press to sabotage negotiations of which they did not approve. Rajiv Gandhi and his colleagues kept their secrets to themselves. It was particularly difficult to keep those with direct interest in Punjab in the dark. Badal and Tohra, Zail Singh, Darbara Singh and Bhajan Lal were all active politicians with contacts in every nook and corner of Punjab and the central-government bureaucracy, but their sources had dried up.

The two Akali leaders were deeply upset when they learnt of the settlement. True to form, they both rejected it, proving Arjun Singh's decision to deal with Longowal was correct. Bhajan Lal could not show his anger when he was told Haryana must accept the terms it had rejected all along. Opposition leaders had conveniently presented Rajiv Gandhi with a long list of corruption charges against the Haryana Chief Minister and so he was in no position to resist. Zail Singh was out of Delhi on a presidential tour when he learnt that the Prime Minister and Longowal were going to meet. Even when he returned to the capital, Rajiv Gandhi studiously ignored his presence in Delhi. No one gave a thought to Darbara Singh who happened to be in Bombay at the time.

When Rajiv Gandhi announced the settlement to cheering Members of Parliament, he said, 'I hope it [the settlement] will be the beginning of a new phase of working together to build the country, to build unity and integrity.' He knew that it was only the beginning of a process of reconciliation between Sikhs and Hindus. He also knew that much needed to be done to reconcile other Indian communities. At that very moment Hindu-Muslim clashes were continuing in Mahatma Gandhi's home state of Gujarat.

Rajiv Gandhi adopted modern crisis management techniques to reach the Punjab settlement. He set up a tight-knit command group, kept his own mind clear by working from brief position papers and maintained secrecy by insisting that documents were only read by those who needed to know. The rumours from all four corners of India which used to waft around Mrs Gandhi's *darbar* were kept out. This new style certainly worked in the case of the Akali settlement. Will it work to solve the much deeper problems which lie behind the Sikh unrest and indeed the communal tension in so many other parts of India?

Communal tension in modern India is often caused by rising expectations. It is at its worst in the more prosperous and advanced parts of the country, showing that mere economic growth is no answer to India's problems. Gujarat and Punjab are the two most progressive states and yet they were the scenes of religious fanaticism and communalism when Rajiv Gandhi came to power, rather than the poor backward areas like Bihar or eastern Uttar Pradesh. The poor of those areas have seen so little change in their surroundings they have no hope of a better life. Punjabis and Gujaratis have seen remarkable progress. Some of them are frustrated because the benefits are passing them by. Others fear that their traditional control over sources of wealth is threatened. Twentieth-century ideologies like progressive capitalism, socialism and even communism exist only in name in India. They have not taken any genuine political form. So those who fear for their traditional privileges and those whose expectations of a better life are frustrated fall back on the ancient divisions of Indian society, caste and creed, to fight their battles.

Rajiv Gandhi's decision to go all out for a political solution in Punjab showed that he realised the police and the army could not provide the answer to communal strife. He found the political courage needed to solve the immediate problem of Punjab; he will need courage and determination of quite a different order if he is to tackle its underlying causes. For that he will have to find ways of modernising every aspect of India's life and thought without destroying the country in the process. He will have to re-create the Congress by making it once again a genuine secular national party, but this time with modern social and economic policies too. He will have to break the stranglehold of the politicians, bureaucrats and contractors, the 'parasitic class' who are sucking the life blood out of the Indian economy. That will mean dismantling the complicated economic controls which they have manipulated for their own ends. He will have to overhaul the ramshackle administration, founding modern institutions which can provide the environment, education, housing and health services needed to change the lives of those Indians still condemned to live in squalid slums or remote and backward villages. There is no doubt that Rajiv Gandhi is committed to modernising India. He made a good start by resolving his differences with the Akalis so quickly and efficiently, but it was only a small beginning.

Notes

1 The Assassination of a Prime Minister

1 Interview with M.J. Akbar, *Sunday* magazine, Calcutta, 10–16th March 1985.
2 Ibid.
3 M.J. Akbar, *India: The Siege Within*, Penguin Books, Harmondsworth, 1985, p. 197.

2 The Sikhs

1 M.A. Macauliffe, *The Sikh Religion*, pamphlet, London, 1910, p. 6.
2 H. Beveridge (ed.), *Tuzuk-i-Jahangiri, or Memoirs of Jahangir*, translated by A. Rogers, Royal Asiatic Society, London, 1909, vol. 1, p. 72.
3 Sita Ram Kohli, 'The Army of Maharaja Ranjit Singh', *Journal of Indian History*, vol. 1:1921–2, Department of Modern Indian History, Allahabad University, published in London.
4 William Francklin, *Military Memoirs of George Thomas*, published for the author by Hurkaru Press, Calcutta, 1803, pp. 71–3.

5 Lord William Godolphin Osborne, *The Court and Camp of Runjeet Singh*, Henry Colburn, London, 1840, p. 72.

6 Emily Eden, *Up the Country*, Curzon Press, London, 1978 (this edition first published by Oxford University Press in 1930), p. 200.

7 Ibid., p. 218.

8 Philip Mason, *A Matter of Honour: An Account of the Indian Army, its Officers and Men*, Jonathan Cape, London, 1974, p. 236.

9 Frederic Cooper, *Crisis of the Punjab*, Smith, London, 1858, pp. 21–2.

10 Khushwant Singh, *A History of the Sikhs*, vol. 2: 1839–1974, Princeton University Press, Princeton, 1966. Indian edition, Oxford University Press, Oxford, 1977 (page numbers from the latter), pp. 112–13.

11 Ibid., p. 160.

12 Mohinder Singh, *The Akali Movement*, Macmillan, Delhi, 1978, p. 14.

13 Ibid., p. 20.

14 Rev. Andrews, articles published in the *Manchester Guardian*, 15th and 24th February 1924.

15 Jawaharlal Nehru, *An Autobiography*, this edition published by Jawaharlal Nehru Memorial Fund, Delhi, 1980, pp. 175–6.

16 Philip Mason, op. cit., p. 514.

3   The Grievances of the Sikhs

1 Ajit Singh Sarhadi, *Punjabi Suba*, U.C. Kapur & Sons, Delhi, 1970, p. 327.

2 Norma Evenson, *Chandigarh*, University of California Press, Berkeley and Los Angeles, 1966, p. 93.

5   The Arrest of Bhindranwale

1 Khushwant Singh and Kuldip Nayar, *Tragedy of Punjab: Operation Blue Star and After*, Vision Books, 1984, p. 24.

2 *Sunday* magazine, Calcutta, 8th–11th August 1982, p. 39.

3 Pramod Kumar, Mahmohan Sharma, Atul Sood and

Ashwani Handa, *Punjab Crisis, Context and Trends*, Centre for Research in Rural and Industrial Development, Chandigarh, 1984.

6 Mrs Gandhi Attempts to Negotiate with the Sikhs

1 Khushwant Singh and Kuldip Nayar, *Tragedy of Punjab: Operation Blue Star and After*, Vision Books, 1984, p. 38.
2 Ibid., p. 50.
3 Amarjit Kaur, Arun Shourie, Lt-Gen. J.S. Aurora, Khushwant Singh *et al.*, *The Punjab Story*, Roli Books International, Delhi, 1984, p. 17.

7 The Asian Games and their Aftermath

1 *Indian Express*, Delhi, 17th November 1982.
2 Amarjit Kaur, Arun Shourie, Lt-Gen. J.S. Aurora, Khushwant Singh *et al.*, *The Punjab Story*, Roli Books International, Delhi, 1984, p. 98.
3 *Illustrated Weekly of India*, Bombay, 10th April 1983.

8 Two Brutal Killings – Mrs Gandhi Acts at Last

1 Amarjit Kaur, Arun Shourie, Lt-Gen. J.S. Aurora, Khushwant Singh, *et al.*, *The Punjab Story*, Roli Books International, Delhi, 1984, p. 39.

9 President's Rule Fails

1 M.J. Akbar, *India: The Siege Within*, Penguin Books, Harmondsworth, 1985, p. 196.

12 Operation Blue Star

1 D.R. Mankekar, *22 Fateful Days*, this edition published by Deep & Deep, Delhi, 1968, pp. 73–4.
2 Amarjit Kaur, Arun Shourie, Lt-Gen. J.S. Aurora, Khushwant Singh, *et al.*, *The Punjab Story*, Roli Books International, Delhi, 1984, p. 13.

3 *Janata Weekly*, Bombay, 23rd September 1984.

13 The Golden Temple, 6th June

1 Amarjit Kaur, Arun Shourie, Lt-Gen. J.S. Aurora, Khush-want Singh *et al.*, *The Punjab Story*, Roli Books Internation-al, Delhi, 1984, p. 28.

14 The Aftermath

1 Amarjit Kaur, Arun Shourie, Lt-Gen. J.S. Aurora, Khush-want Singh *et al.*, *The Punjab Story*, Roli Books Internation-al, Delhi, 1984, p. 28.
2 *Illustrated Weekly of India*, Bombay, 22nd July 1984.
3 Shekhar Gupta, Arun Shourie, Rahul Bedi and Pranoy Roy, *The Assassination and After*, Roli Books International, Delhi, 1985, p. 27.

15 Conclusion

1 *Journal of the Indo-British Historical Society*, Madras, December 1984.

Bibliography

AKBAR, M.J., *India: The Siege Within*, Penguin Books, Harmondsworth, 1985.

ANON, 'A Homage to Amritsar,' *Marg*, vol. XXX, no. 3, Bombay, June 1977.

BRASS, PAUL, *Language, Religion and Politics in North India*, Cambridge University Press, Cambridge, 1974.

COLE, W.H. and SAMBHI, PIYARA SINGH, *The Sikhs: Their Religious Beliefs and Practices*, Routledge & Kegan Paul, London, 1978.

CUNNINGHAM, J.D., *History of the Sikhs: From the Origin of the Nation to the Battles of the Sutlej*, John Murray, London, 1849.

FRANKEL, FRANCINE R., *India's Political Economy 1947–1977*, Princeton University Press, Princeton, 1978.

GULATI, KAILASH CHANDER, *The Akalis Past and Present*, Ashajanak Publications, Delhi, 1974.

JOSHI, CHAND, *Bhindranwale: Myth and Reality*, Vikas Publishing, Delhi, 1984.

KAUR, AMARJIT; SHOURIE, ARUN; AURORA, LT-GENERAL J.S.; SINGH, KUSHWANT; KAMATH, M.V.; GUPTA, SHEKHAR; KIRPEKAR, SUBHASH; SETHI, SUNIL and SINGH, TAVLEEN, *The Punjab Story*, Roli Books International, Delhi, 1984.

KUMAR, PRAMOD; SHARMA, MAHMOHAN; SOOD, ATUL and HANDA, ASHWANI, *Punjab Crisis, Context and Trends*, Centre for Research in Rural and Industrial Development, Chandigarh, 1984.

MACAULIFFE, MAX ARTHUR; *The Sikh Religion: Its Gurus, Sacred*

Writings and Authors, Clarendon Press, Oxford, 1909.

MCLEOD, W.H., *Guru Nanak and the Sikh Religion*, Oxford University Press, Oxford, 1968.

MASANI, ZAREER, *Indira Gandhi: A Biography*, Hamish Hamilton, London, 1975.

MASON, PHILIP, *A Matter of Honour: An Account of the Indian Army, its Officers and Men*, Jonathan Cape, London, 1974.

MORAES, DOM, *Mrs Gandhi*, Jonathan Cape, London, 1980.

NAYAR, KULDIP and SINGH, KHUSHWANT, *Tragedy of Punjab: Operation Blue Star and After*, Vision Books, Delhi, 1984.

SARHADI, AJIT SINGH, *Punjabi Suba*, U.C. Kapur & Sons, Delhi, 1970.

SINGH, HARBANS, *The Heritage of the Sikhs*, Asia Publishing House, New York, 1964.

SINGH, KHUSHWANT, *A History of the Sikhs*, vols 1 and 2, Princeton University Press, Princeton, vol. 1 1963, vol. 2 1966.

SINGH, MOHINDER, *The Akali Movement*, Macmillan, Delhi, 1978.

SURJEET, HARKISHAN SINGH, 'Happenings in Punjab', National Book Centre, Delhi, 1984.

WHITE PAPER ON THE PUNJAB AGITATION, Government of India, 10th July 1984.

Index

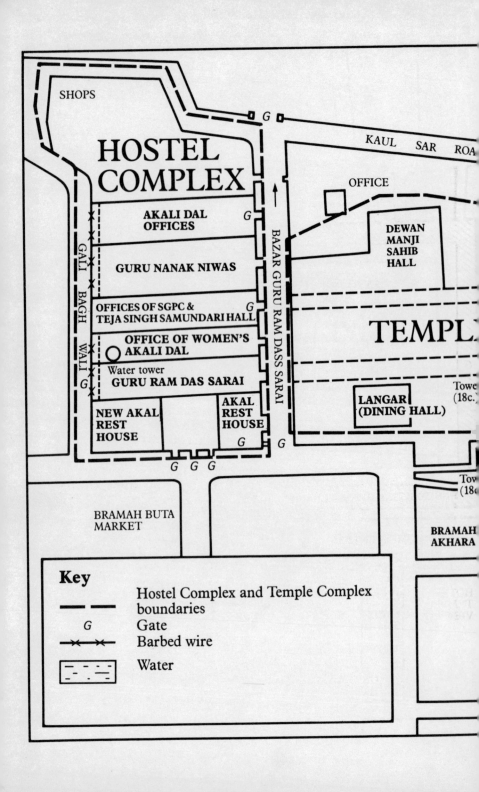